# HOW TO PREPARE FOR THE

# BUSINESS LAW SECTION

# OF THE C.P.A. EXAMINATION

Ellen Grimes

Editor-in-chief

Caryl Ann Russell, Esq.
Trubin Sillcocks Edelman & Knapp
New York

Editorial Review Board

Bruce G. Pritikin, Esq., C.P.A.
Samuel Klein & Company
New Jersey

Richard G. Schneidman, C.P.A.
Seymour Schneidman & Associates
New York

Michael R. Greenberg, Esq.
Prescott Ball & Turben
New York

Jeanette L. Bely, Ph.D.
The Bernard M. Baruch College
 of C.U.N.Y.
New York

Allen H. Brill, Esq.
O'Sullivan Wolff Karabell & Graev
New York

A Trafalgar House Book

McGRAW-HILL BOOK COMPANY

*New York, St. Louis, San Francisco, Auckland, Bogotá, Düsseldorf, Johannesburg, London, Madrid,
Mexico, Montreal, New Delhi, Panama, Paris, São Paulo, Singapore, Sydney, Tokyo, and Toronto*

Material from the Uniform CPA Examinations, Copyright © 1972, 1973, 1974, 1975, 1976, 1977 by the American Institute of Certified Public Accountants, Inc., is reprinted and adapted by Trafalgar House Publishing, Inc. with permission of the AICPA.

0-07-024827-3

1 2 3 4 5 6 7 8 9 10 11 12 13 14 15 16 17 18 19 20 SM SM 7 8 3 2 1 0 9 8


*Library of Congress Cataloging in Publication Data*

Grimes, Ellen.
    How to prepare for the business law section of the C.P.A. examination.

    "A Trafalgar House book."
    1.   Commercial law — United States. I. Russell, Caryl Ann, joint author.
    II. Title.
KF889.5.G73   346'.73'07   77-26920
ISBN 0-07-024827-3

# Contents

# Introduction

The CPA candidate who masters the general concepts, particular points, and definitions presented in this review guide will have no trouble passing the business law section of the Uniform CPA Examination.

The people who construct the questions on the exam look to many different sources and authorities for inspiration. In preparing this volume, I too have looked to those references and have attempted to incorporate into these chapters whatever information past CPA exams imply, and the AICPA Bulletin for CPA candidates suggests, that one have command of.

Obviously, it is almost impossible to cover every single point which can conceivably pop up on an exam, either directly or indirectly, in the multiple-choice questions or in the essay questions. However, because a barely passing grade confers the same benefit on a candidate as a perfect paper does (one receives no more of a passing grade with a 95 than one does with a 75 — a "pass" is a "pass"), a candidate need not be too concerned about not knowing some minor exception to a rule, or about missing a few multiple-choice questions or even part of an essay question. The Institute is concerned with ascertaining whether a candidate has a working knowledge of commercial law, and this volume will certainly offer any candidate the opportunity to acquire that working knowledge.

While most of procedural and substantive business law has not changed very much over the past few years, some areas have seen minor changes. I have done my best to insure that the information contained within is as current as possible. Nevertheless, I must apologize for an occasional time limit or age requirement or whatever which might have been modified between the time this book went to press and the time of the CPA examination.

Sprinkled throughout each chapter are past CPA examination questions which illustrate ways in which the Institute tests a candidate's knowledge of the subject matter. Illustrative questions are true/false, multiple choice, or essay questions. A question which illustrates a particular point covered in one paragraph in a chapter will immediately follow that paragraph; a question which deals with a concept covered in a chapter section will follow that section; and a question which illustrates the broad points covered in the chapter as a whole will follow the chapter.

A statistical analysis of the most recent CPA exams has been done to determine which areas of knowledge are most frequently tested on exams and, in turn, which areas are most frequently tested in objective questions and in essay questions. A sample Business Law examination has been constructed by putting the data which emerged from that analysis to use. It appears at the end of this book. All the questions on the sample exam are from actual past CPA exams and the answers are those which have been approved by the AICPA.

Remember:

Before the exam, make sure you have total command of all the material in this book. At the very least, commit it to memory. Understand it too, if you can.

At the exam, relax. Read every question very carefully (that way you can save precious time by only reading it once), looking out for key words such as: "always," "never," "sometimes," "usually," "and," "or," "except," "including," "probably," "unlikely," and so on. Answer everything you know cold first, and then go back to the more troublesome questions.

Good luck!

Ellen Grimes

# 1 Contracts

The contract is at the heart of every business relationship which a CPA candidate is required to understand. It determines the legal relationship between the agent and principal, between the buyer and seller, between indorser and indorsee, among the partners in a partnership, and so forth. While particular requirements and forms to insure enforcement of the contractual association may vary from relationship to relationship, there are many basics which apply to any and all contracts in order for them to be valid and therefore legally enforceable. This chapter deals with those basics.

For the purposes of this text it will be assumed that there are only two parties to the contract. However, theoretically, there can be an unlimited number of parties to most contracts.

Most contracts do not have to be written to be enforceable; they can be oral instead. The terms can be enforceable whether they are definite (express) or implied. What is crucial to their validity is that contracts contain certain essential elements. There are four questions you must ask yourself before you can determine whether or not a contract is enforceable:

1. Has an offer been made and accepted?

2. Has legally sufficient consideration been exchanged?

3. Do the contracting parties have the capacity to enter into a contract?

4. Is the activity in which the contracting parties have promised to engage legal?

If the answer to all four of these critical questions is yes, then the promises which the parties have made to one another are enforceable in court and a contract between them exists.

**Question 1: Has there been an offer and an acceptance of that offer?**

The contracting parties must mutually agree to the terms of a contract in such a way that their agreement is said to be *objectively manifested*. The word "objectively" is used because, for the most part, what appears to be takes precedence over what one or both parties intended to be, if the two situations contradict one another.

The concept of mutual assent turns on voluntary acceptance by both parties of the terms in question. Often a manifestation of mutual assent may appear to exist when, in fact, it does not. In four such instances in particular, when there is this lack of real consent, the acceptance of an offer does not form a contract or, if one has already been formed, the contract is voidable. These are instances of mistake, undue influence, duress, or fraud.

- *Mistake:* If both parties are victims of a mutual mistake of fact, the contract will most likely be avoided or, in other words, voidable. For example, if the parties enter into a binding promise to exchange, say, a car for a stated amount of money and, unknown to both parties (which assumes without fault of either party) the car has been destroyed, the contract is voidable. (Notice the difference between voidable and void. *Voidable* means that a party may be relieved of his contractual obligations if he so elects; *void* means the contract does not exist, that it is illegal and unenforceable to begin with.) This illustration of the destroyed car is an example of a mutual mistake as to existence of subject matter. An example of mutual mistake as to nature of subject matter, a situation which also allows for avoidance or voidability, would be if the parties were engaged in the sale of what they both believed was an original Picasso and the painting turned out to be a copy. If both parties are aware that they are taking a chance that the car might have indeed been destroyed, or that the painting might have been a copy, then they are both voluntarily assuming risks against which the courts will not protect them. There is a difference, then, between mutual mistakes of fact and mutual agreements to take a chance or mutual agreement that the parties might not know the true value of an item being sold or bought. Mistakes almost always must be mutual for the contract to be voidable. Though there are a few odd cases in which the contract is voidable even though only one party is mistaken, in most cases a contract will not be voidable in such situations. Contracts will also usually not be voidable simply because a party did not understand the legal effect of a contract he voluntarily signed or because he misread or forgot to read a contract which was clearly written.

● *Undue influence:* When the relationship between two contracting parties is characterized by one person having a dominating influence over another or holding the trust and confidence of another — for example, trustee/beneficiary, principal/agent, guardian/ward, lawyer/client, husband/wife — the dominating or trusted party is said to have a fiduciary duty toward the dominated or trusting party such that the former cannot act in a manner which is not in the best interests of the latter. This fiduciary duty is imposed upon the dominating party because, as the illustrative relationships suggest, he is in a position to exercise undue influence upon the subservient party, or to persuade him to do something that will not necessarily be beneficial to him. When a dominating party abuses this fiduciary duty and exercises undue influence upon the subservient party to enter into a contract, that contract is voidable at the victim's option.

● *Duress:* If a party has assented to the terms of an offer because harm has come or threats of harm have been made against him or his family or his property, he will not be held to the terms of the contract. Such acts or threats constitute coercion or duress in that the victim has not exercised his free will. Psychological pressure will lead to avoidance of the contract just as surely as threats of physical harm will. The test to which a court will put a claim of duress is a subjective, as opposed to an objective, test. This means that the effect of the duress will not be measured according to how a reasonable man would have reacted under the same pressures; rather it will be measured according to how the victim in question — given his particular mental and physical condition at the time — could have been expected to and did react.

● *Fraud:* If one party induces another to accept the terms of an offer, and thereby enter into a contract, by *knowingly misrepresenting* a *material fact* upon which the offeree has *relied*, the contract is voidable at the defrauded party's option. Every one of the italicized elements must be present to constitute a successful charge of fraud, whether the charge is of fraud in the inducement (the most common kind) which results in a voidable contract, or fraud in the execution (obtaining someone's signature on a paper he has been told is something other than what it actually is), which results in a totally void contract. The defrauded party's power of avoidance is lost if he waits too long to disaffirm the contract.

. . . *Knowingly misrepresenting* . . . : While it goes without saying that the element of falsehood is essential to establish fraud, it also must be proven that the party who held out the misrepresentation knew of it and intended to deceive the defrauded party. If the alleged defrauder simply made a mistake and did not know that he was in error, or did not intend to deceive anyone, he will usually not be found guilty of fraud.

. . . *material* . . . : If knowledge of a fact induces a party to act or not to act in a way contrary to what he might or might not have done had he not been aware of the fact, that fact is said to be material. In other words, if the fact influenced a decision it is material. Accordingly, unless the fact or facts misrepresented were material, fraud cannot be established.

. . . *fact* . . . : A key element in establishing fraudulent behavior is that a fact was involved as opposed to an opinion. There is a difference between "My old car, which

I want to sell you, has 50,000 miles on it" (fact), and "I think this car of mine is the best buy for your money" (opinion). Courts will not find for a plaintiff charging fraud when opinions are involved; the material misrepresentation must be one of fact. Distinguishing between fact and opinion can often be difficult, because the line that separates them is thin and fuzzy. For example, sales people who exaggerate or stretch the truth are usually not found guilty of fraud. On the other hand, if there is a dominant/subservient relationship between two people, such that one party relies heavily on and does not question what the other party says, statements that might be otherwise characterized as opinions may well become facts when espoused by the fiduciary. Also, except for a very few exceptions, people who misrepresent questions of law to equal parties (not a lawyer to a client) are not liable for committing fraud, because they are both presumed to know the law.

*. . . the offeree has relied . . . :* Finally, even if the statement in question is one in which a material fact was knowingly misrepresented, a plaintiff charging fraud will usually not be granted relief in court unless he can show that he relied on the material misrepresentation and suffered in so doing. Clearly, one cannot prove reliance if he knew of the misrepresentation before entering into the contract, and one cannot prove deception if he did not rely on the material misrepresentation. If the defrauded party relied on a material misrepresentation and happened to have benefited from the arrangement, he should not expect any relief from the courts even though, technically, a fraud has been perpetrated.

**EXAMPLE (True/False):**

Brown, an experienced businessman, has customarily advised Mrs. Weston, a widow without business experience, in connection with business matters. Without making any representations of fact, Brown induced Mrs. Weston to enter a contract of sale with Casey, a business colleague of Brown. Brown and Casey know that the contract is disadvantageous to Mrs. Weston.

    1. Normally an affirmative misrepresentation of material fact is necessary to constitute fraud; i.e., silence is not sufficient.

    2. If Casey were a merchant who knowingly misrepresented a material characteristic of the goods to be sold to Mrs. Weston, the contract would be voidable at Mrs. Weston's option.

    3. If Brown knowing the true facts induced Mrs. Weston to sign on the representation that the document was a mere letter of introduction, the transaction is absolutely void.

    4. If without relying upon Brown's advice Mrs. Weston signed the contract, she would be bound by its terms.

**Solution:** (1) T, (2) T, (3) T, (4)T

**EXAMPLE (Multiple Choice):**

Williams induced Jackson to enter into an employment contract by deliberately telling Jackson certain material facts which Williams knew were *not* true. If there are *no* other relevant facts, on what legal grounds is the contract voidable?

    a. Undue influence     b. Fraud    c. Duress    d. Unilateral mistake of fact.

**Solution:** (b)

Contracting parties most often manifest their mutual assent by means of an *offer and acceptance.*

*Essentials of an offer:*

    1.  An offer must always contain a *promise* on the part of the offeror to do something (or not do something) if and when the offeree does (or does not do) something. As such, preliminary negotiations, or "feelers," do not constitute offers, because there are no

promises involved yet; asking someone if he is prepared to sell his house for $40,000 is not an offer to buy it at that price.

2. The offeror must present *definite terms*. Illusory promises — that is, promises wherein the promisor says he may wish to buy some quantity of something at some price but does not say he will — are indefinite and uncertain. If someone promises to buy all that he needs, this may or may not be an illusory promise. When property or services are involved, the offeror must describe or define the subject matter as clearly as possible and, if he cannot clarify price and/or quantity, he should refer to a reasonably ascertainable standard. When the offer involves the purchase or sale of goods, the "good faith" obligation imposed on contracting parties by the UCC allows for certain particulars — such as price — to be left out of the initial offer; it is understood that such terms will be supplied by the parties later by referring, in good faith, to reasonable practices and commercial standards. For example, output, requirement, and exclusive dealing agreements, where the exact quantities are not mentioned, are enforceable.

### EXAMPLE (Multiple Choice):

Martin, a wholesale distributor, made a contract for the purchase of 10,000 gallons of gasoline from the Wilberforce Oil Company. The price was to be determined in accordance with the refinery price as of the close of business on the delivery date. Credit terms were net/30 after delivery. Under these circumstances which of the following statements is true?

    a. If Martin pays upon delivery, he is entitled to a 2% discount.
    b. The contract being silent on the place of delivery, Martin has the right to expect delivery at his place of business.
    c. Although the price has some degree of uncertainty, the contract is enforceable.
    d. Because the goods involved are tangible, specific performance is a remedy available to Martin.

**Solution:** (c)

3. The offeree must be aware of the offer — that is, the offeror must have *communicated* his offer himself, either through his words or conduct, or authorized his offer to be communicated to the offeree.

Contracts are characterized by the promises behind them: A *bilateral contract* is one in which a promise has been exchanged for a promise; a *unilateral contract* is one in which a promise has been exchanged for an act (not a promise to act); an *inverted unilateral contract* is one in which an act (again, not a promise to act) has been exchanged for a promise.

## *Termination of an offer:*

The offeree can accept an offer at any point up until the time when the offer terminates — that is, up until the time when the offer is no longer available for acceptance. Of course, strictly speaking, the offer terminates (is no longer an offer) when the offeree accepts it. An offer is considered to have been accepted when the offeree mails or dispatches his acceptance, unless the offer stipulates that acceptance must be received as of a particular date.

### EXAMPLE (Multiple Choice):

Unless the offer specifies otherwise, an acceptance is generally effective when it is

    a. Signed by the offeree.
    b. Received by the offeror.
    c. Delivered by the communicating agency.
    d. Dispatched by the offeree.

**Solution:** (d)

The termination of an offer that results from an offeree's acceptance leads to an enforceable contract, assuming the other requirements of consideration, capacity, and legality are also present. An offer can also be terminated in ways other than acceptance, in which cases termination does not lead to an enforceable contract. For example, an offer can terminate:

1. If the *offeror retracts his offer* before it has been accepted.

**EXAMPLE (Multiple Choice):**

Vantage telephoned Breyer on December 18, 1975, and offered to sell a plot of land to Breyer for $5,000. Vantage promised to keep the offer open until December 27, 1975. Breyer said he was interested in the land but wanted to inspect it before making any commitment. Which of the following *best* describes the legal significance of these events?
  a.  Vantage may revoke the offer at will.
  b.  Vantage may *not* revoke the offer prior to December 27.
  c.  A contract was formed on December 18.
  d.  Breyer's response constituted a rejection and counteroffer.

**Solution:** (a)

An offer may be irrevocable, because:

- The offeror has agreed not to revoke it in exchange for consideration, or

- The offer is irrevocable because of a statute, or

- The offeror is a merchant who has made a written offer to buy or sell goods, in which case the offer may not be withdrawn for lack of consideration during the period stipulated in the agreement, or, in the absence of any such stipulation, for a reasonable time, not to exceed three months.

**EXAMPLE (Multiple Choice):**

A written option to buy land generally *cannot* be revoked before acceptance if the offer
  a.  Is supported by consideration from the offeree.
  b.  Allows a specific time for acceptance.
  c.  Is made exclusively to one person.
  d.  By its terms is *not* revocable before acceptance.

**Solution:** (a)

2. If the original offer stated how long it would be effective and the *time period has elapsed* without the offeree having accepted. The offeror has the right to specify any conditions in the offer he wants to, including how long it will remain open. Once the specified time period passes, the offer cannot be accepted, because it no longer exists. If the offeror does not specify how long the offer will be held open, the offeree has the right to notify the offeror of his acceptance within a reasonable period of time. Reasonable is again defined by a good faith judgment of accepted business practices, particular circumstances, and so forth. The phrasing of the restriction and the dating of the offer (if it is written) determine the exact period during which it will remain available for acceptance. For instance, if Mr. X mails Mr. Y an offer dated July 15 and states that the offer will remain open for 15 days, the 15 day period starts as of July 15, even though the offer is not actually effective until Y receives it. Thus, if Y does not receive it until August 2, he cannot accept it. But if X writes instead that Y has 15 days in which to accept the offer, under normal circumstances (that is, no unusual delays in transmission) the period in question will begin on the day Y receives the offer.

3.  If the *offeree rejects the offer,* either by using express or implied language or by virtue of his conduct. Just as an offer, to be effective, must be communicated from the offeror to the offeree, so a rejection, to be effective, must be communicated from the offeree to the offeror. Contrary to an acceptance, which is effective when it is dispatched by the offeree, a rejection is effective when it is received by the offeror, not when it is dispatched by the offeree. Within the realm of rejection comes the *counteroffer.* A counteroffer by an offeree is one which agrees to accept the offer but only if certain terms are changed. A counteroffer is considered to be a rejection, because the offeree has not agreed to the offeror's terms. As such, the original offer is terminated and the offeror/offeree roles are reversed: The offeree becomes the offeror, the rejection becomes his offer, and the offeror becomes the offeree with the option to accept or reject the new offer. If the original offeree simply suggests alternative terms but does not state that he is unwilling to accept the original terms, the offer has not been rejected by means of a counteroffer. A very minor change in the offer's terms does not usually constitute a rejection.

**EXAMPLE:**

On July 1, 1974, Franklin Novelties, Inc., offered to sell Major Toy Marketing Corporation twelve-thousand velocipedes at $6.25 each, delivery FOB Franklin's warehouse not later than December 15, 1974.

Major Toy wired Franklin as follows:

> We accept your offer of July 1, 1974. However, due to the proximity of the Christmas season, we must insist that delivery be made not later than November 1, 1974. This acceptance is expressly made conditional on your assent to the different delivery date.
>
> > (Signed)
> > *Major Toy*

Franklin decided to stick with its original terms and, consequently, sold the twelve-thousand velocipedes to Fremont Toys. It, therefore, ceased entirely its dealings with Major Toy.

Major Toy subsequently learned of the sale to its competitor, Fremont Toys, and promptly dispatched to Franklin the following telegram:

> We hold you liable on your offer of July 1, 1974, re the sale of twelve-thousand velocipedes. Our modification of the terms was a mere proposal, which we herewith waive. In any event, your silence constitutes acceptance of our modified terms. We expect delivery not later than December 15, 1974.
>
> > (Signed)
> > *Major Toy*

**Required:**

What are the legal implications to Franklin Novelties as a result of the above facts? Explain.

**Solution:**

Franklin Novelties is not liable to Major Toy. Although Franklin made a valid offer to sell velocipedes to Major Toy, Major Toy's acceptance varied the terms of the offer and was made expressly conditional upon Franklin's making delivery not later than November 1, 1974. Such a purported acceptance is no acceptance. Instead, it constitutes a rejection and a counter offer by Major Toy. In other words, the original offer is terminated and a new offer has been made by the original offeree, Major Toy. The counter offer must in turn be accepted in order to create a contractual obligation. Since Franklin never responded and since silence would not here constitute acceptance, there is no contract. Furthermore, once an offer is rejected, it can no longer be revived by the party who rejected it. Major Toy's attempt to revive the original offer has no legal merit.

4.  If the *subject matter* to which the offer refers *does not exist,* either because it was destroyed after the offer was made or because the offeror and offeree both thought it existed when, in fact, it did not.

5.  If the offeror or offeree *dies or becomes insane.* Most contracts can be assigned by the original offeree and, as such, insanity or death of the offeror or offeree does not terminate a contract. (An offer contained in an option, then, is not terminated upon the happening of either of these two events, because an option is a binding promise, that is, a contract, and the duties and/or rights therein can pass to an offeror's or offeree's representative or executor.) However, an offer is not assignable; it can be accepted only by the original offeree, so that his subsequent death or insanity does terminate the offer.

6.  If the activities to which the offer refers are legal at the time the offer is made, but are *subsequently made illegal* by a new law.

*Acceptance of an offer:*

An acceptance can be communicated by the offeree to the offeror in any way and can be express (for example, by sending a letter of acceptance, wherein the terms of the offer are precisely restated) or implied (such as performing or not performing specified actions, as in the case of a unilateral contract). For an acceptance to be effective, it must be *positive and unqualified,* and cannot change any of the original offer's terms, or else it will be considered a counteroffer and, as such, a rejection. It must be more than a mere acknowledgment of the offer; it must be an outright acceptance of it. With respect to transactions involving the selling or buying of goods, the UCC modifies and relaxes this constraint to the point where an acceptance can be effective even though it might state "terms additional to or different from those offered or agreed upon, unless acceptance is expressly made conditional on assent to the additional or different terms" and as long as the additional terms do not materially alter the initial offer, the initial offer did not specifically prohibit modifications of its terms, or the offeror has not already objected to them or does not object to them within a reasonable time after receiving notice of them.

**EXAMPLE (True/False):**

On January 2, 1973, West Electronics unconditionally offered in writing to sell a new high-fidelity sound system to Young for $450. Young replied in writing.
1. If West had referred to a reasonable price, in lieu of $450, the offer would be too indefinite to create a power of acceptance in Young.
2. In lieu of an offer of $450, if West had provided that the price was to be set by a third person, its offer would be too indefinite to create a power of acceptance in Young.
3. If West's offer is effective, Young's reply of "I will pay $350" constitutes an acceptance.
4. If West's offer stated that Young must accept on or before January 20, 1973, West could not withdraw the offer prior to that time.
5. If West's offer failed to state the time within which it could be accepted, West could not withdraw the offer before the expiration of a reasonable period of time.
6. If Young paid $10 to West for a written option exercisable for 30 days to purchase the system, West may withdraw the offer only by a written communication to Young.

**Solutions:** (1) F, (2) F, (3) F, (4) F, (5) F, (6) F

REMEMBER: As already mentioned, an offer is not a contract and therefore cannot be assigned. Consequently, it can be accepted only by the offeree.

REMEMBER: Unless the offer has been terminated in one of the previously stated ways, an offer is accepted when the offeree manifests his assent. In other words, when the offeree mails the letter, dispatches the telegram, makes the phone call, etc. If, however, the offer explicitly states that acceptance must be received by a certain date, acceptance is effective when it is received by the offeror, not when it is sent by the offeree.

**EXAMPLE:**

On June 1, 1975, Markum Realty, Inc., offered to sell one acre of land in an industrial park it owned to Johnson Enterprises, Inc. The offer was by mail and, in addition to the other usual terms, stated: "This offer will expire on July 2, 1975, unless acceptance is received by the offeror on or before said date."

Johnson decided to purchase the tract of land and on July 1, telegraphed its acceptance to Markum. The acceptance telegram was delayed due to the negligence of the telegraph company which had admitted that delivery was not made to Markum until July 3. Markum decided not to sell to Johnson because it had received a better offer, but it remained silent and did not notify Johnson of its decision.

When Johnson did not hear from Markum by July 11, its president called the president of Markum and inquired when Johnson might expect to receive the formalized copy of the contract the two companies had entered into. Markum's president responded that there was no contract.

**Required:**

Did a contract result from the above described dealings between Markum and Johnson? Discuss the legal implications of *each* communication between the parties in your explanation.

**Solution:**

No. Markum's offer to Johnson dated June 1, 1975, specifically stipulated that the acceptance must be received by Markum on or before July 2, 1975. Even though Johnson dispatched its acceptance by telegram on July 1, 1975, the offer had expired or terminated on July 2, 1975, because the acceptance had not been received by Markum on that date. The delay by the telegraph company is irrelevant to the relations between Markum and Johnson. Even if Johnson had used the same means of communication (the mails), its acceptance would have had to reach Markum on July 2, 1975, to be a valid acceptance because this was a specific stipulation in the offer.

Under the circumstances, Markum's silence does not constitute an acceptance of Johnson's telegram. The telegram must be considered a counteroffer because it arrived after the expiration date of Markum's original offer. Markum had no obligation to reply, and its actions were legally correct. Hence, because the terms of the offer were not met, no contract resulted from the dealings between Markum and Johnson.

REMEMBER:  Once the offer is accepted, the contract is formed.

## Question 2:  Has legally sufficient consideration been exchanged?

Notice we are not just talking about consideration in general here, but about *legally sufficient consideration.* To be legally sufficient, the consideration which one party gives to the other must be something the former is not otherwise legally obligated to give. Legally sufficient consideration can also be doing something which one is not legally bound to do, or not doing something which one is not legally forbidden to do. In other words, the party giving something must suffer a legal detriment and/or the party receiving the consideration must receive a legal benefit (that is, something which he has no previous legal right to receive in terms of either money, services, and the like). Legally sufficient consideration does not mean the same thing as adequate consideration. If two parties agree to exchange certain services for $10, the consideration is legal (providing the paying party does not owe the receiving party the $10 from a previous debt), although it may not be adequate. If Mr. X agrees to sell a pin to Mr. Y for $10, the contract between the two is enforceable even if X delivers the pin to a third party (at Y's request) or a third party remits payment to X.

Consider the following illustration to further demonstrate the concept of legal detriment and legal benefit:

Suppose that Mr. X performed services for Mr. Y and in exchange received a note for $1,000, which will mature in one year. When the note becomes due, they reach an agreement to the effect that if Y gives X $750, X will accept that sum and cancel the balance due. In fact, X even writes "paid in full" on the note. If afterwards X decides to sue Y to recover the unpaid $250, he will succeed, because legally sufficient consideration had not been exchanged when they agreed that the debt was paid in full at the time the $750 was handed over: Y was legally bound to pay X that $750 (and more) when it came due, so he suffered no legal detriment, and X had the legal right to receive the $750 (and more), so he received no legal benefit when it was paid. If, however, Y paid the $750 two months before it was due and X wrote "paid in full" on the note, legally sufficient consideration would have been exchanged, because Y was under no legal obligation to pay the note early and X had no legal right to receive the money two months early.

Several other concepts with regard to consideration are:

• A promise to give someone a gift is not enforceable; in a gift situation, the promisee gives no consideration to bind the promisor.

• An attempt to use past consideration to bind a promise will not work. You cannot give someone $100 in January and then try to use that $100 as consideration in July.

• A subsequent modification of a contract for the sale of goods can be enforced without subsequent consideration to bind the modification, as long as both contracting parties agree to the modification. The modification of any other kind of contract needs consideration to bind it.

• Consideration may be liquidated or unliquidated. If the promisee has agreed to pay $50 in exchange for what he will receive, the debt is said to be liquidated; both parties know in advance how much the consideration is. A debt is said to be unliquidated if, at the time the contract is entered into, neither party knows exactly how much the debt will wind up being. Nevertheless, an unliquidated debt does involve a definite obligation to pay, although the exact amount will be calculated at some future time.

• A promise to pay a debt which has either been discharged in bankruptcy or is barred by the Statute of Limitations will be enforced without consideration, because both of these promises have definite legal obligations behind them.

• If two contracting parties have not exchanged legally sufficient consideration but, in reasonably expecting it to be forthcoming, one has substantially changed his position, the other is not allowed to claim lack of consideration as a basis for not fulfilling his end of the bargain. The basis of liability lies in the *doctrine of promissory estoppel*; the party is estopped from pleading lack of consideration. A minor change in one's position is not enough to allow him to rely on the doctrine of promissory estoppel.

**Question 3: Do the contracting parties have the capacity to enter into a contract?**

The law does not confer upon everyone the right to enter into a contract; for various reasons an individual's ability to do so might be limited at a particular time in his life. The following classes of people have either permanently or temporarily limited legal capacity to enter into a contract:

1. *Minors:* There is no national definition of minority (also called infancy). Each jurisdiction has its own statutes, which sets its own definition of minority, although 18 or 21 are the most commonly accepted times at which one reaches his majority. An individual can claim the rights of a minor even if he is married and no longer being supported by his parents (if he is *emancipated*), as long as he is within the statutory age limit. In almost every instance, whether the minor is suing or is being sued, a contract which he has entered into can be avoided if he so chooses. It is necessary to have a firm grasp of two concepts in order to have a command over the legal implications of a minor's contract:

a. *Executory/executed contract:* If a contract is executory, it has not been completely performed. From a minor's point of view, he has not received the goods he has purchased, or the services for which he has contracted have not been fully performed. If the contract is executed, the minor has received everything that he is supposed to, either in terms of consideration, goods, services, or the like.

**EXAMPLE (Multiple Choice):**

A contract is said to be executory when
   a. Any of the obligations thereunder remain to be performed.
   b. All of the obligations thereunder have been performed.
   c. It is in writing.
   d. It is informal.

**Solution: (a)**

b. *Necessary/nonnecessary items:* An item which is necessary for the minor to live or to maintain himself in his particular station in life is called a necessary item. If the item is a luxury, it is a nonnecessary. This is a subjective determination; each case must be determined on its own facts. What may be a necessary item for one minor may be a luxury for another in a different situation.

With this in mind, and assuming the minor is being sued for nonpayment, the following rules apply: If an executed contract is involved, the minor is only bound to return the merchandise if it is a nonnecessary item, assuming he has it, no matter what condition it is in. He also has the right to have his consideration returned to him. As far as a necessary item is concerned, the minor has to pay for it, but he only has to pay the price that is considered reasonable, not the price originally agreed upon, should they differ. The merchant has the burden of proving that the item is necessary. If he can, his recovery in this case is not based upon a contract, but upon what is called a *quasi-contract* — that is, a contract wherein liability is implied and then imposed according to what a product or services are reasonably worth. If an executory contract is involved — for either a necessary or a nonnecessary item — the minor can completely avoid the contract, although an adult promisor is bound to complete the contract if the minor wishes him to.

If the minor, however, is suing to disaffirm the contract, the rules are identical except for one case: If the contract is executed and the merchandise sold to the minor has been damaged or lost, a minority of jurisdictions will rule that while the minor can have his consideration returned to him, he will have to pay for damages.

Remember that a minor's contract is not automatically void; it is simply voidable (in most cases) at his option. An adult cannot claim a minor's lack of capacity. If a minor exercises his power of avoidance while he is a minor, he is said to have *disaffirmed* the contract. He can disaffirm through words or conduct either before or after he reaches his majority. When he reaches his majority, a minor may *ratify* a contract, either in an express or implied manner, after which he cannot go back and then disaffirm it. Implied ratification is seen in a minor's continual use of a product or in his not returning the product reasonably soon after having received it.

It becomes apparent, then, that an adult should give careful thought to entering into a contract with someone he knows is a minor. It may happen that he will enter into a contract with someone who actually is a minor but represents himself to be otherwise. There is no uniform agreement in this instance as to how to treat a contract when a minor misrepresents his age. According to the majority view, however, a minor can still rescind his contract; according to the minority view, he cannot.

**EXAMPLE (True/False):**

Fowler, an adult, knew that Youngblood, 19 years old, was very knowledgeable about automobiles.

Fowler orally authorized Youngblood to buy him a second-hand automobile from Best Auto Deals, Inc. for a price not to exceed $400.

   1. The appointment of Youngblood as agent is void because of his infancy.
   2. Fowler and Youngblood may each disaffirm the agency relationship because of Youngblood's infancy.
   3. Fowler may not disaffirm any contract made with Best by Youngblood on his behalf by asserting Youngblood's infancy.
   4. Best may disaffirm the contract made with Fowler, through Youngblood, by asserting Youngblood's infancy.

**Solutions:** (1) F, (2) F, (3) T, (4) F

2. *Drunks:* If a person is so drunk at the time he enters into a contract that he does not understand what he has gotten himself into (whether he got himself drunk or another party got him drunk), he may avoid his contract if he wishes to when he sobers up. He also may choose to ratify it. As in the case of a minor, a person is liable for the reasonable value of any necessary items he purchased while drunk.

3. *Insane people:* If a person has been judged insane by a court before entering into a contract, his contract is void, as opposed to voidable. His contractual capacity is not limited, it is nonexistent and any contract he may have entered into is nonexistent, as well. However, if he was not an adjudicated lunatic, the contract is voidable or ratifiable at his option when he becomes lucid, or by his guardian or a representative after his death. He too is liable in quasi-contract for the reasonable value of any necessaries he purchased while mentally incompetent to understand the legal implications of his actions.

4. Miscellaneous situations involving limited contractual capacity:

   • *Convicts* do not have a limited capacity to enter into a contract. They can legally enter into a contract and seek remedies to enforce one in a court of law.

   • If an *alien* is in this country illegally, he may enter into a contract, but he cannot expect the courts to help him enforce it.

   • *Corporations* may enter into contracts if the state incorporation statutes confer contractual capacity upon them.

## Question 4: Is the activity in which the contracting parties have promised to engage legal?

Illegal contracts are void, and therefore they are not enforceable. A contract will be illegal if it is clearly against the law or if it is not strictly against statutory law but is against public policy in that it tends to be detrimental to the public at large or to the public good. Though public policy cases are each judged independently and on their own merits, a contract will usually fall within this category if it is:

1. A promise by someone not to press charges, to give false testimony, or to conceal evidence in favor of someone who has broken the law. To obstruct justice, it is felt, is to go against public policy.

2. A covenant not to compete which is unreasonably restrictive with respect to time and location. In general, though, convenants not to compete are sanctioned, because they protect a business's goodwill.

3. A promise to "take care of" a public official if he will influence legislation to your benefit. Bribes are illegal, and a promise to bribe is unenforceable.

### The Statute of Frauds:

The Statute of Frauds was written just about three centuries ago. Its original purpose was to prevent a party from defrauding another or from committing perjury in order to prove that certain transactions took place. Two sections of the original statute (sections 4 and 17) pertained to contracts, and their elements have been incorporated into statutory law in almost every state. Both sections stipulate which kinds of contracts must be in writing in order to be enforceable, but section 17 deals exclusively with the sale of goods and, as reenacted in the UCC, with a sale of goods costing $500 or more. Not every type of contract which must be in writing today was covered in the original Statute of Frauds; many jurisdictions have amended the list so that the contract to make a will or to pay a commission to a real estate broker or to authorize an agent to sell real estate must be in writing in many states. Unless some statute in the relevant jurisdiction requires a contract to be in writing in order to be enforceable, an oral contract can be binding. However, if a contract not originally within the statute is brought within the statute through modification, the modified contract must be in writing to be enforced.

The following promises or contracts, then, must be in writing to be enforceable and, as such, are said to be "within the statute":

1.  Marriage settlements. Today these are commonly referred to as marriage contracts or antenuptial agreements. These promises involve some kind of transfer of property or money, though not necessarily to or by the perspective bride or groom. These contracts are quite different from simple promises to marry, which do not have to be in writing but must bear all the other characteristics of an enforceable contract, to be enforced.

2.  Agreements which cannot possibly be fully performed within one year from the time the agreement is made (as opposed to when the activity begins). Obviously, if it can possibly be performed within one year, it is "without," or not within the statute. There is one exception to this rule to keep in mind. If one party to a bilateral contract has completely performed his obligation, the duties of the other party are enforceable even though by the terms of the contract it did not seem possible for performance to be fully completed within one year. For instance, suppose Mr. X orally promises to pay Mr. Y $1,000 in four annual installments of $250 each as consideration for Y's used car (thereby implying a contract which will be fulfilled in four years) and Y delivers the car the day they enter into the agreement. X's promise will be enforced, despite the one-year requirement, that is, despite the fact that the original contract did not seem performable in less than a year, since Y has fully performed his part of the contract.

**EXAMPLE (Multiple Choice):**

On May 1, 1976, James Arthur orally agreed to a contract as a sales representative of Wonder Insurance Company. The contract terminates April 30, 1977, and provides for $10,000 salary plus 1% of the insurance premiums charged by the company on the policies which he writes. Under these circumstances
   a.  Arthur is an undisclosed principal.
   b.  The contract in question is *not* subject to the Statute of Frauds.
   c.  Arthur would be permitted to delegate his performance to another equally competent person.
   d.  Arthur's contract is too indefinite and uncertain to be enforceable.

**Solution:** (b)

3.  An estate executor's promise to use his own funds to pay off some or all of the decendent's debts.

4.  A promise to pay someone else's debt if that party defaults. Notice the effect that the condition "if he defaults" has on this type of promise: The promise involves secondary liability — that is, liability in case the primary debtor defaults. If, however, the person making the promise simply says "I promise to pay his debts" without any conditional "if he defaults" added, the courts will interpret this as an original promise whereby the promisor is making a debt of his own, and this does not have to be in writing in order to

be enforced unless goods costing $500 or more are involved. In addition, based on the concept of the *leading object* or the *main purpose doctrine,* a promise to answer for the debts of another if he defaults does not have to be in writing if the promisor stands to benefit from the arrangement. So, in a situation where X promises to pay Y's debts if Y does not himself, because X wants to buy some merchandise from Y which will be repossessed if Y does not pay his bills, X clearly benefits from this promise to pay. As such, the promise does not have to be in writing to be enforceable.

**EXAMPLE:**

Albert Gideon, Jr., doing business as Albert's Boutique, ordered $480 of mini-skirts from Abaco Fashions. Abaco refused to make delivery, having had previous collection problems with Gideon. Albert's father, Slade Gideon, a prominent manufacturer, called Abaco and said, "Ship the goods my son needs, and I will pay for them." Abaco delivered the mini-skirts, and they were received by Albert's Boutique. Albert's Boutique is in bankruptcy, and Slade Gideon refuses to pay. You are the accountant for Abaco Fashions.

**Required:**

What are Abaco's rights against Slade Gideon?

**Solution:**

Abaco can proceed successfully against Slade Gideon to collect the debt. Slade Gideon created a direct obligation to Abaco (a third-party beneficiary contract) by his statement, "Ship the goods my son needs, and I will pay for them." The Statute of Frauds is not at issue because the debt is for less than $500. Were the Statute of Frauds at issue, it would have been satisfied by the shipment of the merchandise by Abaco and its receipt by Albert's Boutique.

5.  A contract involving a sale of land or interests in that land (including certain easements, leases, mortgages). A concept similar to promissory estoppel, called the *part performance doctrine* plays a role here. According to that theory, if a seller and buyer enter into an oral contract to sell land and, having relied upon the seller's promise, the buyer pays a portion of the amount due and improves the land, the courts will prohibit the seller from disaffirming the contract because it was not in writing. The courts estop the seller from asserting the Statute of Frauds in order to prohibit his unjust enrichment.

6.  An agreement between merchants involving the sale of goods costing $500 or more. The UCC defines *goods* as all things, particularly those that are manufactured, "which are moveable at the time of identification to the contract for sale." If a written agreement leaves out certain terms or states some terms incorrectly, it is not totally unenforceable; however, it is not enforceable beyond the quantity stated in the written contract. There are certain exceptions to this rule that should be remembered. If a contract to sell or purchase goods is valid in all other respects except that it is not in writing, it will be enforced if:

 • The goods are specifically manufactured for the buyer and are not suitable for resale by the seller in the ordinary course of business and, before notice of cancellation, the seller/manufacturer made substantial progress in manufacturing the goods or in procuring the materials used in their manufacture; or

 • The buyer or seller (the party against whom enforcement is sought) admits in court that a contract for sale was made for a particular quantity;

**EXAMPLE (Multiple Choice):**

An oral contract for the sale of goods for a price in excess of $500 is enforceable by the seller if
 a. The goods are generally suitable for sale to others in the ordinary course of the seller's business.
 b. The buyer admits in court that the contract was made.

    c. Payment has *not* yet been made by the buyer.

    d. The goods have been received but *not* accepted by the buyer.

**Solution:** (b)

- Payment has already been made and accepted, or the goods have already been received and accepted; or

- A written confirmation of the transaction has been sent within a reasonable time and is sufficient against the sender, and the other party does not send a written objection within ten days after receipt.

7. A contract for the sale or purchase of stocks and bonds (which does not necessarily have to be between merchants), even if the purchase price is less than $500. Again, as with manufactured goods, payment and acceptance of the purchase price or receipt and acceptance of the stock certificates will render an oral contract enforceable, as will either testimony in court that a contract was entered into or a written confirmation of the transaction that was sent and not objected to within ten days.

8. A contract for the sale of personal property (other than the goods and securities already mentioned), including intangibles, for a purchase price of more than $5,000.

Notice in all these cases that mere evidence of a written contract will not lead to an enforceable contract, unless all other elements necessary to bind a promise are present.

To comply with the Statute of Frauds:

1. The writing may be in pencil or pen, or it may be typewritten.

2. The party against whom enforcement is sought — the defendent — must have signed the written document. (The UCC does not require both parties to sign the document.)

3. The document should be reasonably specific regarding the parties involved, state any material terms, and identify the subject of the transaction.

**Assignment of contractual rights and delegation of contractual duties:**

When the rights of a contract are assigned or the duties of a contract are delegated, contract law is expanded to include the rights and duties of *third parties* — those persons who were not original parties to the contract but who have become parties to the contract by virtue of assignment.

An assignment of a right to a third party, which may be written or oral, has the effect of putting the *assignee* (the third party) in the shoes of the *assignor* (the person assigning the rights). Consequently, the assignee has the same rights against the person owing the obligation as the assignor did, and also takes the assignment with all of its defects or defenses which the other original contracting party had against the assignor. Upon effective assignation of his rights, the assignor gives up those rights with respect to the obligor. Remember: A promise to assign rights is not an assignment of rights. Therefore, if Mr. X promises to assign Mr. Y his right to collect a debt from Mr. Z, but does not, in fact, assign that right, Y cannot collect from Z, although the promise may be enforceable and thereby enable Y to proceed against X. Remember: An offer, which is revocable, is not assignable; a contractual right is irrevocable and thus assignable.

While the rights under a contract are almost always assignable, duties cannot be assigned. Under certain circumstances, though, and with the consent of the person to whom the duty of performance is owing (the obligee), the performance of some duties may be delegated to a third party. They cannot be delegated, however, if the duties involve the performance of services of a highly personal nature (nor can rights to receive very personal services be assigned).

In cases where credit has been extended or risk assumed, duties cannot be delegated either. Accordingly, neither a famous movie star who is supposed to make a personal appearance, nor a person buying on credit, nor a person who has taken out an insurance policy can delegate their contractual duties to a third party. Even in cases where duties have been legally delegated to a third party, the original obligor is liable to the obligee until the duties have been satisfactorily performed or unless the obligor enters into a contract with the third party — and with the consent of the obligee — to effectively discharge him of his duties and substitute the third party in his place. This is called a *novation.*

An assignee's rights against a debtor are lost when the obligor fulfills his obligations. This can be accomplished if the debtor pays the assignee directly, or if he is unaware of the assignment and so pays the assignor — the original creditor. Whereas duties in and of themselves are, in principal, not assignable, an assignee assumes the contractual duties of an assignor and implicitly promises to perform them when he accepts assigned contractual rights. This promise is enforceable by the other original obligee or by the assignor.

Except for the right to have highly personal services performed by the original obligor, the owner of legally assignable contractual rights — whether he is the original owner or a subsequent assignee — has complete control over those rights. He can break the rights up and assign separate portions to any number of assignees; an assignee can, in turn, in an action called a *subassignment,* reassign the rights to still another assignee or group of assignees, who will then have all the rights and duties of the original assignee. An assignee can even assign the same rights to more than one assignee and, though this is fraudulent, it is often done. The problem resulting, of course, is to whom does the debtor pay his obligation when there is more than one assignee? The prevailing view is that the first assignee — not the first one to give notice to the debtor, but the first one to whom the fraudulent assignor assigned his rights — is entitled to the proceeds.

When two parties enter into a contract which stipulates that a particular third party — who is not one of the contracting parties — will benefit, the question is no longer one of assigned rights to an assignee, but one of a *third party beneficiary.* Thus, if X owes an obligation to a creditor and enters into a contract with Y such that Y promises to satisfy that outstanding debt in exchange for agreed upon consideration from X, X's creditor becomes a third party creditor beneficiary. (Notice the difference between a contract involving a third party beneficiary, who exists at the time the contract is entered into and is known to all contracting parties, and an assignee, who does not necessarily exist at the time the contract is entered into.) Both the original debtor and contracting debtor are liable to a third party creditor beneficiary, and the latter can sue both parties separately if neither one performs.

If the third party is to receive something from a beneficiary contract to which he has no prior legal right, such as a gift, he is a *third party donee beneficiary.* A third party has no right to sue his donor for nonperformance, but he can go against the other party who contracted to act as a conduit for the donor. A third party donee beneficiary cannot be divested of his rights without his consent.

If a third party is simply an *incidental beneficiary,* he has no rights under the contract. For example, if X and Y contract to build a motel on a plot of land which happens to be adjacent to Z's gas station, Z is merely an incidental beneficiary and cannot go against either X or Y, regardless to what extent he may have changed his position in relying on the coming event, should their contract be revoked or breached.

**Termination of contractual duties:**

The duties imposed upon contracting parties terminate when the contract is discharged. A contract can be discharged in many ways, some of them legal and some of them illegal. When a contract is illegally breached, the victim can look to the courts for a remedy.

1. *Methods of discharging contracts:*

    a. *Performance:* Full performance of contractual duties by one or both contracting parties discharges one or both parties from all obligations. Partial performance will not result in a full discharge, although it will prevent the other party from claiming nonperformance as an excuse for his not performing his duties or obligations.

    b. *Preventing a party from performing his duties:* If one party prevents the other from performing his contractual duties or prevents the occurrence of a condition upon which performance is based, the party whose performance has been interfered with is discharged from his contractual obligations.

    c. *A contract is entered into to end the contract:* This is known as *mutual recision.* It discharges contractual duties when the parties agree to terminate the prior contract and support their agreement with mutually agreed upon consideration. The conventional consideration furnished is each party's giving up his legal rights as stipulated in the rescinded contract. Unless otherwise stated in the former contract, or unless the former contract was within the Statute of Frauds, the subsequent contract can be oral, just as long as all the elements of an enforceable contract are present.

    d. *Breach:* If one party does not perform, without having any legal basis for not doing so, he breaches the contract. The obligations which the contract had imposed upon the victim are consequently terminated. Keep in mind that there is a difference between nonperformance of contractual duties, in which case the victim may seek damages in a court of law, and the nonoccurrence of a condition upon which performance is based, in which case the victim cannot seek damages unless the condition was prevented from happening by the nonperforming party. For example, if Mr. X promises to pay Mr. Y $3,000 for Y's boat and Y delivers the boat but X does not deliver the $3,000, X is liable to Y for breach of contract. But if X promises to pay $3,000 for Y's boat only on the condition that the boat wins its next race and, in fact, it comes in second, X is not liable to Y for breach of contract unless X in some way prevented the boat from coming in first.

    If one party knows before his obligation is due that he will not perform, the nonrepudiating party is discharged from his obligations and, in addition, may sue immediately for breach of contract, even though he is only faced with an *anticipatory breach.* If the nonrepudiating party has not materially changed his situation because of the anticipatory breach, or has not discharged the contract, the repudiating party can rescind his repudiation, although he may be required to sign a statement to the effect that he assures performance.

    e. *Change in the material provisions of the contract:* Any material alteration of the contract by one of the contracting parties discharges the other from performing his duties under the original contract.

    f. *The contract subsequently becomes illegal:* If the subject of the contract was legal when entered into, but subsequently becomes illegal, both parties are excused from performing their contractual obligations.

    g. *The contract becomes impossible to perform:* If the contract becomes impossible for both parties to perform their contractual duties, the contract is discharged and they are both relieved of any liability to the other party. If only one party cannot possibly perform his duties, he will generally not be liable for nonperformance if the duties are *objectively impossible* to perform — that is, if no one else could perform the duties either. An example of a duty objectively impossible to perform would be if a race car driver contracts to drive a particular car in a race and the car blows up before the race. If, however, the duty is *subjectively impossible* to perform (that is, the obligor personally cannot perform, but someone else might be able to), then the obligor will be held liable for nonperformance. An example of such a situation would be that of a debtor who assigns his wages to a creditor in satisfaction of a debt, and is then fired from his job. Such a debtor will still have to meet his financial obligation to his creditor.

h. *A debtor becomes an adjudicated bankrupt:* If a debtor complies with the Bankruptcy Act and is judged bankrupt in court, he is discharged from paying certain kinds of debts. This type of discharge and the kinds of debts which can be discharged in this manner, are fully discussed in Chapter 5, Bankruptcy.

2. *Remedies of breach:* In determining the remedies which an aggrieved party can get, a court will attempt to put that party in the same position he would have been in had the breaching party fully performed his contractual duties. With this in mind, courts offer the following remedies for breach of contract:

a. The best remedy a plaintiff could hope to get, and one which the courts sometimes award, is that of *specific performance* — that is, the defendant is required to do exactly what he had contracted to do originally. Certain types of contracts are always specifically enforceable and other never are. Examples of the former and latter respectively are contracts to buy and sell land and contracts involving personal services. The remedy of specific performance is usually decreed only when the contractual promise relates to some unique property (real or personal) and the terms of the promise are clear.

**EXAMPLE (Multiple Choice):**

The remedy of specific performance is available where the subject matter of the contract involves

    a. Services.      b. Goods with a price of $500 or more.     c. Fraud.     d. Land.

**Solution**: (d)

b. Another remedy is that of awarding money to the plaintiff. This remedy is always available for almost any breach of contract. If the court awards a sum such that upon receiving that amount the plaintiff is put in the same or similar financial position he would have been in had all the contractual obligations been fully performed, the court has awarded *compensatory damages*. If the plaintiff cannot show that he has suffered a loss as a result of the breach, but he wants to sue the defendant for breach anyway, the court may allow him to recover a very small amount — such as $1.00 and costs — and, as such, will have awarded the plaintiff *nominal damages*. *Exemplary or punitive damages* are usually awarded in a tort case involving malicious acts, and not in a breach of contract case. In awarding punitive damages, a judge's purpose is to impose upon the defendant a financial burden much greater than just the loss the plaintiff has suffered, in order to teach the defendant a lesson and set an example for others to see as a means of discouraging similar torts in the future.

c. Sometimes a contract will specifically state a sum to be paid by a nonperforming party if he should breach the contract. This sum is called *liquidated damages*. The contractual provision for them will be enforced in court only if the stipulated amount is reasonable and the loss caused by the breach would be very hard to estimate under normal circumstances. If the amount of liquidated damages is unreasonable — that is, if it does not represent a fair estimate of a probable loss in the event of a breach — the provision for liquidated damages will not be enforced.

d. Another remedy available for breach of contract is *restitution*, in which case the defendant must return to the plaintiff the consideration, or its value, which the latter gave to bind the promise. In this case, then, the court attempts to put the plaintiff back in the position he was in before he entered into the contract, as opposed to the position he would have been in had the contract been fully performed.

## Parol evidence rule:

As already mentioned, any contract that does not fall within the Statute of Frauds is enforceable even if it is oral, as long as the requisite elements are present. Despite the fact that most oral contracts are enforceable, many contracting parties prefer to have all the terms of the contract — whether material or not — set down in writing and signed by both parties, attesting to the fact that the document is their complete contract wherein all the terms both parties want in the contract are written down. Such an agreement is called an *integrated contract*. The parol evidence rule says that in the case of an integrated contract, no evidence, whether oral or written, which is extrinsic to the written integrated agreement will be allowed to change or modify or alter any of the terms of the contract. As with any rule, there are several exceptions. The rule does not apply:

1.  To an oral recision of the original contract or an oral modification, as long as the oral modification is subsequent to the written integrated contract, and the original contract was not within the Statute of Frauds.

**EXAMPLE (Multiple Choice):**

The parol evidence rule
- a. Requires that certain types of contracts be in writing.
- b. Precludes the use of oral testimony to show that a written contract was fraudulently obtained.
- c. Eliminates the requirement of consideration if the rule is satisfied.
- d. Does *not* prohibit a subsequent oral modification of a written contract.

**Solution:** (d)

2.  To substantiate the fact that a written agreement is void or voidable because one of the parties lacks contractual capacity. (That is, one of the parties was intoxicated or insane when he entered into the contract.)

3.  If the original contract was partly oral and partly written.

4.  If there is an obvious gross error in the written contract.

5.  To prove a lack of real consent, as in cases of undue influence, duress, fraud, or to prove illegality of the written contract's subject matter.

**EXAMPLE:**

Your client, Super Fashion Frocks, Inc., agreed in writing to purchase $520 worth of coat hangers from Display Distributors, Inc., with payment terms of net/30 after delivery. Delivery was to be made within five days from the signing of the contract. Two days prior to the due date for delivery, Display Distributors called and offered a flat $25 discount if payment were made upon delivery instead of the original net/30 terms. Super Fashion Frocks agreed and tendered its check for $495 upon delivery. Display Distributors cashed the check and now seeks to enforce the original contract calling for payment of $520 (i.e., seeks to recover $25 from Super Fashion). It bases its claim upon the following arguments:

1.  The Statute of Frauds applies to the contract modification.

2.  The Parol Evidence Rule prohibits the introduction of oral evidence modifying the terms of a written agreement.

3.  There was no consideration given for Display's promise to take a lesser amount.

**Required:**

Discuss the validity of each argument.

**Solution:**

1. The Statute of Frauds is not applicable because the dollar amount is less than $500 after the modification. Since the contract as modified is not included under the Statute of Frauds, the statute has no impact upon the contractual adjustment made by the parties. The Uniform Commercial Code provides that if a modification is agreed upon, it need not be in writing as long as the contract is not within the Statute of Frauds.

2. The Parol Evidence rule has no application to the facts stated. It prohibits the contradiction of the written terms of a contract by any prior oral agreement or a contemporaneous oral agreement. It is not applicable to a subsequent oral modification of a written contract.

3. Under the Uniform Commercial Code an agreement to modify a contract for the sale of goods requires no consideration. But, even if consideration were necessary, Super Fashion provided consideration by paying earlier than required by the terms of the original agreement. Thus, Super Fashion prevails under either rule.

REMEMBER: Forty-nine states and the District of Columbia have adopted the Uniform Commercial Code. However, in some instances the jurisdictions have altered or eliminated certain sections to accommodate their legal philosophies. If there are contradictions in applicable contract law from one jurisdiction to another, the contract law of the state where the contract was entered into will govern, even if a court action regarding that contract takes place in another jurisdiction with contradicting laws. Where a contract involves real property, however, the law of the jurisdiction in which the property is located will govern. In both cases, if the contract specifies the state to have jurisdiction, then the state in which the contract was entered into or where the real property is located becomes unimportant; the governing state will be that one specified in the contract.

# 2 Sales

A major part of the law which applies to sales is covered in the previous chapter on general contract law. This is because a sale transaction is basically a contract between a buyer and seller. There are some rules, however, which apply specifically to sales of goods or contracts between merchants (those people who regularly deal in selling goods as an occupation), and it is those exceptions to or modifications of general contract law which this chapter covers. Most of the information in this section comes from Article 2 of the Uniform Commercial Code, which is simply entitled Sales. (In an attempt to present the material as concisely as possible, points made in the previous chapter which refer specifically to a contract for a sale of goods have not been repeated here. The reader is advised to reread Chapter 1 after having finished this chapter and focus again on those particular points in order to integrate the subject matter.)

The key concept around which the law of sales revolves is that of transfer of title to the goods in question from the seller to the buyer, in exchange for consideration transferred from the buyer to the seller. In the area of sales, consideration is almost always synonymous with selling price. The transfer of title is an important element in determining which party to the sale transaction bears the risk of loss or the burden of paying for damage. While delivery of goods and transfer of title are intimately connected, they do not always necessarily go hand in hand. There are no specific laws that determine at which point in time title must pass from the seller to the buyer; the two parties can determine between themselves when they intend for title to pass, with or without referring to when the goods are delivered. Title can pass at any time, on any conditions, and in any way to which they agree. The seller and buyer do not necessarily have to make that determination at the time the contract is entered into, unless they are entering into a *conditional sales agreement*. The seller and buyer do not always explicitly state in an ordinary sales contract when title will pass from one to the other. Accordingly, the UCC fills in this void when it exists by stipulating that title to the goods passes from seller to buyer:

- When and where the *seller completes his performance* by delivering the goods.

- When and where the *seller ships the goods*, if the contract authorizes or requires the seller to send the goods, but does not require him to deliver them to the buyer at a particular destination.

- When the *seller tenders the goods* to the buyer at a particular destination, if the contract requires delivery there.

- When and where the *seller delivers a document of title*, if the contract requires delivery of title without requiring delivery of goods.

- When and where *the contract is entered into*, if the contract requires neither delivery of a document of title nor the moving of goods.

In all cases, title can be transferred only if and when the goods in question exist and are specifically indentified in the contract.

Up until the time the buyer accepts the goods — at which point he owns and takes title to them — he can reject them or, if he has already accepted them, he can revoke them if he finds that they don't conform to the contract. The buyer, however, must notify the seller of his rejection or revocation and do so within a reasonable time in order for it to be effective. A proper or legal rejection or justified revocation of the goods passes title back to the seller if it had already passed to the buyer.

If the seller must assume risk of damage to or loss of goods, he loses his right to collect the purchase price from the buyer; if the buyer must assume it, he must pay the full purchase price regardless of the fact that the goods may have been damaged or lost. The risk of damage or loss is imposed on the party who has title to the goods.

Besides the rules already mentioned, the other major provisions in the UCC with regard to title and the assumption of risk of damage or loss are as follows:

1.  A *sale on approval* is where the buyer takes possession of the goods, without taking title, for a specified or reasonable period of time, during which he decides if he will ultimately buy them or not. The seller assumes the risks. Title passes, as does imposition of risk, when the buyer manifests his approval explicitly, by failing to notify the seller within a reasonable or stipulated period of time that he does not approve them, or by actually using the goods.

**EXAMPLE (Multiple Choice):**

Under a contract for sale on approval, unless otherwise agreed, what happens to "risk of loss" and "title" upon delivery to the buyer?
  a.  Risk of loss but *not* title passes to buyer.
  b.  Title but *not* risk of loss passes to buyer.
  c.  Risk of loss and title pass to buyer.
  d.  *Neither* risk of loss *nor* title pass to buyer.

**Solution:** (d)

2.  A *sale or return* is a sale wherein title and imposition of risk passes to the buyer in exchange for consideration, even though he has the option to return the goods to the seller. If he decides to exercise that option, the imposition of risk and title return to the seller only after the goods are actually returned — not when the buyer notifies the seller that he will be returning the merchandise. During transit from returning buyer to seller, the risk and title remain with the former.

3.  *F.O.B.* means *free on board*. Goods may be shipped *fob shipping point*, in which case title and imposition of risk passes to the buyer, who also pays for transportation, when the goods are shipped from the seller's warehouse. On the other hand, goods may be shipped *fob destination*, in which case title and assumption of risk pass to the buyer when the goods arrive at his warehouse, and the seller pays the freight costs.

As the buyer and seller can form their own agreement as to when title passes, so can they also form their own agreement as to who shall bear the risks at which point in time. They can, if they wish, agree to transfer title without transferring the imposition of risk or, regardless of their agreement as to title, they can share the risk between themselves. The point here is that the UCC provisions are applied only when the sales agreement does not include the appropriate provisions.

A *contract to sell* is distinguished from a *sale* in that the former involves a usually enforceable agreement or promise to transfer title at sometime in the future, while the latter is an actual transfer of title taking place in the present. Not every transfer of goods from one party to another involves a transfer of title, and not every transfer of title involves a sale. A transfer of goods which does not involve a transfer of title is a *bailment*. (Leaving your shirts at a laundry is an example of this.) A transfer of title which does not involve a sale, because no consideration has been exchanged, is a *gift*. When personal property is transferred as security for an outstanding debt, but title to it is not, the property is said to be *pledged*. However, if title to that property is transferred as security and, as such, it has been *conditionally transferred* (because title will vest in the transferee only on the condition that the debt is not repaid), the instrument of transfer is a *chattel mortgage*. A *conditional sale contract* is one in which the seller transfers the goods, but the buyer has not paid the full purchase price. As such, the seller retains title until the conditional event happens upon which the full purchase price will be paid. The seller thus retains title as security. Unless otherwise mentioned in the contract, when title has not been transferred but the goods have been, the title holder can demand the return of his goods by *replevin*. In like manner, if consideration has been paid but the goods have not been delivered, the buyer can demand the delivery of his goods by replevin. Should the seller refuse to deliver the goods without a justifiable reason, the buyer is under the obligation to try to find similar goods elsewhere and to attempt to purchase them — that is, he is obligated to try to cover his original purchase. If the buyer succeeds in covering the purchase, he can sue the first seller for *consequential damages* — for the difference between the price he originally contracted to pay and the price he ultimately paid a subsequent seller.

**EXAMPLE (Multiple Choice):**

If a seller repudiates his contract for the sale of 100 radios with a buyer, what recourse does the buyer have?
   a. He can cover, i.e., procure the goods elsewhere and recover the difference.
   b. He can obtain specific performance by the seller.
   c. He can recover punitive damages.
   d. He must await the seller's performance for a commercially reasonable time after repudiation.

**Solution:** (a)


## Express and implied warranties:

When a seller transfers goods to a buyer in exchange for consideration, he assumes certain obligations with regard to those goods, which he owes the buyer. Some of the obligations are imposed by law, and some he assumes voluntarily. Certain obligations may be expressly stated in the contract and others are implied. These obligations are called *warranties*, and if the seller does not live up to them, whether they are express or implied, he can be sued for breach of contract, because a warranty is a contractual obligation.

   1. *Express warranties:* Express warranties are promises made by the seller to the buyer, with respect to the condition and quality of the goods, which are explicitly stated. Express warranties form a basic part of the agreement. If such promises are made before the actual contract of sale, they may be incorporated into the eventual contract. If they are made after the contract is entered into, they may become express warranties only if they are considered modifications of the original agreement. However, if the express warranties are brand new promises, they must be supported by consideration to be enforceable, as they are thus part of a new and separate contract.

The UCC states that express warranties are created by the seller as follows:

   a. If the seller affirms a fact or promise made to the buyer with respect to the goods in question and that affirmation is basic to the bargain, then the seller has expressly warranted that the goods will conform to the fact or promise.

   b. If the goods are actually described in the bargain and the description is basic to the bargain, the seller expressly warrants that the goods will conform to that description.

**EXAMPLE (Multiple Choice):**

In a contract for the sale of goods, express warranties by the seller are created by any
   a. Reasonable implication based upon the seller's acts.
   b. Description of the goods which is made part of the basis of the contract.
   c. Expression of the value of the goods.
   d. Statement of seller's opinion.

**Solution:** (b)

   c. If a sample or model of the goods in question is basic to the bargain, the seller expressly warrants that the goods will conform to the sample or model.

These warranties are enforceable only if the buyer has relied on them in entering into the agreement. However, if they are basic to the bargain, the courts will assume that they have been relied upon.

A seller's statement that he is selling a buyer the best transistor radio around is not an express warranty. A certain amount of latitude is allowed a salesperson who indulges in the common practices of salesmanship. If, however, a salesperson states that the radio's battery is good for 50 hours (which is fact, not opinion) and that statement is basic to the bargain, he has made an express warranty, the breach of which will enable the buyer to successfully sue for damages. If the batteries turn out to be good for only 25 hours, but the seller honestly thought they would be good for 50 hours, he will still be liable for breach of warranty. He is not excused because he made a good faith mistake.

2. *Implied warranties:* Implied warranties are not explicitly spelled out by the seller; they are obligations which are imposed upon him by law, whether expressly stated or not (that is, whether written or oral).

    a. If the seller is a merchant, he automatically warrants *merchantability*. As such, he promises the buyer that the goods he is selling are reasonably fit for their normal use and that they are of average quality.

    b. Any seller (merchant or not) impliedly warrants *fitness for a particular purpose* if he has been told by the buyer or is otherwise aware that the buyer plans to use the goods in a particular way which differs from the normal way the goods are used. The warranty of fitness for a particular purpose must be relied upon by the buyer in order for it to exist and be enforceable.

**EXAMPLE (Multiple Choice):**

Carter purchased goods from Dunn for $450. Dunn orally made an express warranty of fitness of the goods for the particular purpose described by Carter. In addition, Dunn orally disclaimed "all warranty protection." The express warranty of fitness

    a. Is irrelevant in any event, because it is superceded by the Uniform Commercial Code section which creates an implied warranty of fitness.
    b. Is valid even though *not* in writing.
    c. Is effectively negated by the general disclaimer clause assuming both the warranty and disclaimer are in writing.
    d. Coupled with the disclaimer, effectively negates all Carter's implied warranty protection.

**Solution:** (b)

3. *Warranty of title:* The code stipulates that a seller warrants that title to the goods in question is good, that its transfer is rightful, and that the goods will be delivered free from any security interest or any other encumbrance of which the buyer is not aware at the time he enters into the contract.

While a buyer is not required to inspect the goods he is purchasing, he may do so. If he does, and in so doing finds glaring defects, an express warranty will not apply to those defects. There will also be no implied warranty regarding defects which a normal inspection should have revealed. This is so because in both these cases the element of reliance no longer exists. As such, if the buyer does not examine the goods, all existing warranties are usually effective.

A seller may exclude express warranties by simply taking care not to make any promises or references to any samples, models, and the like, with respect to the goods in question. An implied warranty of merchantability and/or of fitness for a particular purpose can be excluded by a seller if he expressly disclaims either one in writing and the disclaimer stands out conspicuously in the contract. In addition, to be effective, a disclaimer of an implied warranty of merchantability must mention the word merchantability. In most cases, simply including, in a conspicuous manner, the phrase "with all faults," or "as is," will effectively disclaim the implied warranty. A warranty of title may be excluded or modified only by specific language and only under special circumstances.

**EXAMPLE:**

Your annual examination of the financial statements of Mars Distribution Corporation revealed that Colossal Computer Co. sold Mars 1,000 desk computers. The contract stated in bold type:

> **The buyer hereby purchases these computers with all faults, and all warranties are hereby expressly excluded.**

After Mars has sold approximately 200 of the computers, three significant problems arose.

- First, Major Computer Components sued Mars for conversion in that one of the major components in Colossal's computers had been stolen from Major's warehouse.

- Second, B.M.I. Computers has indicated that the computers in question infringe its existing patents.

- Third, 90% of the computers sold have proven to be defective.

Mars' customers have claimed that the computers are nonmerchantable. Colossal, when informed of the various problems encountered by Mars, said, "That's your tough luck, we rely on the disclaimer in the contract."

**Required:**

What are the rights of Mars against Colossal? Explain.

**Solution:**

Mars has no right against Colossal for the quality of the goods because of the bold disclaimer in the contract, i.e., that Mars accepted the "computers with all faults." However, Mars may have a right against Colossal on the warranty of title and warranty against patent or other trade infringements implicit in any transaction between merchants. In spite of the general disclaimer, Colossal warranted that it had good title and that the transfer was proper. It also warranted against title impairment resulting from patent and other trade infringements. These warranties may be excluded only by specific wording including knowledge by the customer that the seller is not representing that he has title or by agreement, that title may be impaired by patent or other trade infringements.

# *3* **Secured Transactions**

Secured transactions are covered by Article 9 of the UCC. Most of the definitions in this chapter are taken right from that article.

A *secured transaction* is one which offers a creditor a form of insurance such that, if his debt is not repaid or an obligation not met, he will receive satisfaction by taking possession of certain personal property which belongs to the debtor or obligor. The personal property is called *collateral*, and the protected party is said to be *secured*. There are usually two types of secured transactions, both involving a buyer who does not have, or does not want to spend, his own money to purchase something, or does not have very good credit.

In the first case the seller of the goods lends the buyer the purchase price and retains an interest in the goods that have been sold as security. This interest is called a *security interest* or, more specifically, a *purchase money security interest*.

In the second case the buyer borrows money from an outside party (for example, a bank) and that outside party takes a security interest in collateral. If the buyer borrows money to purchase goods and puts those goods up as collateral, the third party is said to have a purchase money security interest in the collateral, just as the seller does in the first case. However, if, instead of putting up the newly purchased goods as collateral, the buyer puts up something that he already owns outright, the third party has a *nonpurchase money security interest* in the collateral.

In both cases the terms to which both parties agreed are incorporated into a document called a *security agreement*, and the agreement — except in the case of a pledge (see Chapter 2) — must be in writing.

### Perfecting the security interest:

In most situations only the buyer and seller, or the buyer and the outside third party, are aware of the existence and terms of the security interest. For purposes of protection, either or both parties may want the general public to be aware that the collateral is encumbered by a security interest. For example, if X borrows money from Y (who could be either the seller or a bank) to buy certain goods, and Y takes a security interest in those goods, it would be wise for Y to inform the public of this encumbrance, just in case X should decide to resell those goods to a subsequent buyer.

To inform the public of the existence of a security interest — that is, to *perfect the security interest* — one must usually file a *financing statement*.

As noted, a state may adopt UCC provisions at its option. Accordingly, rules for perfecting a security interest by filing a financing statement may very well differ from one jurisdiction to another. As such, it is very important for the parties involved to check carefully the applicable statutes to insure compliance. Nevertheless, it can be safely said that all jurisdictions require that a financing statement include a reasonable description of the collateral, the names and addresses of the parties involved, and at least the signature of the debtor, although the signature of the secured creditor is almost always on the statement too.

**EXAMPLE (Multiple Choice):**

Waldo Washing Machine Co. sold a Zippo Super Suds washing machine to Franklin. Waldo took a promissory note, a security agreement, and a financing statement. Waldo filed only the financing statement. The financing statement is invalid if
    a. Not filed within five days from the time of execution.
    b. Not signed by two witnesses and appropriately notarized.

27

c. Not signed by the debtor.

d. The property involved is a "consumer good."

**Solution:** (c)

Remember that the security agreement and the financing statement are not one and the same. The former may be much more detailed than the latter, particularly with reference to descriptions of the collateral, terms of the arrangement, and maturity date of the obligations. While the financing statement may be detailed, it may not have to be in order to comply with the appropriate statute. The statement is filed for the sole purpose of informing the public that an encumbrance exists, not necessarily to describe the exact nature of the encumbrance. If a third party wishes to have more detailed information than is covered in the statement, he should look at the security agreement itself.

In most cases, if a financing statement is properly filed, the secured party's interest will be good against all third parties, including trustees in bankruptcy, if the debtor should become bankrupt before having satisfied his obligation to the creditor in full. Of course, there are exceptions to the rule insisting on the filing of a financing statement in order to perfect a security interest. These exceptions are discussed in the following section on collateral.

**EXAMPLE (True/False):**

Sullivan leased a commercial printing press to Hanes under a written agreement providing for 60 monthly payments of $250. The agreement further provided that after the last lease payment is made, title to the press will vest in Hanes without a further bill of sale.

1. The arrangement between Sullivan and Hanes is a secured transaction under the Uniform Commercial Code.

2. If the arrangement between the parties is a secured transaction, then the lease agreement must be signed by both parties to be effective as a security agreement.

3. The lease agreement may be filed as a financing statement if it complies with the requirements set forth for a financing statement in Article 9 of the Uniform Commercial Code.

4. A financing statement must state a maturity date to be valid.

**Solutions:** (1) T, (2) F, (3) T, (4) F

## Types of collateral:

Just about any type of personal property can be used as collateral in a secured transaction. What is important is that the debtor have some rights in the collateral and that the collateral is satisfactory to the creditor. Some types of property are offered and accepted as collateral more often than other types, however, and they are listed below:

1. *Consumer goods:* Goods are called consumer goods if they are bought primarily for personal, family, or household purposes. Because consumer goods will most likely not be resold by the consumer to a third party, a financing statement usually does not have to be filed to perfect a purchase money security interest in them. The purchase money security interest, then, is said to be *automatically perfected*. However, in general, automatic perfection will not be good against a third party who has bought the goods for his own use, does not know of the encumbrance, and gives consideration for it. A security interest must be perfected in order for it to be good against an *innocent purchaser*. Therefore, if the consumer goods involved are likely to be resold by the buyer to an innocent third party, a financing statement should be filed. Once it is filed, no third party can claim innocence; the statement is a matter of public record. In particular, automatic perfection does not apply to cars or to personal property which has been attached to land or to a building (that is, *fixtures*). In these two cases, some kind of public notification to perfect a security interest is required, with the particular steps to be taken spelled out in the applicable statute. In any event, automatic perfection of consumer goods is good against a trustee in bankruptcy.

In the case of nonpurchase money security interests, a financing statement must always be filed to perfect the interest. In the case of a *pledge*, though, in which instance the creditor actually takes possession of the collateral and, as such, is said to have a *possessory interest* in the collateral, filing is not necessary to perfect the nonpurchase money security interest.

**EXAMPLE (Multiple Choice):**

Carter Corporation loaned $500,000 to Devon Corporation pursuant to an oral agreement granting a security interest in certain shares of stock held by Devon. Carter sought to have Devon sign a security agreement granting a security interest in the shares. Devon refused to sign any agreement, but instead delivered the stock certificates in question to Carter.

    a. The security interest of Carter is *not* perfected until Devon signs the security agreement or Carter files a financing statement, whichever first occurs.

    b. Carter must file a financing statement, or a copy of a security agreement, signed by the debtor to perfect its security interest.

    c. Carter has a perfected security interest in the collateral.

    d. Carter must sign the agreement, and a financing statement, and file either one of them to perfect its security interest in the shares of stock.

**Solution:** (c)

2. *Inventory:* Inventory is the general term applied to goods held by a person for sale or lease, including raw materials, work in process, finished goods and other materials used or consumed in a business. (The same car which would be a consumer good in one case can be part of inventory in the case of a car salesman. The particular situation most often determines the classification.) In order to facilitate the smooth flow of business transactions, third parties are able to purchase goods from retailers' or manufacturers' inventories in the normal course of business, free of any encumbrance on the items, even if the third party knows of the security interest (that is, even if he is not an innocent purchaser). The creditor enforces his security interest in the inventory by means of a *floating lien*, which is a security interest in collateral that is composed of elements which constantly change. Floating liens are most often associated with inventories because of the constant turnover rate associated with these types of goods; but they can apply to any type of collateral which changes from day to day. When floating liens are involved, the creditor's security is in the debtor's inventory — or proceeds from their sale — at the time of the loan and thereafter. In other words, as the debtor sells off old inventory and purchases new inventory to replace it, the creditor's interest moves from the old items to the new ones automatically. As such, a floating lien allows for a *continuously perfected interest*.

**EXAMPLE:**

On January 14, 1976, Thelma Corporation sold and delivered to Dey Corporation inventory goods priced at $5,000 on terms which required payment within 30 days after delivery. Because of business reverses, Dey found that it was unable to pay the amount due Thelma. On February 9, 1976, Thelma's credit manager validly filed a properly signed financing statement. On February 19, 1976, he met with Dey's officers to effect a plan of repayment. At this meeting, Thelma obtained a $5,000 promissory note and security agreement signed by Dey and secured by Dey's presently existing and thereafter acquired inventory.

**Required:**

Does Thelma have a perfected security interest?

**Solution:**

Yes, Thelma has a perfected security interest in the inventory as of February 18, 1976.

According to the Uniform Commercial Code, a security interest is not enforceable (or does not attach) against a debtor with respect to the collateral unless (1) the debtor has signed a security agreement that contains a description of the collateral (or the collateral is in the possession of the security party pursuant to agreement), (2) value has been given by the creditor, and (3) the debtor has rights in the collateral. Attachment or enforceability generally occurs as soon as all of these events occur. Here, Thelma Corporation has given value by delivering the $5,000 in goods to Dey Corporation. Dey, having taken title to the goods, has rights in them. Dey signed a security agreement providing that any obligation covered by the security agreement is to be secured by after-acquired collateral. Thus, Thelma has a security interest that has attached to Dey's present inventory and that will continue to be a floating charge on Dey's subsequently acquired or changing stock of inventory.

Generally, a financing statement must be filed to perfect all security interests except where the collateral is in the possession of the secured party. The Code provides that a security interest is perfected as soon as filing plus all the events required for attachment have occurred. If the filing is effected before the security interest attaches, it is perfected at the time when it attaches. Thus, a financing statement may be filed before a security agreement is made or a security interest otherwise attaches. Here, the filing on February 9, 1976, of the financing statement prior to reaching an agreement on the secured transaction on February 18, 1976, was proper. Thelma is a secured party with a perfected security interest generally enforceable against Dey and against third parties.

3. *Equipment:* Goods are referred to as equipment if they are used or bought for use primarily in business (including farming or a profession) or by a debtor who is a nonprofit organization. In other words, equipment is not intended to be resold. Typical examples of equipment are machinery used by a manufacturer to produce his goods, the equipment in a dentist's office, and so on. In order to perfect a security interest in equipment, a financing statement must be filed. Again, if the equipment is pledged, no financing statement need be filed to perfect the interest. (Of course, it is highly unlikely that a debtor will pledge his equipment as security.) And, again, the situation determines what classification the goods in question receive: That same car which was a consumer good in one case and part of inventory to be sold in another, may be equipment under totally different circumstances — if, say, a doctor uses it to make house calls.

**EXAMPLE (Multiple Choice):**

Baker Loan Company made secured loans to Smith, Jack, and Roe. Smith gave Baker a security interest in his household furniture. Jack delivered Baker his rare-coin collection as a pledge. Roe's loan is evidenced by his promissory note, payable over three years in monthly payments and secured by a security interest in the inventory of Roe's Clothing Store, a sole proprietorship owned by Roe. Proper security agreements were made and financing statements were duly executed and filed with respect to all of these transactions on the dates of the transactions.

  a. A filing of a financing statement was *not* required to perfect the security interest in Smith's household furniture.
  b. Baker's security interest in Jack's coin collection was perfected before a financing statement was filed.
  c. On filing a financing statement covering Roe's inventory, Baker's security interest therein was perfected for a maximum period of one year.
  d. The financing statement for Roe's inventory must include an itemization and valuation of the inventory if the financing statement is to be valid.

**Solution:** (b)

4. *Intangible collateral:* There are several types of intangibles in which a creditor may have a security interest:

  a. *Contract rights:* Contract rights usually evolve out of installment contracts where the owner has the right to receive payments in stipulated amounts, at regular intervals, over a stated period of time. The actual contract right is the right to the future payments that will be earned when a service is rendered or performance completed or, possibly, just when time passes. In order to perfect a security interest in contract rights, a financing statement must be filed.

b. *Accounts receivable:* If Mr. X agrees to sell merchandise to Mr. Y on credit, but insists on some collateral, a security interest arises in X's favor. As already described, it will be a purchase money security interest if the collateral is the merchandise bought, and a nonpurchase money security interest if the collateral is some element of Y's personal property that he already owns. However, if X sells the merchandise to Y on credit, but without any collateral of any sort as security, an account receivable arises in X's favor. At some later point in time, if X — in the role of buyer — needs credit from a seller or a loan from a third party, he may offer his accounts receivable as collateral. Then, whoever has loaned X money or extended him credit will have a security interest in the intangible collateral. Again, to perfect a security interest in accounts receivable, a financing statement must be filed.

c. *General intangibles:* These are other intangible items which are often offered and accepted as collateral, but that do not fall into the two broader categories just discussed. Some examples might be interests in goodwill or interest in trademarks. As with other intangibles, security interests in general intangibles will be perfected only by the filing of financing statements.

## Default:

A creditor usually acquires a security interest in a debtor's property because there is some question in his mind as to the debtor's ability to meet his obligation in full or on time or both. Hopefully, then, this security interest will protect the creditor should the debtor default. If the debtor does default, both parties must look to the security agreement and to Article 9 of the UCC to determine the appropriate rights, obligations, and remedies.

Most often the creditor takes title to the collateral, at which point he can usually do whatever he wants to with it. Occasionally a security agreement will specify methods by which the collateral may be disposed of or will specifically prohibit certain means of disposal. If the value of the collateral is less than the unpaid balance of the debt at the time of default, the debtor must usually make up the difference. If the collateral's value is greater than the unpaid balance he is usually entitled to a "refund." The provisions of the security agreement control.

It is not unusual for a person to look to more than one source to finance his acquisitions, particularly in the cases of large purchases of inventory or office and warehouse equipment, where initial outlays can be tremendous. If such a situation exists, the question of which creditor has priority in case of a debtor's default comes up. The following guidelines usually apply:

1. A debtor has put up the same personal property as collateral for a loan from more than one creditor and all of the creditors have filed financing statements. The first creditor who filed will have priority, even if he actually advanced the funds after a second creditor did.

2. A creditor has a floating lien on all of a debtor's office equipment. The debtor has to replace one large unit and does so by means of a purchase money financing of that unit (that is, the seller of the unit has a purchase money security interest in that unit alone). The second secured creditor will have priority provided that he files a financing statement either before the goods are delivered or within ten days after the buyer/debtor receives them, and provided that he notifies the previous creditor of the arrangement he is entering into with the debtor. If the second creditor fails to comply with any of these provisions, the first creditor will have the prior claim.

# 4 Suretyship

Basically, a *surety* is a third party who guarantees that if a debtor fails to pay a creditor an outstanding debt due, he, as the surety, will pay it. In more general terms, the surety promises the creditor that he will do whatever the debtor has contracted to do, according to the terms of the *suretyship agreement.* The original debtor is called the *principal debtor.* Upon the creation of the suretyship relationship, the surety's obligation is to the creditor, not to the debtor, to do or pay something in case he does not. As the relationship between a surety and a creditor is a contractual one, all the elements of a contract must be present if the surety's promise of satisfaction is to be enforced. In addition, as pointed out in the Statute of Frauds section in Chapter 1, the contract must be in writing to be enforced, because the surety is guaranteeing payment if the principal debtor defaults. (Remember the exception, though: If the surety benefits by assuming the principal debtor's obligation, the contract need not be in writing.)

Although the surety is a secondary debtor, he is nevertheless *primarily liable* to the creditor and usually signs, but does not have to, the same instrument that the principal debtor does. Because he is primarily liable, the surety can be looked to for satisfaction when the debt matures, whether the principal debtor was looked to first or not, and whether the principal debtor has been sued for breach or not.

A *guarantor,* as distinct from a surety, is *secondarily liable* on the instrument; accordingly, his liability exists only if and when one of the primarily liable parties (the principal debtor or the surety) dishonors the instrument or defaults on it.

**EXAMPLE (Multiple Choice):**

Barnes has agreed to become the conditional guarantor of collection on credit extended by Ace Supply Company on a contract for the sale of goods by Ace to Wilcox not exceeding $5,000.
   a. If Wilcox defaults, Barnes is immediately liable for the amount of the debt outstanding.
   b. A discharge in bankruptcy obtained by Wilcox will discharge Barnes.
   c. Upon default, Barnes must proceed against Wilcox on Ace's behalf if Ace so requests.
   d. Ace must first proceed against Wilcox before it is entitled to recover from Barnes.

**Solution:** (d)

A *subsurety* is a secondarily liable surety for a primarily liable surety; if he is looked to for satisfaction by the creditor, he can enforce his right of reimbursement against the original, primarily liable surety. *Cosureties* share primary liability. The cosuretyship relationship is between the several sureties; each one (along with the principal debtor) is primarily liable — usually jointly and severally — to the creditor. Each cosurety may be liable to the creditor for equal or unequal amounts and may be gone against by the creditor for equal or unequal amounts, depending upon the terms of the suretyship agreement. In any event, unless the suretyship agreement states otherwise, each cosurety is liable for the full amount of the outstanding debt until the debtor has fully satisfied the creditor. If, however, one cosurety pays a creditor a higher proportion of the debt than he agreed to with the other cosureties, he can collect the excess from the other cosureties. He cannot refuse the creditor full payment, even if he knows that it will be impossible to be reimbursed for any excess paid by one or all of the other cosureties. Cosureties do not necessarily have to know of the existence of each other when they enter into the suretyship relationship with the creditor.

**EXAMPLE:**

Fox Construction Corporation obtained a $20 million contract from the United States government to construct a federal office building. The contract required Fox to obtain a surety (or sureties) guaranteeing performance of the contract. After contacting several surety companies, Fox learned that no one company would write a bond for that amount. However, Fox was able to obtain a $10 million bond from Ace Surety Company and a $5 million bond each from Empire Surety and the Excelsior Surety Company. Fox breached the contract and, as a result, the United States government suffered a $2 million loss.

**Required:**

1. What are the rights of the United States against the three surety companies? Explain.

2. When finally settled, for what amount will each surety company be liable? Explain.

**Solution:**

1. The United States could proceed against one or more of the cosureties to collect the $2 million damages resulting from Fox's having breached the construction contract. The three surety companies are cosureties on the Fox Construction Corporation obligation. As such, they are jointly and severally liable. Assuming Ace pays the entire amount ($2 million), it will have a right of contribution from the other sureties as discussed below.

2. Ace will be liable for $1 million, Empire for $500,000, and Excelsior for $500,000. In the event that a cosurety pays more than its proportionate share of the surety obligation, it has a right of contribution from its fellow sureties in proportion to the several undertaking. Thus, if Ace were to pay the $2 million liability, it would have the right to receive $500,000 each from Empire and Excelsior.

As noted, the suretyship relationship with the creditor is a contractual one and all elements of a contract must be present for the creditor to enforce the surety's promise. The following rules apply to the legally sufficient consideration which a creditor must transfer to a surety to bind the latter's promise:

1. If the suretyship contract is entered into before the principal debtor's obligation comes into existence, the creditor need not transfer additional legally sufficient consideration to the surety to bind him and thereby hold him liable. The law views this situation as one in which consideration will "automatically" be transferred at the time the debtor's obligation actually arises, because the creditor will have relied on the surety in extending credit to the principal debtor.

2. If the suretyship contract is entered into at the time the principal debtor's obligation comes into existence, no consideration need be transferred to bind the surety, for the same reasons as mentioned above.

3. If the suretyship contract is entered into after the principal debtor's obligation comes into existence, the creditor must give the surety legally sufficient consideration in order to bind him and hold him liable for the outstanding debt.

**EXAMPLE (True/False):**

Agor, a clock dealer, placed an order for 100 grandfather clocks costing $20,000 with Chimes, Inc. The latter requested a surety to protect itself from loss. Hayes and Tilden signed the contract as sureties without receiving any consideration.

1. The surety relation arises by operation of law.
2. Hayes and Tilden are not liable as sureties since they received no consideration.
3. If Hayes and Tilden are liable, each is liable to the creditor for the full amount of the debt.
4. If a cosurety pays the full amount of the debt, he has a right to contribution from his cosurety.
5. A suretyship relation may be created by the parties after the principal's obligation arises.

**Solutions:** (1) F, (2) F, (3) T, (4) T, (5) T

## Valid defenses to a suretyship contract:

A surety may avoid liability to a creditor if any of the following situations exist:

1. If the agreement between the principal debtor and the creditor is illegal, a surety cannot be held liable to the creditor.

2. If the principal debtor has a valid defense, the surety is relieved of liability. Put more generally, if the principal debtor is not liable, the surety is usually not liable either.

**EXAMPLE (Multiple Choice):**

Young, a minor, purchased a car from Ace Auto Sales by making a down payment and signing a note for the balance. The note was guaranteed by Rich. Subsequently, Young sought to return the car and *not* pay off the note because Ace made false representations concerning the car's mileage at the time of sale. Which of the following *best* describes the legal implications in these circumstances?

    a. *Neither* Young *nor* rich is liable on the note solely because Young is a minor.
    b. Young's attempt to return the car, in and of itself, released Rich of any liability.
    c. The fraud perpetrated upon Young is a valid defense to Rich's guaranty.
    d. There are *no* valid defenses for Rich and Young and the only recourse is to seek to reduce the amount owed based upon a counterclaim for fraud.

**Solution:** (c)

3. If the principal debtor fully performs or tenders payment, the surety is no longer liable.

4. If the collateral which the creditor holds is subsequently changed without the surety's knowledge or consent, the surety can disclaim all liability.

5. If the Statute of Limitations has run out, the surety cannot be held liable.

6. If the principal debtor and creditor modify their agreement in any way (including the creditor's release of the debtor) — and without the surety's knowledge or consent — the surety can usually disclaim all liability. If a surety's occupation is such that he regularly enters into surety contracts and gets paid to do so (perhaps a flat fee per contract or a percent of the outstanding debt), he is said to be a *compensated surety*. If he receives no compensation for entering into such contracts, he is said to be a *noncompensated surety*. When a contract between the principal debtor and creditor is modified without the knowledge or consent of a noncompensated surety, this rule applies as stated. However, when the unaware or nonconsenting surety is compensated, his release extends only as far as he suffers by the modification.

**EXAMPLE:**

Superior Construction Company, Inc., submitted the successful bid for the construction of your client's new factory. As a part of the contract, Superior was required to obtain a performance bond from an acceptable surety company. Ace Surety, Inc., wrote the surety bond for the proposed building.

After the project was about one-third completed, Superior suggested several major changes in the contract. These included the expansion of the floor space by 10 percent and construction of an additional loading platform.

**Required:**

1. What problem does your client face if it agrees to the proposed changes? Explain.

2. What advice would you suggest in order to avoid this problem?

**Solution:**

1. The suggested changes represent material alterations of the original construction contract. If the client agrees to the proposed changes, it faces the loss of the surety company's protection. Material alteration of the contract affords the surety a defense against recovery on its undertaking.

2. The client should either obtain a consent to the changes from the surety company in writing or reject the proposed changes.

**Invalid defenses to a suretyship contract:**

A surety may not be discharged of his liability to a creditor in the following circumstances:

1. If the principal debtor lacks the capacity to enter into a contract, becomes insolvent or bankrupt, or dies, a surety cannot legally disclaim his liability to the creditor. (In fact, most creditors get involved with sureties to protect themselves against just such possibilities.)

2. A surety cannot be relieved of his liability if a principal debtor defaults and the creditor forgets or fails to give the surety notice of the default.

**EXAMPLE (True/False):**

Clifford sued Hatfield as surety for Buckley on a $200,000 contract. Hatfield advised Care, his accountant, that no notice had been given or demand made upon him, Hatfield, prior to the commencement of the action.

  Hatfield was legally entitled to notice of Buckley's default before commencement of the action.

**Solution:** F

3. A surety cannot raise as a defense the argument that the creditor went against the surety before he went against the principal debtor, or that the creditor failed to foreclose against or liquidate the principal debtor's collateral before going against the surety.

4. Proof that the surety's contract was obtained as a result of the principal debtor's *fraudulent* behavior will not serve to relieve the surety of his liability to the creditor. Proof that the creditor and principal debtor conspired together to defraud the surety, however, will.

It is important to keep in mind that these defenses are available or are not available only in the absence of any specific terms in the suretyship agreement. Accordingly, if the contract specifically states that the creditor's collateral can be changed or modified at any time without the surety's consent, a surety cannot raise the defense that the collateral was changed. Likewise, if the suretyship contract specifically states that a creditor must liquidate the collateral before going against the surety, the surety may validly disclaim all liability if the creditor does not act in accordance with the terms of their agreement.

**Collateral:**

The collateral which a principal debtor offers is usually pledged (that is, the debtor transfers the property, but not title to it). Pledged collateral may be held by either the surety or the creditor.

When it is held by the surety, the creditor still has a legal interest in it. As such, if the principal debtor defaults, the creditor may look to the surety to satisfy the debt due by having him transfer the collateral to him, plus any difference between the balance of the debt due and the present value of the collateral. If the creditor demands and receives satisfaction in cash from the surety, the surety's legal interest in the collateral is no longer shared with the creditor; it is the surety's property alone. If cosureties are involved, each one has an appropriate proportionate interest in the collateral, even if it is held by only one of the cosureties.

If the collateral is held by the creditor and the principal debtor defaults, the creditor may liquidate or foreclose against the collateral or, if he prefers, go directly against the surety and demand cash, as if the collateral did not exist. If the creditor elects the second alternative, and the surety satisfies the principal debtor's obligation, the surety is then said to be *subrogated* to the creditor's rights against the principal debtor. This means that the surety "steps into the shoes" of the creditor, thereby assuming all rights the creditor had to the collateral and against the principal debtor. The original creditor is responsible for protecting the collateral, and if he destroys or ruins it, he may be held liable to the surety for the difference between its value and when the principal debtor transferred it to the creditor and its value when transferred by the creditor to the surety. The creditor is also liable to the surety for the full amount of the collateral's value in its original state if the creditor goes against the surety and the surety finds that the creditor returned the collateral to the principal debtor without having first gotten the surety's consent to do so. In all events, a surety must return to the principal debtor all amounts he has received (either from the creditor or upon his own liquidation of or foreclosure against the collateral) which are in excess of what he has paid to the creditor.

**EXAMPLE (Multiple Choice):**

The surety's right of subrogation
- a. Is *not* available in a bankruptcy proceeding.
- b. Must be explicitly stated and defined in the surety undertaking.
- c. Does *not* apply to situations where the creditor holds security sufficient to satisfy the debt.
- d. Allows the surety, upon satisfying the obligation, to succeed to the creditor's rights.

**Solution:** (d)

Once a surety has paid a creditor, he has the right to indemnification or reimbursement from the principal debtor on the theory that the principal debtor is ultimately responsible for the debt, regardless of the suretyship contract between the creditor and the surety.

### Surety bonds:

There are various suretyship relationships which create rights, duties, and obligations that are similar to those created by ordinary suretyship contracts but that are also different in certain respects.

1. *Fidelity bonds:* A surety who is party to a fidelity bond guarantees an employer that the employees named or bonded will perform their duties as expected. In the case of a fidelity bond, the employer assumes the rights and duties of a creditor, the employee assumes the rights and duties of a principal debtor, and embezzlement, outright theft, and the like are tantamount to default. Employers usually warrant that, to their knowledge, no bonded employees have ever defaulted. Breach of such a warrant discharges a surety from his duties under the terms of the bond. Similarly, if an employer finds out that a bonded employee has defaulted and yet continues to employ him, a surety will be able to disclaim all liability to the employer. If a bonded employee's duties change without the surety's knowledge or consent, the surety will be able to successfully raise this development as a defense.

2. *Judicial bonds:* The most common judicial bond is a bail bond. Sureties who are parties to judicial bonds guarantee that the appropriate obligations will be met and duties performed in connection with judicial proceedings.

3. *Performance bonds:* This might be seen as a general, all-encompassing term for a suretyship contract. A performance bond is defined as one whereby the surety guarantees that the principal debtor will perform his duties according to the terms of the contract he has entered into.

# 5  Bankruptcy

While most people who incur debts do so with the intention of being able to repay them, they sometimes cannot because in between the date the debts were incurred and their maturity dates, the debtor becomes *insolvent*. There are two concepts of insolvency: One describes a person whose assets are less than his liabilities, and the other describes a person who is unable to meet his obligations as they become due. The former is the legal meaning of insolvency and the latter is the equity meaning. The Federal Bankruptcy Act, whose purpose is to satisfy a bankrupt's creditors in the most equitable way possible, as well as to put the bankrupt in a position that will enable him to "wipe his slate clean" and start over again, deals with the legal meaning of insolvency.

A person may be declared bankrupt either as a result of an *involuntary petition* of bankruptcy being filed against him, or as a result of his own filing of a voluntary petition of bankruptcy.

An involuntary petition of bankruptcy can be filed against an insolvent debtor under the following two circumstances:

If the debtor owes outstanding debts to a total of less than 12 creditors, any 1 of those creditors can file a petition if his claim equals at least $1,000.

If the debtor owes outstanding debts to 12 or more creditors, any 3 or more creditors can file a petition if their total debts due equal at least $1,000.

An involuntary petition may be filed against anyone except against a wage earner, a farmer, a building and loan association, or a municipal, railroad, banking, or insurance corporation. These debtors can only become voluntary bankrupts.

**Acts of bankruptcy:**

Once the involuntary petition has been filed, the case goes to a federal bankruptcy court (see below) to be decided. At this point, the debtor will be *adjudicated* bankrupt if he so consents or if it can be proved that he committed an *act of bankruptcy* within four months before or after the petition has been filed. There are six acts of bankruptcy:

1. *Fraudulent conveyance:* A debtor is guilty of fraudulent conveyance if he tries to deceive his creditors as to the true value of his total assets. This can be done by hiding the assets or by transferring property to a third party for inadequate consideration — and usually under the assumption that it will be returned at some later date to the debtor/transferor — to keep the creditors from attaching the property to satisfy their debts due.

2. *Preferential Transfer:* A preferential transfer is one made by the debtor to one creditor to satisfy a debt due without giving value in proportionate amounts to any other creditors he may have. For this kind of transfer to be considered an act of bankruptcy, the debtor must intentionally mean to prefer one creditor over another. This kind of transfer is voidable if the creditor knows or has reason to know that the debtor is insolvent, and if the transfer is made within four months before or after the involuntary petition is filed. If the creditor accepts the payment/transfer in good faith (that is, if he does not know of the debtor's insolvency), the transfer is not voidable, although it is still an act of bankruptcy. A debtor who engages in a bona fide sale for adequate consideration at any time during his insolvency is not committing an act of bankruptcy, and the transfer is not voidable even if it is to a creditor who is aware of the debtor's insolvency.

**EXAMPLE (Multiple Choice):**

A creditor who receives a preference payment from a bankrupt debtor will
    a. Be barred from any recovery on his claim.
    b. Lose it if he knew or had reason to know that the debtor was insolvent in the bankruptcy sense.

      c. Have a priority even if the preference is voidable.
      d. Have committed a bankruptcy offense.

**Solution:** (b)

3. *Judicial lien:* If a debtor allows a creditor to obtain a lien on any of his property ("allow" in the sense that he cannot prevent it from happening) and the lien is not discharged within 30 days, the debtor commits an act of bankruptcy.

4. *General assignment:* This refers to making a general assignment to benefit the creditors of the debtor.

**EXAMPLE (Multiple Choice):**

Your client is insolvent under the federal bankruptcy law. Under the circumstances
      a. As long as the client can meet current debts or claims by its most aggressive creditors, a bankruptcy proceeding is *not* possible.
      b. Such information, i.e., insolvency, need *not* be disclosed in the financial statements reported upon by your CPA firm as long as you are convinced that the problem is short lived.
      c. An assignment for the benefit of creditors will constitute an act of bankruptcy.
      d. Your client *cannot* file a voluntary petition for bankruptcy.

**Solution:** (c)

5. *Appointment of a receiver:* If the bankrupt allows (again, this means that he cannot prevent) a receiver or trustee to be appointed to administer the debtor's assets, an act of bankruptcy is committed.

6. *Written admission:* An act of bankruptcy also results from a debtor's admission in writing that he cannot pay his outstanding debts and he is willing to be judged bankrupt. Though this sixth acts falls within the discussion of acts of bankruptcy with regard to involuntary petitions, it is tantamount to a voluntary petition in bankruptcy. As a result of a written petition, then, a debtor becomes a voluntary bankrupt.

In order to be considered an act of bankruptcy, a preferential transfer, judicial lien, and appointment of a receiver or trustee must occur when the debtor is insolvent. If the acts occur when the debtor is not legally insolvent, they will not be considered acts of bankruptcy. The debtor need not necessarily be insolvent at the time of a fraudulent conveyance, general assignment, or written admission in order for these particular occurrences to be considered acts of bankruptcy. However, to repeat, all acts — whether insolvency is required at the time they are committed or not — must be committed within four months before or after the petition is filed, in order to be held as acts of bankruptcy.

**EXAMPLE:**

In the course of examining the financial statements of Superior Systems, Inc., the financial vice president discloses that the corporation has a serious collection problem with one of its customers, Vizar Components, Inc. Vizar is approximately $10,000 in arrears; its checks have been returned for insufficient funds. Other creditors have similar claims against Vizar.

You have also learned that the principal creditors, including Superior, have held a meeting to consider possible alternative courses of action. During the meeting, an examination of the financial statements of Vizar revealed that it was in a difficult current position, but that it had sufficient assets to meet liabilities in the event of a bankruptcy proceeding. The meeting also revealed that Vizar's problems had built up over the past two years due to poor management. The company appears to have significant potential to return to profitability if properly managed.

**Required:**

What are the chief objections to proceeding against Vizar in bankruptcy? Explain.

**Solution:**

To proceed successfully against Vizar in bankruptcy by Superior and the other creditors, they must establish that Vizar has committed an act of bankruptcy. This may be difficult to do. Three of the six possible acts of bankruptcy would require that Vizar be insolvent, which it is not. A fourth act would require Vizar to admit in writing that it is unable to pay its debts and that it is willing to be adjudged a bankrupt; such an admission by Vizar is highly improbable. The fifth act involves a concealment or removal of assets to the detriment of creditors, which is not evident in the facts presented. The sixth act, making a general assignment of assets for the benefit of creditors, if done equitably for all qualified creditors, would probably preclude a bankruptcy action by the creditors.

Another significant objection to using the bankruptcy alternative is that bankruptcy is a costly and time-consuming procedure for all parties. In circumstances such as those described in the question, instituting bankruptcy proceedings should be considered as a last resort.

## Court proceedings:

As mentioned above, the insolvent debtor has the right to have his case heard in court and to have a jury decide if he is in fact legally insolvent, if he has committed an act of bankruptcy, and so forth. The court in which bankruptcy proceedings are carried on is the U.S. District Court — in particular, a bankruptcy court. District Court judges appoint *referees* who are sort of surrogate or substitute judges, and who preside over the bankruptcy proceedings with varying degrees of authority. Their orders, findings of fact, and conclusions are subject to review by the presiding judge.

If the court determines that the debtor is, indeed, bankrupt, he is so adjudged. The court then takes over the adjudicated bankrupt's affairs with the intent of satisfying his creditors' outstanding claims.

If the insolvent debtor has filed a voluntary petition of bankruptcy, however, an order of adjudication is not necessary for the court to take over whatever assets he may have and to administer his affairs. If the involved parties make the requisite application, the court will appoint a *receiver* to take possession of the adjudicated bankrupt's assets and temporarily administer his affairs.

Between 10 and 30 days after the court has adjudged the debtor bankrupt, all his creditors must meet with the judge or referee, at which time they have the opportunity to submit and prove their claims under oath. A claim will be allowed only if it is "provable." All the creditors do not necessarily have to submit all their claims at this first meeting, but they must do so within six months of this first meeting if they want any satisfaction from the court.

**EXAMPLE:**

Marco owns all the shares of stock of Digits Corporation. Digits is currently short of cash and has had to default on some of its current liabilities. Marco loaned Digits $2,000 to tide it over its crisis and obtained a note from Digits for the amount of the loan. If Digits is petitioned into bankruptcy, what is the status of Marco's loan?
   a. It is a provable and allowable claim against the bankrupt's estate which is superior to the claims of other general creditors.
   b. It is a provable and allowable claim against the bankrupt's estate together with the claims of all other general creditors.
   c. It is invalid because the loan by Marco constituted an act of bankruptcy.
   d. It is worthless because Marco is personally liable for the debts of Digits since he owns all of its stock.

**Solution:** (b)

The creditors usually appoint a *trustee in bankruptcy* at their first meeting. This trustee then takes over from the court-appointed receiver in administering the bankrupt's affairs and satisfying the creditor's claims as equitably as possible. In the event the creditors do not appoint a trustee themselves, the court will. In any event, once the trustee is appointed, the bankrupt must turn over title to all his assets to the official.

## Payment of claims and discharge:

The Bankruptcy Act stipulates that certain claims have priority, and it is these claims which the trustee will attempt to satisfy out of the bankrupt's estate before all others. The priorities and their order are:

1.  Expenses incurred in administering the bankruptcy proceedings and in the collecting and preserving the bankrupt's assets.

**EXAMPLE (Multiple Choice):**

Of the following items, the highest priority for payment in full before general creditors' claims in a bankruptcy proceeding is assigned to
    a. Wages, in a limited amount, if earned within three months preceeding bankruptcy.
    b. Wages owed to an insolvent employee.
    c. Administration costs of bankruptcy.
    d. Unpaid federal income taxes.

**Solution:** (c)

2.  Wages which the bankrupt owes these employees (whether they work for him in a personal or professional capacity), and which have been earned within three months before the bankruptcy proceedings began. While various employees may have more than $600 coming to them, and while they may eventually receive a large proportion of their total due, they have a prior claim on only up to $600 in accrued wages per employee.

3.  The expenses which the creditors have incurred in bringing the bankruptcy case to court.

4.  All taxes due to the federal government, as well as to any state, municipal, or local jurisdiction.

5.  Any other claims which can claim priority by virtue of federal and/or state statutes.

**EXAMPLE (Multiple Choice):**

Your client is entitled to a rent priority in bankruptcy; as such he
    a. Will have his claim satisfied prior to those of general creditors even though the general creditors receive little or nothing.
    b. Ranks equally with all other parties entitled to priorities.
    c. Has a claim superiór to the claims of secured creditors.
    d. Is precluded from asserting the priority if it was obtained within three months of the filing of the petition in bankruptcy.

**Solution:** (a)

6.  Though not specifically provided for in the Bankruptcy Act, one could consider sixth in this order of priorities any secured creditors' claims over those of unsecured creditors. A secured creditor can either take title to the collateral in which he has a secured interest and then, if the value of that security is less than the total debt, attempt to prove his claim for the balance still outstanding, or waive his secured interest in the debtor's assets and attempt to prove his claim for the full amount of the debt. If he opts for the second alternative, his priority as a secured creditor will be lost and satisfaction of the debt will be accorded him as it would be accorded any ordinary unsecured creditor. In no case can he do both — that is, claim the secured property and then try to recover the entire debt.

**EXAMPLE:**

During the examination of the financial statements of Delta Corporation, you note that as of September 30, 1972:

- Current liabilities exceed current assets.

- Total assets substantially exceed total liabilities.

- Cash position is poor and current payables are considerably in arrears.

- Trade and secured creditors are pressing for payment and several lawsuits have been commenced against Delta.

Further investigation reveals the following:

- On August 31, 1972, Delta made a $1,000 payment to Oliveros on a $20,000 mortgage indebtedness over one year in arrears. The fair-market value of the mortgaged property is $35,000.

- On September 20, 1972, a trade creditor, Miller, obtained a judgment against Delta which under applicable law constitutes a lien on Delta's real property.

- On September 22, 1972, Delta paid a substantial amount to Helms, a supplier, on an account over one year old.

- On September 27, 1972, Delta executed and delivered a financing statement to Honea, a vendor, from whom Delta had purchased some new machinery six months earlier. Honea duly filed and perfected the financing statement.

**Required:**

1. As of September 30, 1972, did any of the above transactions legally constitute acts of bankruptcy? Explain.

2. As of September 30, 1972, could the creditors of Delta file an involuntary petition in bankruptcy against Delta if a sufficient number of them having a sufficient amount of claims decide to do so? Explain.

3. Independent of your answers to parts 1 and 2, assume the same facts set out above except that Delta's total liabilities exceed total assets and that on October 2, 1972, Delta filed a voluntary petition in bankruptcy, and a Trustee has been appointed.

    a. What are the rights, if any, of the Trustee against each of the creditors involved in the four transactions stated in the problem? Explain.

    b. What are the general requirements for creditors to be entitled to vote on and participate in a bankruptcy proceeding? Explain for each of the four creditors involved whether he meets these requirements. Why?

**Solution:**

1. No. Before any of the given transactions can be acts of bankruptcy, the debtor must be insolvent. On the facts given, the debtor, Delta, is not insolvent for purposes of the Bankruptcy Act. In bankruptcy law, insolvency exists only when the aggregate of the property owned by the debtor is insufficient to pay his debts. Although Delta's current liabilities exceed its current assets, its overall assets exceed its overall liabilities. Hence, Delta is not insolvent and thus has committed no act of bankruptcy.

2. No. Although a voluntary petition can be filed by the debtor at any time, the debtor must have committed an act of bankruptcy before an involuntary petition may be filed by the creditors. As discussed above, Delta has not committed an act of bankruptcy.

3a. The transfers to Helms and Honea would be considered preferential transfers because they were made to creditors on account of an antecedent indebtedness at a time when other creditors were not paid. The Trustee can void such transfers provided that they had been made within four months of the filing of the petition and that the creditor receiving the preference knew, or had reason to know, that he was receiving preferential treatment.

Since both of these transfers occurred within four months of the filing, the Trustee can void the transfers if it can be shown that either Helms and/or Honea knew, or should have known, that the transfers were preferential. If the transfers were voided, the Trustee could recover the payment made to Helms and set aside the lien given to Honea.

The payment on the mortgage would not be considered as preferential treatment since the creditor is secured. Thus, the Trustee could not void the transaction.

The lien arising from the judgment obtained by Miller would be voided because it was obtained within four months preceding the filing.

3b. Generally speaking, only general (i.e., unsecured) creditors may vote to accept or reject plans of arrangements and participate in dividends. Secured creditors may do so only if they waive their security or if, on foreclosure, there is a deficiency. A creditor with a voidable security interest that has been avoided is, of course, a general creditor. Thus, with respect to the creditors involved.

- Oliveros would not be able to vote or participate unless he waived his security or if, on foreclosure, there was a deficiency.

- Miller would be allowed to vote and participate because the Trustee would void his lien as described above.

- Helms would be allowed to vote and participate because he is an unsecured creditor.

- Honea's right to vote and participate would depend on the Trustee's ability to set aside his lien as described above. If the lien were voided, Honea would be able to vote and participate as an unsecured creditor; if not, Honea would not be able to vote and participate unless he waived his security or if, on foreclosure, there was a deficiency.

Miscellaneous federal and state laws exempt certain of the bankrupt's assets from being turned over to the trustee for the purpose of satisfying creditors' claims. The bankrupt should check the appropriate statutes in effect at the time the voluntary or involuntary petition was filed in order to know to which property he may retain title in the event he is adjudicated as bankrupt.

Once a debtor becomes an adjudicated bankrupt, he is automatically discharged from all debts, except those specifically nondischargeable, as long as there are no objections registered by the trustee or creditors or U.S. district attorney, and as long as he has not been found guilty of certain crimes which are enumerated in Section 14c of the Bankruptcy Act.

**EXAMPLE (Multiple Choice):**

A discharge in bankruptcy
   a. Relieves the debtor from all provable debts.
   b. Is *not* available if the debtor was previously discharged within ten years prior to the present bankruptcy.
   c. *Cannot* be revoked.
   d. Is barred if the debtor commits a bankruptcy offense.

**Solution:** (d)

Specifically nondischargeable debts include:

- Taxes due.

- Legal liabilities arising out of judgments against the bankrupt, based on fraud, embezzlement, and intentional (not negligent) torts.

- Alimony, wife and child support.

- Debts which the bankrupt did not list.

- Wages due employees which were earned within three months before the bankruptcy proceedings began.

### Out-of-court settlements:

The Federal Bankruptcy Act is usually depended upon to enforce creditors' rights and oversee debtor relief. However, often the statute will not have to be looked to; court proceedings and their high costs can be avoided if the parties involved can work out an acceptable agreement among themselves.

The debtor and his creditors may work out an ordinary contractual agreement whereby the creditors receive proportionate shares of the debtor's assets. By virtue of his having fewer assets than liabilities, the debtor cannot pay his obligations in full; nevertheless, his debts will be considered fully satisfied if such a *composition agreement* is entered into by both sides.

**EXAMPLE:**

Which of the following statements *best* describes a composition agreement unanimously agreed to by all creditors?
   a.  It provides for the appointment of a receiver to take over and operate the debtor's business.
   b.  It is subject to approval by a federal district court judge.
   c.  It provides for a discharge of the debts included in the composition agreement upon performance by the debtor.
   d.  It binds only those creditors who do *not* subsequently withdraw from the agreement prior to its consummation.

**Solution:** (c)

As a composition agreement is basically an ordinary contract, all the essentials of a contract must be present for it to be binding. The offer on the part of the debtor and the acceptance on the part of the creditors are clearly evident. Consideration under these circumstances is seen in the creditors' offering to forgive the balances of their claims to which they are legally entitled. If any creditor refuses to participate in the composition agreement (participation is voluntary; it is not an "all or none" proposition), he can attempt to collect the full outstanding debt at some other time.

Instead of apportioning his assets among his creditors himself, a debtor can assign — that is, voluntarily transfer — title to some or all of his property to a third party or trustee. That third party will then liquidate the assets and pay the creditors proportionately. This arrangement is called a *nonstatutory general assignment.*

# *6* **Commercial Paper**

The area of commercial paper, or negotiable instruments, is covered in Article 3 of the Uniform Commercial Code.

There are basically two kinds of commercial paper: notes and drafts.

1. *Notes:* Notes are instruments which initially involve two parties: the *maker* of the note and the *payee* or *bearer* of the note. The maker promises to pay the payee/bearer a particular sum of money at a particular time. That time can be either whenever the payee wishes to collect (in which case the maker has issued a *demand note*) or at some specific future date (in which case the maker has issued a *time note*). *Promissory notes* usually provide for the payment of interest, either at a rate specifically stated apart from the principal, or added onto the principal, such that one lump sum (principal plus interest) will become due. A note of the latter type is called a *discount note.* A simple promissory note is the most common kind of note, but there are other types with which one should be familiar:

- *Certificates of deposit,* or CDs, are notes which are issued by a bank (the maker) after having received money from the payee. In issuing a CD, the bank promises to repay the money to the payee/depositor according to the arrangement agreed upon by the two as stated in the terms of the note.

- *Installment notes* allow for the maker to pay the payee the agreed upon principal and interest in installments over a predetermined period of time. The interest due at each installment is usually on the remaining unpaid principal at that time.

- *Real estate mortgage notes* are notes secured by a mortgage on some specific real property which is owned by the maker.

- *Collateral notes* are notes secured by the maker's personal property. The property is pledged to the payee and, as such, remains in his possession until the note is fully paid. If the maker defaults, the payee/pledgee takes title to the property, usually liquidates it, and then applies the value received toward the outstanding debt.

2. *Drafts:* Drafts are instruments which involve three parties: a *drawer*, a *drawee*, and a *payee*. The drawer orders the drawee to pay a certain sum to the payee. Drafts, as notes, can be payable on demand (in which case the drawer has issued a *sight draft*), or at some specific future date (in which case the drawer has issued a *time draft*). A simple check with which everyone is familiar is the most common type of draft. Other frequently used drafts include:

- *Cashier's checks,* which are drafts drawn by a bank upon itself. In other words, the bank is both the drawer and the drawee.

- *Bank drafts,* which are drafts drawn by one bank on another bank. Bank drafts are sometimes called *remittance drafts.*

If either notes or drafts are payable on demand, they are, for all intents and purposes, simply substitutes for money; if they are payable at some future date, they are more in the nature of instruments of credit.

**Is the instrument negotiable?**

Commercial paper is widely used because it allows transactions that would normally involve money to be completed without exchanging actual cash and yet without disrupting the normal flow of business. Commercial paper, then, derives its value from the fact that it can be used as a substitute for money which is either presently due or which will be due in the future. However, these instruments will be valuable as cash substitutes only if they are *negotiable*. Whether or not a draft or note is negotiable depends entirely on its *form*. This is so because in order to facilitate the free flow of business, parties to commercial paper should not have to look beyond the tangible document itself to determine their obligations and rights. Having to look beyond the four corners of a document would slow down the normal course of business. Thus, if a reference to any other document besides the instrument itself is necessary to determine the terms to which the parties have agreed, the instrument is not negotiable.

This is not to say that commercial paper cannot be transferred from one party to another unless it is negotiable. For instance, a nonnegotiable instrument can simply be assigned by the payee to a third party. However, as an assignee, the third party's rights in the case of a nonnegotiable instrument will be much more limited than those of a holder in due course in the case of a negotiable instrument. The assignee's rights are identical to the assignor's, whereas the rights of a holder in due course of a negotiable instrument can be broader than those of the original payee. (The characteristics and rights of a holder in due course will be detailed further on in this chapter.)

Article 3 of the UCC spells out the essential elements of form which an instrument must take in order for it to be negotiable:

1. The draft or note must be in writing. Any kind of writing is acceptable — it can be handwritten in pen or pencil; it can be typewritten or professionally printed. It can also be written on any material. However, in drawing up the instrument, the maker or drawer should understand the importance of the instrument's being able to circulate among many people over a long period of time. Consequently, although it is perfectly legal to do so, one should not carve the terms on a tree trunk.

2. The draft or note must be signed by the drawer or maker. Again, the law allows a broad interpretation of this requirement; the instrument need not necessarily be signed at the bottom, and any form the signature takes is valid as long as the signer's intention to sign is substantiated. An instrument can be issued in the name of a business or even in an alias or fictitious name. In the latter case, parol evidence would be introducible to determine the signer's true identity. If the maker or drawer is illiterate, he may use any mark he wants to, as long as he intends that mark to be his signature. The signature should be handwritten in pen, but it is perfectly valid if it is typed, written in pencil, or even affixed by means of a signing machine.

3. To be negotiable a draft or note must contain an actual intention or promise to pay. Mere recognition that a debt is outstanding — such as in the case of "I.O.U. $1,000" — is not a promise to pay the $1,000, but merely corroboration that the $1,000 is owed. In the same way, "Please pay Mr. X" is not a definite promise to pay. In the case of a draft, the word "promise" does not actually have to be written on the instrument, as long as the key phrase "pay to the order" or "pay to bearer" is written. Thus, though the above Mr. X example is not a definite promise to pay, "Please pay to the order of Mr. X" is. In the case of a note, the word "promise" is usually used, but need not necessarily be to render the note negotiable. What is crucial, however, is that the maker evidence his absolute intention to pay the payee.

4. The drawer's or maker's promise to pay must be unconditional. As such, any use of the word "if" or phrase "but for" or any such variation indicating that payment will be forthcoming only if some conditional event takes place, will render an instrument nonnegotiable.

If the instrument is one which grew out of a previous contract or arrangement, the instrument will not lose its negotiability if the prior contract is simply referred to on the note or draft, as in the phrases "as per" or "in accordance with" a previous agreement. However, if the terms of that previous agreement are referred to in the instrument in such a way that the payee or subsequent indorsees have no way of knowing whether the amount due will be forthcoming without referring to the prior contract, then the instrument will be nonnegotiable. Consequently, if the phrase "subject to our previous agreement" or any similar combination of words appears on an instrument, such instrument will be nonnegotiable for two reasons: it renders the note conditional, and it forces holders to look beyond the four corners of the instrument to determine their rights.

**EXAMPLES (Multiple Choice):**

1. A promise or order is conditional if the instrument states
     a. That it is secured by a mortgage or other security device.
     b. The purpose for which it was given.
     c. That it is subject to the provisions of another agreement.
     d. The account which is to be charged.

2. An instrument is nonnegotiable if it
     a. Is payable in a foreign currency.
     b. States it is secured by a mortgage.
     c. States that it is subject to any other agreement.
     d. Is issued by a partnership and limited to payment from partnership assets.

**Solutions:** 1 (c), 2 (c)

In addition, if the instrument states that the payment must come from a particular fund, its negotiability is destroyed. Notice the difference between "pay to the order of Mr. X $2,000 out of the interest received on the loan to Mr. Y," (which is conditional because it refers to a particular fund that may or may not be sufficient to cover the amount owed to Mr. X) and "pay to the order of Mr. X $2,000 and in so doing, debit Account A and credit Account B" (which is just a bookkeeping procedure and does not suggest that payment is conditional).

Notice that the additional phrases which do not impair negotiability are descriptive in nature, while those that do impair negotiability are conditional in nature.

5.   The payment must be stated in terms of money. The amount does not necessarily have to be stated in terms of U.S. currency, but it does have to be stated in terms of a currency authorized by an officially recognized governmental body. Therefore, if payment is stated in terms of something like dollars, francs, yen, or marks, the instrument will be negotiable. But if the amount to be paid is stated in terms of, say, head of cattle — a form of currency which is not officially sanctioned by any domestic or foreign government — the instrument will be nonnegotiable. If payment is stated in terms of $1,000 plus two dozen head of cattle," the instrument will be nonnegotiable also. However, if the instrument is merely secured by those head of cattle, its negotiability will not be affected.

6.   The amount to be paid must be a sum certain. This provision is required so that the payee can tell just by examining the note how much — in terms of minimum principal — will be forthcoming. The following examples illustrate the concept of sum certain:

     • Assume an instrument calls for a payment of $1,000 in two years. Assume also that the terms call for no interest charge if the $1,000 is paid within three months, 6% interest charged if it is paid after three months expire, and an additional ½% interest for every additional month after the first year expires. The payee may not know exactly how much interest he will collect when the entire debt is paid off, but the sum certain element is still present, because he knows exactly how much principal he will receive — that is, $1,000.

- Because there is always a possibility of default, most notes include a provision whereby, if the maker defaults, he will pay the collection fees. If this provision is not included, the burden of collection fees will probably fall on the payee, so that if he does not know what the collection will cost (which is usually the case), the payee cannot know how much principal he will net. Accordingly, most notes include a provision — "plus legal fees for collection" — to insure the instrument's negotiability. True, the maker does not know what those fees will be either, but the sum certain must be ascertainable by the payee only, not necessarily by the maker of the note.

- Interest does not necessarily have to be stated explicitly in a promissory note. If the terms are for "$500 plus 6 percent interest" for one year or just for "$500 plus interest," the note is negotiable. In the second case, the statutory legal interest rate will be automatically applied.

- An installment note does not render an instrument nonnegotiable because a total sum certain is not explicitly stated; a payee can easily calculate the minimum principal he will receive.

7.   The sum certain must be payable at a definite time for the instrument to be negotiable. A demand note or sight draft, which allows a holder to collect payment whenever he wants, is payable at a certain time. The holder determines that time himself. Therefore, demand notes or sight drafts do not necessarily have to be dated in order to be negotiable. If they are, though, the stated date controls. Thus, if demand paper is issued June 1 but is dated July 1 (in other words, it is *postdated*), it becomes time paper, because it will not be payable until July 1.

Time notes usually must be dated, because reference to the date is almost always necessary to determine when the note is due. If the instrument is payable "two years from now," the due date cannot be determined unless the instrument is dated. If the time of payment is ascertainable in the body of the instrument without reference to its date of issue, the instrument need not be dated to be negotiable.

If time paper is payable "on or before" a certain stated date, it meets the definite date terms of negotiability, because the holder knows the latest he may receive payment. Likewise, terms stating the note is payable "on or after" a certain date — with the extension at the maker's option — do not impair negotiability either, as long as the potential extension is not indefinite. Thus, terms calling for payment "in two years, with the right to extend time for payment to three years" will not affect negotiability. But terms calling for payment "in two years with the right to extend time for payment" will impair negotiability, because the payee cannot determine the latest time he can expect payment by examining the instrument. If the extension is at the option of the holder, however, the time limit need not necessarily be spelled out in the instrument.

If the instrument is payable when an event occurs, it is not negotiable. Thus, if the note is payable "when I graduate from school" or "one week after my grandfather dies," it will not be considered negotiable. Even if a stipulated event is certain to occur, a note is still nonnegotiable if a holder cannot determine, from the instrument alone, when the event will occur. If the note is payable "when my grandfather dies, or on January 1, 1978 — whichever comes first," it will be negotiable, because the holder can ascertain the latest possible time he will receive payment (January 1), even if he has no idea when the maker's grandfather may die.

**EXAMPLE (Multiple Choice):**

An otherwise valid negotiable instrument is nonnegotiable if it is
   a. Postdated.
   b. Undated.

   c. Payable thirty days after a stated date but with the right of the holder to demand immediate payment at his option.

   d. Payable only upon the happening of an event which is uncertain as to the time of occurrence.

**Solution:** (d)

8. The magic words of negotiability must be present to make any note or draft negotiable. Those magic words are "pay to the order of" or "pay to bearer." These words allow the holder to subsequently negotiate the note himself to another holder. A holder's ability to negotiate an instrument is at the heart of the concept of negotiability. As such, "pay Mr. X" renders an instrument nonnegotiable, whereas "pay to the order of Mr. X" or "pay to Mr. X's order," or "pay to bearer" results in a negotiable instrument.

**EXAMPLE (Multiple Choice):**

Arthur Fox purchased a large order of business supplies from Spencer & Company by paying 10% in cash and giving Spencer & Company the following instrument to cover the balance due:

Los Angeles, Calif.
February 2, 1977

   For value received, I, Arthur Fox, hereby promise to pay my debt of One thousand thirty and 26/100's dollars ($1,030.26) to Spencer & Company or to their order. The instrument is due not later than March 2, 1978, but the maker may at his option pay within one month of the date of this instrument and receive a 1% discount.

(signed) *Arthur Fox*

Which of the following is true with respect to this instrument?

   a. The instrument is a trade draft.

   b. Since Fox can pay earlier than the due date, the instrument is thereby rendered nonnegotiable.

   c. The language "For value received" is necessary in order to satisfy the requirements of negotiability.

   d. The instrument is negotiable.

**Solution:** (d)

Sometimes people who intend to create a negotiable instrument and who are familiar with the elements of negotiability, leave an instrument incomplete in one way or another. For example, a maker may forget to date an instrument when dating is necessary, or he may forget to sign it or state the sum certain. Such incomplete instruments are nonnegotiable — regardless of the maker's or drawer's intent to create a negotiable instrument — until they are completed. If the maker or drawer does not complete the instrument himself, but authorizes his agent or even the payee to do so, the instrument will be enforceable once completed. If it is completed, but the completion is unauthorized, no one except a holder in due course may enforce the terms of the instrument. Unauthorized completion may occur when an unauthorized person completes the instrument, as well as when an authorized person completes it, but in an unauthorized way.

When there is a contradiction of terms in two different areas of the instrument and in one place the terms are handwritten and in the other they are typewritten, the handwritten terms control. Similarly, amounts written out in words control those written out in numbers.

**EXAMPLE (True/False):**

Your client, Mortgage Discount Service, Inc., purchased the following piece of commercial paper from Martin Gross. Gross had received it in connection with the sale to Charles Lamb of certain real property he owned in Illinois. Martin Gross indorsed it in blank and received $14,750 from Mortgage Discount.

$15,000.00                                                                New York, New York
                                                                          February 2, 1973

Sixty days after date, I promise to pay *to the order of* Martin Gross *Fifteen Thousand + 00/100 Dollars* at the *Second National Bank of Wabash, Illinois.*

Value received with interest at the rate of 7½% per annum. This instrument arises out of the sale of real estate located in the State of Illinois. It is further agreed that:

    1. This instrument is subject to all implied and constructive conditions.

    2. The instrument is secured by a first mortgage given as per the sale of the real estate mentioned above.

    3. It is to be paid out of funds deposited in the *Second National Bank of Wabash, Illinois.*

No. 60                    Due _____                  *Charles Lamb*
                                                                          Signature

Having been sued on the instrument, Charles Lamb claims that he may assert all defenses (real and personal) against Mortgage Discount Service, Inc., in that the instrument is nonnegotiable.
    1. Since the instrument is drawn in New York and payable in Illinois, it is a "foreign" instrument.
    2. The instrument was intially bearer paper.
    3. The instrument is a demand note.
    4. The fact that the due date was not filled in at the bottom renders the instrument nonnegotiable.
    5. Clause No. 1 of the instrument renders it nonnegotiable.
    6. Clause No. 2 of the instrument renders it nonnegotiable.

**Solutions:** (1) F, (2) F, (3) F, (4) F, (5) F, (6) F

## Has the instrument been properly negotiated?

An instrument needs to conform to the format of negotiability only if the payee intends to transfer it to a third party — that is, to a subsequent holder. Before determining whether or not an instrument has actually been transferred, it is necessary to be aware of who can negotiate an instrument to a third party — that is, who can be a payee.

An instrument may be made payable to the order of the drawee, the maker or drawer; an office (such as the American Embassy); a named person with a title (such as John Doe, Secretary); an officer, without naming him (such as Treasurer of the City Council), and so forth. An instrument can also be made payable to the order of "Mr. John Doe or Mr. Ed Brown" (in which case either of the *alternate payees* may indorse the instrument to negotiate it), or to "Mr. John Doe and Mr. Ed Brown" (in which case both of the *joint payees* must indorse the instrument to negotiate it). If an instrument is made "payable to bearer" or "payable to the order of bearer" or "payable to cash," it need not necessarily be indorsed to be negotiated.

Any person can become a transferee of an instrument by virtue of that instrument being transferred to him. A holder's rights, however, will be determined by the manner of transfer. Negotiation of an instrument is a special kind of transfer. A transferee of a negotiated instrument who has fulfilled certain specific requirements is a *holder in due course.*

In order for an instrument to be validly negotiated to any holder, the transferor must deliver it to the transferee voluntarily. In addition, if the instrument is made payable to a party other than bearer, the transferor must indorse it. Thus, if the instrument is payable to bearer or to cash, only voluntary delivery by the transferor to the transferee is necessary for a valid negotiation, although an indorsement by the transferor could not hurt.

### Indorsements:

An indorsement is customarily written on the back of the instrument, with each subsequent indorsee signing under the previous one. Occasionally an instrument has been negotiated so often there is no more room for indorsements on the original instrument. In such instances indorsements can be written on an *allonge* — an additional piece of paper which must be very securely attached to the original instrument for the indorsements thereon to be valid. If a signature appears in an ambiguous place on the instrument, it will be assumed that it is an indorsement.

An indorsement does not have to be dated. Nor does it have to contain the magic words of negotiability "pay to the order of" for it to be negotiable in the hands of the indorsee, as the face of the original instrument must. Minimally, all that is needed is the bare signature of the indorser.

An indorser of an instrument calling for payment of $2,000 cannot indorse the note with directions to pay only $1,000 to the indorsee, without causing an invalid negotiation in so doing. He can, however, indorse the instrument to joint or alternate indorsees, just as long as he does not purport to direct how the principal shall be split up.

Every indorsement has three characteristics which affect how or whether the instrument can be further negotiated, as well as what rights future holders have against the indorser:

1. Every indorsement is either blank or special. If the indorser signs his signature without specifying the person or entity to whom he is negotiating the instrument, the indorsement is said to be *blank*. An instrument becomes bearer paper (if it is not so already) by means of a blank indorsement and can then be transferred just as easily as cash would be. If the indorser specifies — above his signature — the entity to whom he is making the instrument payable, the indorsement is said to be *special*. If a holder receives a blankly indorsed instrument, he may himself convert it to a special indorsement by writing directions to the effect that the instrument is payable to him, over the signature of the indorser.

2. Every indorsement is either qualified or nonqualified. If an indorsement is amended with the words "without recourse," it is said to be *qualified*. Absent those or similar words, the indorsement is *nonqualified*. A qualified indorser disclaims his liability to future holders — that is, he does not guarantee that he will pay the amount of the instrument. A qualified indorser does have some obligations to future holders, however, which are imposed upon him by the UCC in the form of warranties. By indorsing the instrument, a qualified indorser warrants that he has good title to it, that it has not been altered in any material way, that all signatures are authorized or genuine, that he has no knowledge of any insolvency proceedings against a maker or drawer, and that he has no knowledge of any defense of any party against him.

If an indorsement is unqualified, the indorser guarantees payment. The warranties which are imposed upon an unqualified indorser are also imposed upon a qualified indorser, except that instead of warranting that he has no knowledge of any defense of any party against, the unqualified indorser warrants that there is no defense of any party against him.

**EXAMPLES (Multiple Choice):**

1. The transferor of a bearer negotiable instrument who transfers without indorsing but for full consideration
    a. Is liable to all subsequent holders if there exists a personal defense to the instrument maintainable by the primary party and the transferor was aware of the defense.
    b. Warrants to his immediate transferee that he has good title.
    c. Makes *no* warranty that prior signatures are genuine or authorized.
    d. Engages that he will pay the instrument if his immediate transferor is unable to obtain payment upon due presentment and dishonor because of insufficient funds and due notice is given the transferor.

2. When the holder of a negotiable instrument transfers it for consideration by indorsing "without recourse," he
    a. Makes *no* warranty as to title as to any subsequent holder.
    b. Prevents further negotiability.
    c. Makes the same warranties as an unqualified indorser except that he warrants that he does *not* have knowledge of a defense of any party good as against him rather than that there is *no* such defense.
    d. Becomes immune from recourse to him by a subsequent holder.

**Solutions:** 1 (b), 2 (c)

An unqualified indorser is liable to subsequent holders for payment, as well as for breach of any of the warranties, whereas a qualified indorser is liable only for breach of warranty. In both cases, these warranties on transfer run only to the immediate transferee.

3. Every indorsement is either restrictive or nonrestrictive. If an indorsement is *nonrestrictive,* the indorsee's rights are not abridged in any way. However, if the indorsement is *restrictive,* the indorser has attempted to protect his interests by limiting the rights of the indorsee with regard to future negotiability. By means of a restrictive indorsement, an indorser attempts to insure that the instrument will be put directly into a bank for deposit or collection (the indorsement may read "for deposit — or collection — only") or can condition payment on the happening of a certain event (the indorsement may read "Pay Bill Smith only if the Yankees win the 1978 World Series") or see to it that the proceeds go to a third party (the indorsement may read "Pay Bill Smith for David White"). It is incumbent upon subsequent holders to see that payment is applied in accordance with the directions of the restriction. In actuality, a restrictive indorsement cannot prevent the subsequent negotiation of an otherwise valid negotiable instrument; however, such an indorsement can direct the use to which funds must ultimately be put, or when the funds can be paid to the indorsee.

**EXAMPLE (Multiple Choice):**

Kenneth Nelson has a negotiable check in his possession. It was originally payable to the order of Donna Baker. The back of the instrument contained the following indorsements:

> *Donna Baker*
>
> *Harold Sharp, without recourse*
>
> *Pay Kenneth Nelson*
> *Judy Lally*
>
> *For deposit only*
> *Kenneth Nelson*

Which of the following statements is true with respect to these indorsements?
    a. Kenneth Nelson's restrictive indorsement "for deposit only" does *not* prevent further negotiation.
    b. Kenneth Nelson *cannot* be a holder in due course because of Sharp's indorsement.

c. Harold Sharp eliminates all potential liability to himself via the "without recourse" indorsement.

d. Once Donna Baker signed the instrument in blank, it became a bearer instrument and remained so despite the subsequent indorsements.

**Solution:** (a)

REMEMBER: Negotiability is not destroyed if an indorsement does not include the words "pay to the order of" or "pay to bearer," or if it does not guarantee payment (qualified indorsement), or if it conditions the rights of the indorsee to collect (restrictive indorsement). Negotiability is destroyed, however, if any of these elements characterize the actual instrument itself.

### Is the transferee a holder in due course?

The unique value associated with the holder-in-due-course status is found in the fact that a holder in due course takes possession of the negotiable instrument free of all claims of ownership asserted by other parties and, except for a few limitations, free of all defenses to the instrument. In contrast with the rights of a holder in due course are those of a holder, whose rights are no more than those of a mere assignee. A transferee attains the status of a holder in due course if the instrument is negotiable in the first place, if it is properly negotiated in the second place, and if the indorsee (soon-to-become holder in due course) meets all of the following requirements:

1.  To be a holder in due course, a transferee/indorsee must give value for the instrument. An indorsee who has received a negotiable instrument as a gift has not given value and so is not a holder in due course. A holder does not necessarily have to give value in the face amount of the note; sufficient value is whatever the transferor and transferee agree to. However, if the holder gives less than the agreed to value, his holder in due course status protects him only to the extent that the value he gives bears to the amount agreed upon. If, at the request of the transferor, a holder agrees to forgive a loan owed to him by the transferor or by any other party, value is given by the holder even though forgiveness of a previous debt is not necessarily valid consideration under ordinary contract law. In addition, value is said to have been given if the holder gives the transferor a negotiable instrument of which he is the maker or drawer, or if he makes an irrevocable commitment to a third party at the request of the transferor.

2.  The holder must take the negotiable instrument in *good faith*. Whether or not the holder has taken the instrument in good faith is determined on a subjective basis. It will be assumed that a holder has not taken the instrument in good faith if, at the time he purchases it, he knows or has reason to know that:

    a.  There is an outstanding claim or defense against the instrument, which will allow one of the parties to it to avoid his obligation. If a holder has constructive notice of a defense, his good faith position will not necessarily be destroyed. If a purchaser learns of a claim of defense before he actually purchases the instrument, but for some reason it is too late for him to act on that knowledge, his holder in due course status will not be lost.

    b.  There is something highly irregular about the instrument's appearance that would cause a prudent man to question its validity.

    c.  The instrument is overdue. In the case of a demand note or sight draft, of course, the instrument cannot be overdue, unless it has been outstanding for an unreasonable period of time. But a purchaser cannot claim holder in due course status if, on December 15, he buys an instrument which is marked payable on December 1.

    d.  The instrument has already been presented for payment once and has been refused.

**EXAMPLE**:

Harry Fisk operates a local tuna cannery. On May 31, 1975, your client, Fair Food Wholesalers, Inc., purchased 100 cases of tuna for $12 per case, FOB Fisk's warehouse. The contract expressly stipulated that the tuna was to be first quality and all white meat in "solid chunks." It was further agreed that Fair Food had until June 10, 1975, to inspect the tuna before the transaction became final. Consequently, on May 31, 1975, Fair Food gave Fisk the following instrument:

No. <u>1625</u>

FAIR FOOD WHOLESALERS, INC.

$\dfrac{1\text{-}12}{210}$

*June 10, 1975*

Pay to the
order of  *Bearer* _____   *$1,200.00*

*Twelve hundred & no/100's* _____   Dollars

Fair Food Wholesalers, Inc.

By ___*James Duff*___
James Duff, President

CENTURY BANK
2 Broadlane
Providence, R.I.

*For tuna purchase from*
*Harry Fisk per contract dated May 31, 1975*

Fisk had orally agreed not to transfer the above instrument until June 10 or at the time final acceptance was manifested by Fair Food if this was earlier.

Fisk disregarded this agreement and promptly transferred the instrument to one of his creditors, Ross, who was threatening to force Fisk into bankruptcy. Ross took the instrument in good faith and without notice of any claim or defense in satisfaction of indebtedness arising from previous sales to Fisk which were overdue. The instrument was not indorsed by Fisk.

On June 10, 1975, Fair Food sample tested the tuna and found that it was not first quality and that it was not all white meat in solid chunks. Fair Food promptly notified Century Bank to stop payment on the instrument. Century did so and Ross is seeking recovery against Fair Food. In addition, Fair Food notified Fisk that it rejected the shipment and that it was holding the tuna on Fisk's behalf awaiting instructions from Fisk for disposition.

**Required**:

What are Ross's rights, if any, against Fair Food and Century Bank on the instrument? Explain.

**Solution**:

Ross qualifies as a holder in due course and, as such, takes the instrument free of any and all personal defenses, i.e., in this case, breach of warranty. First, the instrument is negotiable despite the postdating of the check and the fact that it recites the transaction out of which it arose. Furthermore, because it is payable to bearer, no indorsement by Fisk is necessary to negotiate it to Ross. Nor can Fair Food rely upon the fact that no new value was given in exchange for the instrument at the time of negotiation. The Uniform Commercial Code recognizes an antecedent debt as value for satisfying the value requirement to qualify as a holder in due course. As indicated in the facts, Ross took the instrument in good faith and without notice of any claim or defense. Thus, Ross takes the instrument free of any personal defenses assertible by Fair Food against Fisk.

Fair Food's stop order was proper under the circumstances and the bank correctly refused to make payment. However, since the instrument is in the hands of a holder in due course, Ross, he may proceed directly against Fair Food and collect the face amount of the instrument.

If a bona fide holder in due course subsequently transfers an instrument to another holder, that subsequent holder will automatically acquire the rights of the transferor/holder in due course, although he, himself, may not be a holder in due course. For example, if a holder in due course named A gives an instrument he has purchased to a friend named B, as a gift, B will enjoy the rights of the donor A, even though B himself is not a holder in due course, because he has not given value for the instrument. To repeat: B is not a holder in due course — he just has the rights of a holder in due course. Consequently, if B transfers the note to someone named C, C must comply with the requirements of a holder in due course in order to take the instrument free of all claims and defenses, because C has not gotten the note from a holder in due course.

Similarly, suppose A complied with all the rules and became a holder in due course, on December 1, of an instrument that is payable on December 15. If he transfers that instrument to B on December 20, B will enjoy the holder in due course status that A did, even though B took the note after it was due. However, again, B himself is not actually a holder in due course, and any subsequent purchaser could not automatically attain the preferred status.

It is the *shelter provision* which allows a transferee receiving an instrument from a holder in due course to take on that preferred status automatically.

As mentioned earlier, a holder in due course's preferred position allows him to take possession of a negotiable instrument free of all claims of possession and most defenses against the instrument. Those defenses which are not good against a holder in due course — but which are good against any other holder or assignee — are referred to as *personal defenses*. Personal defenses include:

- Lack of consideration.

- The charge that goods given as consideration do not comply with what was ordered (that is, failure of consideration).

- Unauthorized completion of an instrument.

- Breach of contract.

- Fraud in the inducement.

These are the most common, but not the only examples of personal defenses.

### EXAMPLE (Multiple Choice):

Carter fraudulently misrepresented the quality and capabilities of certain machinery he sold to Dobbins. Carter obtained a check for $2,000, the amount agreed upon, at the time he made delivery. The machinery proved to be virtually worthless. Dobbins promptly stopped payment on the check. Carter negotiated the check to Marvel in satisfaction of a prior loan of $600 and received $1,400 in cash. Marvel, who had accepted the check in good faith, presented the check for payment which was refused by Dobbins' bank.

    a. Even if Marvel is a holder in due course, Dobbins has a real defense.

    b. Marvel can only collect for $1,400 cash in that he did *not* give new value beyond that amount.

    c. Marvel will be able to collect the full amount from Dobbins.

    d. Dobbins' timely stop order eliminates his liability on the check.

**Solution:** (c)

The only defenses which are good against a holder in due course are called *real defenses.* They include all defenses which automatically make any contract null and void. Thus, if a defense is such that an underlying contract is voidable at someone's option, the defense is no good as against a holder in due course. But if a defense is such that the underlying contract would be rendered void, the defense is good against a holder in due course. Real defenses include:

- Minority, to the extent it is a defense to a simple contract.

- Illegality of subject matter.

- Adjudicated insanity.

- Discharge of debts in bankruptcy.

- Fraud in the execution.

- Duress and undue influence to the extent that they would render a contract null and void in a given jurisdiction.

- Material fraudulent alteration.

- Forgery.

**EXAMPLE**:

Barton Fashion, Inc., was in poor financial condition and desperate for cash. Wilcox, its major owner and president, contacted Marvel Department Stores, Inc., and offered to sell them 2,000 genuine alligator handbags at a bargain price. Wilcox showed several of the bags to Marvel's chief purchasing officer. These were duly examined and found to be of first quality in every respect. Marvel's chief purchasing officer placed an order with Barton for the 2,000 handbags. Payment was to be made upon delivery and inspection by Marvel. In fact, Barton had about 100 real alligator bags, the rest were clever imitations. Wilcox had the cartons packed in such a way that the genuine alligator bags were on the top of each carton. The shipment was made, and Marvel's initial inspection revealed that everything was apparently in order. Marvel delivered a check to Barton's agent who turned it over to Wilcox. Wilcox as president of Barton promptly negotiated the check to Walker, one of Barton's creditors who was threatening to file bankruptcy proceedings against Barton. Barton received $3,000 in cash and full credit against its debt to Walker for the balance of the check. Upon discovery of the fraud, Marvel promptly notified its bank, First Commerce, to stop payment on the check. When the check was presented for payment the next day, payment was refused.

**Required**:

Answer the following, setting forth reasons for any conclusions stated.

     1. What are the rights of Walker against First Commerce?

     2. What are the rights of Walker against Marvel?

**Solution**:

1. Walker has no rights against First Commerce. First Commerce validly obeyed its customer's stop order. Hence, under the circumstances it had no potential liability to Walker.

2. Walker, as a holder in due course, has a valid claim against Marvel. The defense in question is a mere personal defense and as such is not available against a holder in due course. Furthermore, Walker may collect in full; both the cash and antecedent indebtedness constitute "value" under the Uniform Commercial Code.

## Who is liable on the instrument?

Once a party's signature is on a negotiable instrument, he runs the risk of being held liable for payment. Certain signers run higher risks than others, of course, but the idea here is that if someone's signature is somewhere on the instrument — whether it is written personally or by an authorized agent or representative — liability is possible unless specifically disclaimed in one way or another. A person whose signature is not on the instrument (including a person whose signature has been forged) cannot be held liable to any party, regardless of any connection he may have had with the instrument's origination or subsequent negotiation.

A party may be primarily liable for payment or secondarily liable for payment. A *primarily liable* party is one who is unconditionally committed to pay the holder according to the terms of the instrument. A *secondarily liable* party is conditionally committed to pay — that is, there are certain events which must occur before a secondarily liable party must pay. Those conditions are *presentment, notice of dishonor,* and, sometimes, *protest.* Unless they have disclaimed their liability or have been otherwise released from it, a drawer (in the case of a draft) and indorsers (in the case of both notes and drafts) are secondarily liable on negotiable instruments.

With respect to notes, the party with primary liability is the maker of the note. With respect to drafts, there is no primarily liable party at the time it is drawn up. Once it is presented for payment to the drawee and the drawee accepts the draft, the drawee becomes primarily liable for payment. To restate then: The maker of a note is primarily liable when the note is initially drawn up. The drawee of a draft will become primarily liable only when — in the role of acceptor — he accepts the draft for payment. Upon acceptance, the drawee/acceptor is in a position identical to that of a maker of a note.

**EXAMPLE (Multiple Choice):**

Fenster has a negotiable trade acceptance in his possession. It is signed by Edwards and orders Wilberforce, a trade debtor of Edwards, to pay Fenster ten days after acceptance. Wilberforce has *not* yet accepted the instrument.

    a. The instrument is *not* negotiable until acceptance.
    b. Wilberforce *cannot* refuse to accept the instrument without incurring liability to Fenster.
    c. *No* one presently has primary liability on the instrument.
    d. A mere refusal to accept as contrasted with a refusal to pay will *not* constitute a dishonor.

**Solution:** (c)

The drawee is not bound to the payee to accept the draft; he is bound in a contractual agreement only to the drawer. If the drawee refuses to accept the draft for payment, his liability extends to the drawer for breach of contract — unless told by him not to accept the draft — and not to the payee. However, once the drawee accepts the draft, his liability for payment, as the acceptor, extends to the payee. Accordingly, a maker or acceptor who does not pay according to the terms of the instrument is in a position to be sued by the holder/payee/indorsee for breach of contract.

A holder of a sight draft does not have to bring it to the drawee for acceptance before payment; once it is presented it must be paid. A time draft, though, must be accepted to be paid. If the drawee refuses to accept and pay a draft, he is considered to have *dishonored* it.

Because it is essentially a sight draft, a check does not have to be first accepted in order to be paid. However, it may go through the process of acceptance in which case it is said to be *certified.* But because it need not be certified in the first place, a drawee's refusal to accept does not constitute dishonor of the check. Certification of a check at the request of a holder discharges the drawer and all prior (but not subsequent) indorsees from secondary liability. Certification at the request of the drawer does not. In both instances, certification renders the drawee bank primarily liable.

**EXAMPLE (Multiple Choice):**

Certification of a check by the drawee bank
    a. Is obligatory if demanded by a holder in due course.
    b. Is the drawee's signed engagement to honor it when presented.

   c. Where procured by a holder discharges all prior indorsements, but does *not* affect the drawer's liability.
   d. Is ineffective regarding any indorsement made after certification and creates *no* liability for the subsequent indorser.

**Solution:** (b)

**EXAMPLE:**

John Ford signed a check for $1,000 on January 25, 1975, payable to the order of Charles Benson Manufacturing, a sole proprietorship. The check was dated February 1, 1975. Benson indorsed the check to Francis Factoring, Inc., by writing on the back of the check: "Pay only to Francis Factoring, Inc., Charles Benson." After Benson delivered the check to Francis Factoring, Francis Factoring immediately took the check to First National Bank, the drawee, and had the check certified. Francis Factoring then indorsed the check in blank to Hills Brokerage Corporation in payment of materials purchased.

**Required:**

1. Can Hills Brokerage qualify as a valid holder of the check with all the rights of a holder in due course? Explain.

2. Assuming Hills Brokerage qualifies as a holder in due course, can it successfully sue First National Bank if the bank refuses to honor the check on February 1? Explain.

3. Assuming Hills Brokerage qualifies as a holder in due course, can it successfully sue Ford for the proceeds of the check if the bank refuses to honor it on February 1? Explain.

4. Assuming Hills Brokerage qualifies as a holder in due course, can it successfully sue Benson for the proceeds of the check if the bank refuses to honor it on February 1? Explain.

5. Assuming Hills Brokerage qualifies as a holder in due course, can it successfully sue Francis Factoring for the proceeds of the check if the bank refuses to honor it on February 1? Explain.

**Solution:**

1. Yes. The elements of a holder in due course will not be affected by the restrictive indorsement, by the fact that the check was certified, or by the fact that the check was postdated. Hills gave value, took it in good faith, had no knowledge of defenses, and the check had been properly indorsed by Benson and Francis.

2. Yes. In certifying the check the bank promises to honor the check when presented within a reasonable time after the date payable, February 1, 1975.

3. No. While a drawer of a check is normally liable to pay the amount of the check if it is dishonored by the drawee-bank, this secondary liability of the drawer, Ford, was terminated when the check was certified at the request of a holder of the check, Francis Factoring.

4. No. Benson would also be released from the secondary liability he had as an unqualified indorser by the later certification of the check by Francis Factoring.

5. Yes. Certification of a check releases all parties who signed or become secondarily liable on the check before the certification, but all indorsers after the certification remain liable to pay on the check if the bank does not.

An acceptance cannot be oral; it must be written, and it must be written on the instrument itself — not on a separate piece of paper. It can be typed, stamped, handwritten, or whatever; and any word or phrase indicating the drawee's intention to accept the draft will constitute acceptance.

A drawee can accept a draft no matter what condition it is in. Needless to say, if he accepts a partially or suspiciously completed draft, he will have trouble recovering from the drawer if the drawer did not authorize completion, etc. Thus, it behooves a drawee to exercise due care before accepting a draft, because once he accepts it he becomes primarily liable to a holder in due course for its face amount, regardless of unauthorized completion. If a drawee accepts a draft on which the drawer's signature has been forged, or a draft which has been altered without authorization by the drawer, the drawee cannot expect reimbursement from the drawer. The drawee will have to take the loss — unless he can successfully pursue the defrauder. If the forgery or alteration came about because of the drawer's own negligence, however, the drawer will have to reimburse the drawee for the funds the latter paid out.

After presenting a draft for acceptance, a draft is presented for payment. The difference between these two activities or points in time is that, when a holder presents a draft for acceptance, he is getting the drawee's promise that the draft will be paid. When he presents it for payment, however, he is actually making the demand for — and receiving — the funds.

Remember that a *note* does not have to be presented for acceptance; it is just presented for payment when it is due. Presentment of any instrument for payment is necessary to charge the indorsers. Failure to present does not usually discharge the drawer.

A holder in possession of an instrument accruing interest might well be tempted to refrain from presenting it for payment on the date it matures, in order to accrue more interest. (While a maker is committed to pay the note on the day it is due, a holder is under no obligation to present a note for payment at any particular time.) Needless to say, a maker would be at a great disadvantage with respect to this ever-accruing interest in the face of a holder who refuses to present the note for payment. The UCC has attempted to protect a maker from such circumstances. If the maker *tenders payment* (that is, tries to pay the note) when it becomes due, interest on the note will stop accruing, although the principal amount due will not change.

A holder must present an instrument at the bank at which it is made payable on the day it is due, if so noted on the instrument. If there is no mention of a specific date of maturity, it must be presented within a reasonable time. Though the definition of "reasonable" can vary from case to case, it is usually thought to be one month after the date of issue with respect to the liability of the drawer, and one week after indorsement with respect to the liability of an indorser. Of course, the discharge of one indorser based on this passage of time does not effect or lead to the discharge of any subsequent indorsers.

If, upon presentment to the primarily liable parties, either acceptance or payment is refused, the instrument is said to have been *dishonored*. (If a drawee simply requests some additional time to assure himself that the holder and draft are legitimate, he will not be charged with dishonor of the draft.) At this point, the holder must give prompt notice of the dishonor to all parties who are secondarily liable. Once he does so, he has an immediate right of recourse against all drawers and/or unqualified indorsers.

Notice of dishonor is considered to have been given if the holder apprises all secondarily liable parties of the dishonor himself, or if he just tells the last indorser — for it is incumbent upon this last indorser to notify the indorser immediately preceding him if he is to have a right of recourse himself. Graphically stated, suppose the situation is such:

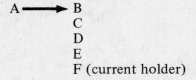

A has made the note payable to B, the payee. B has indorsed it to C, who has indorsed it to D, who has indorsed it to E, who has endorsed it to F, who is now the holder. If A refuses payment, F can either notify all secondarily liable parties (B, C, D, E) or just E, because in order to protect his right of recourse against D, E will have to give him notice. Accordingly, by virtue of a sort of domino theory, all secondarily liable parties will get notice of dishonor once the last indorser does. If, however, F chooses to notify an indorser other than E — say he notifies C only — all subsequent indorsers (D and E) will be discharged. Prior indorsers, however, are not discharged in this event.

After having given notice of dishonor, a formal protest may be required in rare instances. The UCC has virtually eliminated this requirement, except in the cases of international drafts which are payable outside of the United States.

A holder need not go through presentment, notice of dishonor, and protest in order to charge secondarily liable parties, in the following situations:

- If it is clearly written on the note that any or all of the preliminaries are waived.
- The secondarily liable party has previously dishonored the instrument.
- The secondarily liable parties cannot be located.

All liable parties — both primarily and secondarily — are discharged with respect to the holder once the instrument has been satisfactorily paid. In addition, the liable parties are discharged with respect to the holder:

- If the holder intentionally physically destroys the instrument.
- Or if the holder strikes out an indorser's signature, in which case that indorser is — and all subsequent (but not prior) indorsers who have a right of recourse against the discharged indorser are — discharged from liability.

# 7 Agency Law

The law of agency is based largely on general contract law. In other words, the relationship between an agent and principal is a contractual one. Though the actual contract is between two parties, there are usually three parties involved in this kind of relationship: the *principal* (who authorizes another to act on his behalf), the *agent* (the party so authorized), and a *third party* (the party with whom the agent deals on behalf of the principal and to whom the agent binds the principal).

**The principal-agent relationship:**

A principal-agent relationship can be brought about by means of the two parties entering into a written or oral contract, in which case all the elements necessary for a valid enforceable contract must be present. As in the case of general contract law, a principal-agent contract entered into by a minor or nonadjudicated insane principal is voidable. However, if the agent is a minor or is insane, the contract between the two is still voidable, but the principal may still be bound to a third party because of the agent's acts.

Agency may also be created by estoppel or by a principal who subsequently ratifies contracts entered into by an unauthorized agent. An agent's authority may be express, implied, or apparent. *Express* or *implied authority* is that which has actually or ostensibly been given by the principal to the agent. *Apparent authority* arises when the circumstances are such that a third party can reasonably conclude that the agent has authority to bind a principal.

**EXAMPLE (True/False):**

Opel, a poultry dealer, represented himself as Farmer Jones' agent and agreed to sell all of Jones' old hens to Bennett. Jones, who was present during this conversation, remained silent although he had not authorized Opel to act as his agent. Later Jones refused to perform and Bennett sued Jones.
    1. Opel had actual authority to sell the hens.
    2. Opel had apparent authority to sell the hens.
    3. The stated facts create an agency by estoppel.
    4. Agency by estoppel is imposed by law rather than created by the mutual consent of the parties.

**Solutions:** (1) F, (2) T, (3) T, (4) T

As a result of entering into a principal-agent relationship, the parties have certain obligations which they owe to one another. The obligations which a principal owes to an agent are:

- To fulfill his responsibilities as stipulated in the particular contract.

- To not interfere with the agent's ability to perform his duties.

- To keep records of and to keep the agent informed of payments or other obligations due to the agent.

- To make the agent aware of any physical dangers or financial risks involved in his work.

- To reimburse the agent for any money which the principal has expressly or impliedly authorized him to lay out on the principal's behalf.

**EXAMPLE (Multiple Choice):**

Farber, a principal, engaged Waters for six months as his exclusive agent to sell specific antiques.
    a. The creation of such an agency must be in writing.
    b. If the principal sells the antiques through another agent, he will be liable to Waters for damages.
    c. The principal does *not* have the legal power to terminate the agency since it is an agency coupled with an interest.
    d. Waters has impliedly guaranteed that he will sell the antiques within the six month period.

**Solution:** (b)

The obligations which an agent owes to a principal are:

- To fulfill his responsibilities as stipulated in the contract.

- Loyalty. The agent has an implied fiduciary duty imposed on him by law to act in the best interests of the principal at all times, even if and particularly when it means subordinating his own interests to those of his principal. As such, an agent cannot compete with the principal, he cannot act on behalf of anyone whose interests conflict with those of the principal or on behalf of the third party against the principal. He also cannot buy, as an undisclosed purchaser, that which the principal has employed him to sell. Because the principal and third party usually do not deal with each other directly, but only between the agent, the agent is often in the unique position of being the only one completely aware of all the facts. Thus, in meeting his fiduciary duty, an agent must disclose all the facts to the principal. An agent is liable for breach of his fiduciary duty just as surely as he is liable for breach of the express contract.

- To perform his duties with reasonable care and skill.

- To act only as authorized.

- To keep records and to keep the principal informed of any expenses he has incurred or money he has paid out on behalf of the principal.

## The principal-third party relationship:

As already noted, the principal has the right to receive certain things from and owes duties to third parties by virtue of the acts of an agent acting within express, implied, or apparent authority. Unless he subsequently ratifies it, a principal is not bound to fulfill the duties of any contract to which an unauthorized agent has bound him.

### EXAMPLE (Multiple Choice):

Walker made a contract for and on behalf of his principal which was legally unauthorized. What is the status of this contract?

  a. It is illegal.
  b. It can be ratified only by a written affirmation of the contract.
  c. It can *not* bind the third party regardless of the principal's subsequent action.
  d. It can be ratified by the principal by his silence and the receipt and retention of the benefits of the contract.

**Solution:** (d)

If an agent has express, implied, or apparent authority to delegate his duties to another person (a subagent), the principal is bound to a third party by the acts of the subagent. However, if the original agent does not have the authority to appoint a subagent, the principal will not be bound by the subagent's actions (unless he subsequently ratifies them) even though he would have been bound to a third party had the acts been those of the original agent.

A third party dealing with a principal through an agent has the right to assume:

- That any knowledge or notice he relays to the agent will, in turn, be relayed to the principal.

- That an agent with the authority to buy property for or sell property of the principal also has the authority to agree to the terms; to make the usual and customary warranties; to pay or receive the appropriate amount of the purchase price to be exchanged at the time the property is transferred; to give up or take possession of the property. (An agent does not usually have the authority to bind a principal to a contract to sell land, though. His authority usually extends only to finding a buyer.)

- That an agent directing the principal's business has the authority to engage in all activities necessary to run that business.

In addition to the liabilities which contract law imposes upon a principal for the acts of his authorized agent with respect to third parties, there are liabilities which the law of torts imposes upon a principal with respect to third parties. (A *tort* is any wrongful act which injures another's person, property, or reputation. Relief usually depends upon whether a tort has been negligently or intentionally committed.)

As such, if a principal authorizes his agent to commit a tortious act, the principal is definitely liable to the victim/third party. If the agent commits a tortious act he was not authorized to commit, the principal will still usually be held liable if the agent did so while in the principal's employ, during the ordinary course of business. If the agent is not in the principal's employ when he commits a tort (that is, if he is not under contract to the principal, or if he is under contract but is not "on the job" at the time), the principal will not be held liable to the third party.

**EXAMPLE (Multiple Choice):**

Jackson is a junior staff member of Stutz & Harris, CPAs. He has been with the firm for one year working with the audit staff.
   a. If Jackson is injured while auditing one of the firm's clients, the client's workmen's compensation insurance will cover him.
   b. The federal wage and hour laws do *not* apply to Jackson.
   c. Stutz & Harris will be liable for the torts committed by Jackson within the scope of his employment.
   d. Clients will be liable for the torts committed by Jackson since he and his principal (Stutz & Harris) were engaged by them.

**Solution:** (c)

These same rules apply to the common employer-employee relationship. The reasoning behind imposing such liability on the principal or employer is found in the doctrine of *respondeat superior*: Let the superior respond. Whether the principal or employer will be found liable to a third party for the torts committed by an agent or employee has no bearing on the agent's or employee's liability: The person who actually committed the tort (that is, the *tortfeasor*) will always be liable to the victim.

**EXAMPLE (Multiple Choice):**

Harper was employed as a carpenter by the Ace Construction Company. He negligently constructed a scaffold at one of Ace's construction sites. The scaffold collapsed and injured Dirks (a fellow employee), Franklin (a supplier), and Harper.
   a. Ace Construction Company is *not* liable to Franklin if Harper disobeyed specific instructions regarding construction of the scaffold.
   b. Ace Construction Company is liable to Franklin even though Harper was grossly negligent.
   c. Harper is *not* personally liable to Dirks or Franklin.
   d. Harper *cannot* obtain workmen's compensation.

**Solution:** (b)

If the authorized duties of an agent call for him to sign a document, the liability of the principal and/or agent to a third party will depend upon the manner in which the agent signs the document. If the agent signs "Mr. X, principal, by Mr. Y, agent," the principal — who is thereby said to be *disclosed* — is liable and the agent is not. If an agent just signs his own name, he alone will be held liable. However, if the third party is or becomes aware that the agent is representing a principal, the principal will usually be held liable, as well. The third party usually has the option to hold either the principal or the agent — but not both — liable. If an agent signs a negotiable instrument without disclosing the principal's name, or signs a document without having the authority to do so, and the principal does not ratify it, the principal will not be held liable to a third party under any circumstances. Where a principal and/or agent is liable on a contract to a third party, so is that third party liable to the principal and/or agent.

**EXAMPLE (Multiple Choice):**

Filmore hired Stillwell as his agent to acquire Dobbs' land at a price *not* to exceed $50,000; the land is badly needed to provide additional parking space for Filmore's shopping center. In order to prevent Dobbs from asking for an exorbitant price, Filmore told Stillwell *not* to disclose his principal. Stillwell subsequently purchased the land for $45,000. Under these circumstances

    a. Stillwell and Filmore committed fraud when they did *not* disclose the fact that Stillwell was Filmore's agent.

    b. Absent an agreement regarding the compensation to be paid Stillwell, he is entitled to the difference between the $50,000 limitation and the $45,000 he paid for the land; i.e., $5,000 based upon quasi contract.

    c. Dobbs may rescind the contract upon his learning the truth as long as the conveyance has *not* been accomplished.

    d. Dobbs may sue either Filmore or Stillwell on the contract in the event of default by Filmore.

**Solution:** (d)

## Termination of the agency relationship:

As in the case of any ordinary contract, the legal relationship between a principal and agent can end in many ways. An agent's authority to bind the principal can terminate if:

• The purpose or terms of the contract have been satisfactorily fulfilled.

• There is a breach of contract, including — but not only — the agent's breach of fiduciary duty.

• The principal revokes his authority or the agent renounces the authority the principal has given him.

• Performance is impossible.

• The principal or agent dies, becomes insane, or goes bankrupt.

• The subject matter of the contract or the relationship itself subsequently becomes illegal.

**EXAMPLE:**

An agent's power to bind his principal to a contract is generally terminated

    a. Automatically upon the commission of a tort by the agent.

    b. Instantly upon the death of the principal.

    c. Upon the bankruptcy of the agent.

    d. Without further action by the principal upon the resignation of the agent.

**Solution:** (b)

In some of the above-mentioned circumstances, the contract may have terminated illegally, so that the principal or the agent can sue the other for damages. Whether the contract has been terminated legally or not, the ability of the agent to bind his principal to a third party terminates if any of these events come to pass and when proper notification is given to third parties who might not otherwise be aware of the end of the relationship.

If the principal wants to insure that he will not be subsequently liable to any third parties for the actions of an agent whose authority has been terminated, he must:

• Give actual notice — by means of phone calls or letters, for example — to any third parties with whom the agent had previous dealings, and

● Give constructive notice — that is, place an ad in a trade journal or well-read newspaper — to third parties with whom the agent did not have dealings but who may have reason to assume the agent's authority is still authorized.

**EXAMPLE (True/False):**

The examination of the financial statements of the Franklin Grocery Company revealed the following dispute relating to a balance due on open account. The item in dispute was a certain quantity of canned goods allegedly purchased by the Birch Steamship Company. On October 10, 1972, Arthur Snead, one of Franklin's salesmen, called upon Birch Steamship to solicit business. He had done business for several years with Ken Small, one of Birch Steamship's purchasing agents. Upon asking for Small at the receptionist's desk, he was told that Small was not there. The receptionist then called James Drew, another purchasing agent. She informed Drew that Arthur Snead of Franklin Grocery was looking for Small. Drew told the secretary that Small was at pier 30 supervising the loading of provisions. Snead found Small at pier 30 and took the disputed order for the canned goods, which were duly shipped to Birch Steamship. Unknown to Snead, Small had been relieved of his position as purchasing agent due to incompetency. Small obtained possession of the canned goods shipped to Birch Steamship and sold them. Birch refuses to pay.

1. Small had no express authority to make the purchase on Birch Steamship's behalf.
2. Small had the apparent authority to bind Birch Steamship.
3. To defeat Franklin Grocery, Birch Steamship must show knowledge by Franklin of Small's dismissal as a purchasing agent.
4. A publication in local papers and trade publications of the removal of Small as a purchasing agent would give effective notice to new suppliers of Birch Steamship.
5. Birch Steamship is liable on the contract made by Small as its purported agent.
6. Had Birch Steamship learned of the unauthorized contract made on its behalf by Small, it could have ratified the transaction.

**Solutions:** (1) T, (2) T, (3) T, (4) T, (5) T, (6) T

If an agent attempts to bind a principal after the principal has given actual and constructive notice of termination of the agency relationship, the purported agent will be in the position of trying to bind a nonexistent principal. If such is the case, that agent alone will be held personally liable on any contracts he enters into on behalf of the nonexistent principal.

**EXAMPLE:**

In examining the financial statements of Plover Corporation, you learn that Plover hired Amber to manage its farm and gave him authority to purchase seed up to a maximum of $500 per year. Amber was also given authority to hire employees' to help operate the farm. Plover also gave Amber authority to buy for Plover, a forty-acre tract, adjacent to the farm, if it became available, and to collect the monthly rental of a house located on the farm.

Amber purchased seed from Supplee as authorized but exceeded his authority by contracting in Plover's name with Supplee for fertilizer in the amount of $600. Amber hired Mans to operate a farm tractor. While operating the tractor in a negligent manner, Mans destroyed a boundary fence belonging to Naybor. Meanwhile, Amber had entered into a contract to purchase the forty acres from Honer, its owner, without revealing that he was purchasing for Plover.

Plover, on learning of the Mans incident, discharged Amber. Amber, who had been collecting the rents on the house, promptly collected the rent then due for the current month from the lessee and disappeared. The lessee did not know of Amber's discharge.

**Required:**

1. Discuss Plover's liability to Supplee on the order for fertilizer.

2. To what extent, if any, is Plover liable to Naybor for Mans' actions?

3. What are Plover's rights under the agreement for the forty acres?

4. Discuss Plover's liability on the contract for the purchase of the land if it wishes to avoid the obligation.

5. Discuss Plover's rights to recover from the tenant of the house for the last rental payment made to Amber.

**Solution:**

1. Amber had actual authority to carry on major management duties in connection with the farm and would be deemed to have had apparent authority to purchase normal farming supplies. Supplee could reasonably believe that Amber, as farm manager, could contract for the fertilizer as well as the seed. The fact that the contract was in the amount of $600, or in excess of Amber's actual authority, would not permit Plover to avoid liability thereon because this would also reasonably appear to be within the scope of Amber's apparent authority.

2. Plover is probably liable to Naybor for the damage to Naybor's fence as a result of Man's negligence. Amber had authority to hire employees to help operate the farm, and Plover would be responsible for the act of his employee-agent acting within the scope of his employment.

3. Although Plover was an undisclosed principal, it has the right to enforce the contract made by its agent within the scope of the agent's authority.

4. The fact that Plover was an undisclosed principal gives it no right to avoid a contract made by its agent for the principal within the scope of the agent's authority.

5. The tenant, having made payment to Amber, is not liable to Plover. Plover, the principal, did not give the tenant notice that Amber's authority had been terminated. The tenant, having paid the rent to Amber on prior occasions and without notice of any lack of authority on the part of Amber to make the collection, is protected under the apparent authority doctrine, and payment to the agent is deemed effective payment to the principal.

# *8* Partnerships

When a person decides to go into business with someone else, there are several legal forms which their relationship can take. All of them are basically variations of either a partnership or a corporation. This chapter deals with partnerships, and the second with corporations. [Note: As the Uniform Commercial Code deals with contracts and various forms of contractual relationships, so the Uniform Partnrship Act (UPA) deals with partnerships and the Model Business Corporation Act (Model Act) with corporations.]

## Creation of the partnership:

A partnership can be formed very informally or by means of a formal contract. (As is the case in general contract law, contracts between partners where one has limited contractual capacity are voidable, and between partners when one has no contractual capacity are void.) A partnership is just as legal if it is formed by a simple handshake as it is if it is formed in a methodical, formal way. Regardless of how the relationship is formed, people will be deemed to be partners and to have formed a partnership if they co-own a business which is operated for the purposes of making a profit.

Tests of determining the existence of a partnership include establishing that each of the partners has invested capital in the business or has contributed their services, that they co-own the assets of the business, that they share in the profits and losses, and that they each have the right to manage and control the business. Generally all these elements must be present. A business which is not carried on for the purposes of making a profit (such as a nonprofit organization) is not a partnership; if a person helps manage a business and even shares in the profits, he is not necessarily a partner if he does not co-own the partnership assets; if a person's share in the profits comes from his receiving wages, interest on a loan to the partnership, repayment of a debt, or the like, he is not necessarily a partner; if two or more people co-own assets, share in their management and share profits and losses, a partnership does not necessarily exist if they are not carrying on a business.

If all the elements of a partnership are present, a partnership will be deemed to exist by means of estoppel, even if the people involved do not hold their relationship out as such. Similarly, an individual can be deemed a partner by estoppel if he appears to be one, even if he is not an official member of the partnership.

### EXAMPLE (Multiple Choice):

Charles Norman and Walter Rockwell did business as the Norman and Rockwell Company. This relationship was very informal and neither party considered himself to be a partner of the other. Their stationery was printed with the name of Norman and Rockwell Company. Donald Quirk loaned Rockwell $10,000 for and on behalf of the business. Norman was informed of this but stated to Rockwell, "That's your responsibility; I had nothing to do with it." Rockwell defaulted and Quirk seeks to hold both Norman and Rockwell liable on the debt. Under these circumstances

    a. Quirk *cannot* recover against Norman because of Norman's statement to Rockwell, "That's your responsibility; I had nothing to do with it."
    b. Norman and Rockwell are partners by estoppel.
    c. Absent a signed partnership agreement, Quirk *cannot* recover against Norman.
    d. The fact that neither party considered their relationship to be a partnership precludes recovery against Norman.

### Solution: (b)

A partnership is a very personal relationship. Existing partners cannot be forced to take in a partner against their will, and a nonpartner cannot be forced to become a partner against his will. As such, partnership by estoppel does not create a legal partnership relationship between people where none exists. However, if a nonpartner holds himself out through his words or actions to be a partner, or if he knows that bona fide partners are representing him to be a partner and does nothing to change that impression, the duties, liabilities, and obligations of a partner will be imposed upon him by means of partnership by estoppel if a third party relies on the impression given and, as a result, changes his position accordingly. Similarly, if the bona fide partners know that a nonpartner is representing himself as a partner and they do nothing to correct that impression, they will be held liable for the actions of that nonpartner, as if he were a bona fide member of the partnership.

A partnership is not a legal entity; it does not have an existence separate and apart from the partners. As such, a suit cannot usually be brought against or by a partnership, but only against or by the individual partners. A partnership does not pay taxes on the profits it earns, although it must file an information return with the IRS. Rather, the profits pass through the partnership to the individual partners who pay personal income taxes on their share of the profits.

**EXAMPLE (Multiple Choice):**

For federal income tax purposes, a partnership is
    a. A taxable entity similar to a trust or an estate.
    b. Considered to be a nontaxable entity but which must file an information return.
    c. Treated the same as an association for tax purposes.
    d. Required to pay a tax upon its profit which in turn must be assumed by its partners.

**Solution:** (b)

Nevertheless, in order to carry on business, a partnership is considered an entity for the purposes of being able to own partnership assets. A distinction, then, is made between partnership property owned by the partnership and personal or real property owned by the individual partners. A partnership can be declared bankrupt although the individual partners may be personally solvent, and vice versa.

A person may be a *real partner* (in which case he is an actual partner in law and in fact); an *ostensible partner* (in which case he is not a partner in law but only in fact — that is, a partner by estoppel); a *general partner* in a general or limited partnership (in which case he has unlimited liability); a *limited partner* in a limited partnership (in which case he has limited liability); a *silent partner* (a real partner who does not participate in managing the partnership business); a *secret partner* (a real partner who the public is not aware of is a member of the partnership); or a *dormant partner* (a real partner who is both silent and secret).

A partnership can be general or limited. A *general partnership* is composed solely of general partners and can be formed either formally or informally. A *limited partnership* is composed of one or more general partners and one or more limited partners and can be formed only by complying with the limited partner statutes of the controlling jurisdiction. The statutes usually require, at the least, that a certificate be filed or recorded with the appropriate public official and that public notice of the existence of the limited partnership be given. Limited partnerships are dealt with in the Uniform Limited Partnership Act (ULPA).

**EXAMPLE (Multiple Choice):**

A valid limited partnership
    a. Created pursuant to state law **cannot** be treated as an "association" for federal income tax purposes.
    b. *Cannot* be created unless there is an enabling statute in the jurisdiction.
    c. Is exempt from all Securities and Exchange Commission regulations.
    d. Must designate in its certificate the name, residence, and capital contribution of each general partner but need *not* include this information to limited partners.

**Solution:** (b)

The virtue of being a limited partner in a limited partnership is that liability extends only to the amount invested in the limited partnership, whereas a general partner's liability can extend to his personal assets if the partnership assets are not sufficient to satisfy outstanding claims on the partnership. (Partnership assets must be attached first, however, before a general partner's personal assets can be attached.)

In order to enjoy that protected position, a limited partner cannot participate in the management or operation of the business and cannot have his last name included in the name of the partnership, unless it coincidentally happens to be the name of one of the general partners. If a limited partner violates either of these two rules, his liability will automatically become unlimited.

**EXAMPLE:**

Fletcher, Dry, Wilbert, and Cox selected the limited partnership as the form of business entity most suitable for their purpose of investing in mineral leases. Fletcher, the general partner, contributed $50,000 in capital. Dry, Wilbert, and Cox each contributed $100,000 capital and are limited partners. Necessary limited-partnership papers were duly prepared and filed clearly indicating that Fletcher was the sole general partner and that the others were limited partners.

Fletcher managed the partnership during the first two years. During the third year, Dry and Wilbert overruled Fletcher as to the type of investments to be made, the extent of the commitments, and the major terms contained in the leases. They also exercised the power to draw checks on the firm's bank account. Finally, Fletcher withdrew and was replaced by Martin, a new and more receptive general partner. Cox did not join his fellow partners in these activities. However, his name was used without qualification and with his general knowledge and consent on the partnership stationery as part of the firm's name.

**Required:**

Discuss the legal liability of Martin, Dry, Wilbert, and Cox, as individuals, to creditors of the partnership.

**Solution:**

Martin, Dry, Wilbert, and Cox are all liable as general partners. Martin is an incoming general partner, and, as such, he would have the same liability as a general partner in an ordinary partnership. In effect, the law states that he has unlimited joint and several liability. However, as to obligations incurred prior to his entry into the partnership, his liability cannot exceed his capital contribution.

Dry and Wilbert are liable as general partners because, in addition to the exercise of their rights and powers as limited partners, they also took part in the control of the business.

Cox's liability as a general partner rests upon the doctrine of estoppel or a specific provision under the Uniform Limited Partnership Act. The act provides that a limited partner whose name appears in the partnership name is liable as a general partner to partnership creditors who extend credit to the partnership without actual knowledge that he is not a general partner. Hence, unless a creditor knows of Cox's true status, Cox has unlimited liability to that creditor.

Another difference between a general and limited partner is that the former's contribution to the partnership can be in the form of capital, property and/or services, while the latter's can only be in the form of capital and/or property. A limited partner, then, is essentially like a shareholder/investor in that he contributes capital to the organization, participates in the profits, but has no say in its management.

Aside from general and limited partnerships, other partnership-type associations of which people can become members include:

- *Joint ventures:* These are partnerships organized for a specific, limited period of time and/or to complete a specific project.

- *Trading partnerships:* These are partnerships which make profits by buying and selling goods.

- *Nontrading partnerships:* These are partnerships which make profits by rendering services. Doctors, lawyers, CPAs, and the like, organize into nontrading partnerships.

As already noted, a partnership can be created by the people involved conducting themselves as partners (that is, by estoppel), or by oral or written contract. Contracts between partners do not have to be in writing unless the partnership is to continue for longer than a year, in which case the contract falls within the Statute of Frauds and must be written to be enforceable. However, whether the Statute of Frauds applies or not, it is usually a good idea to reduce the agreement to writing and, in so doing, to clarify the name of the partnership (which may consist of the partners' real names or be fictitious), the names of the partners, the way in which profits and losses will be shared, the purpose of the partnership/business, each partner's initial capital contribution, and any other information or terms which the partners consider worth their while to have in writing. When the partnership contract is reduced to writing, the contract is called the Articles of Partnership.

**EXAMPLE (Multiple Choice):**

The Statute of Frauds requires a written partnership agreement when the partnership
    a. By its terms has a duration of more than one year.
    b. Has assets in excess of $5,000.
    c. Is engaged in the real-estate business.
    d. Contains members who reside in different states.

**Solution:** (a)

## Partnership property:

One characteristic of a partnership is co-ownership of the partnership property by all the partners. When people co-own property as partners, they are said to be *tenants in partnership*. Tenancy in partnership confers upon each co-owning partner certain rights and limitations:

- A tenant in partnership may not assign his interest in partnership property to a non-partner (which includes a partner by estoppel).

- A tenant in partnership may not utilize his share in partnership property in any nonpartnership-related activity.

- Nonpartnership creditors of an individual partner may not initially go against the debtor/partner's share of partnership property.

Partnership property may be real or personal. No special problems arise with respect to personal property. However, in order to enable the partnership to carry on its business, certain rules which generally apply to real property are somewhat modified when real property is held by a partnership. For example, title to real property normally passes to a decedent's widow or to his heirs at law. However, while a partner's right to his share of the partnership's profits can pass to his heirs, his interest in specific partnership assets cannot. The interest in partnership property passes to surviving partners. To overcome these two opposing concepts, the courts allow real property to be considered as personal property when it is held by tenants in partnership. As such, by means of this doctrine of *equitable conversion,* a deceased partner's interest in real property held by the partnership passes to the surviving partners.

**EXAMPLE:**

Dowling, a partner of Lazor, Bassett, Dowling, & Lamb, died on February 2, 1976. The four partners were equal partners in all respects (i.e., capital accounts, profit and loss sharing, etc.). The partnership agreement was silent on the question of the rights of a deceased partner upon his death. Dowling's Last Will and Testament bequeathed his entire estate to his "beloved wife." His widow is now claiming the right to 25% of all partnership property.

**Required:**

1. What rights does Dowling's widow have in respect to specific partnership property or against the partnership or surviving partners? Explain.

**Solution:**

Mrs. Dowling has no rights to any particular partnership property nor to a share thereof. Pursuant to the Uniform Partnership Act, the surviving partners have a right of survivorship in all partnership property, and such property is not subject to the surviving spouse's award. The property passes according to this law regardless of any provisions contained in a deceased partner's last will and testament.

However, Mrs. Dowling does have the right to compensation for her husband's partnership interest. At a minimum, this would consist of a return of his capital contribution plus accumulated and current profits to the date of death. However, if the partners wish to continue the firm without a "winding up" and under its existing name, then the aspect of goodwill and the fair market value of the decedent's interest becomes more complex. If the problem cannot be solved amicably by negotiation between the remaining partners and the widow, then an independent appraisal or litigation or both would be necessary.

Another modification relating to real estate is one of common law as changed by the UPA. Under common law, title to real property could only be transferred to an individual partner or partners; it could not be transferred to the partnership as an entity. The UPA has changed the common law in this area and allows title to real property to be in the name of the partnership, or, as was always the case, in the name of an individual partner as a member and representative of the partnership. Once title to the property has been acquired by and in the name of the partnership, it can only be subsequently transferred by and in the name of the partnership. If title to real property has been acquired for the partnership and with partnership funds, each partner has a right to possess an appropriate portion of that real property, even if title happens to be in one individual partner's name.

**The relationship between the partners:**

When a person becomes a partner, he has certain rights to which he is entitled from the other partners, as well as certain obligations which he owes to them.

1. *Rights:*

   a. A partner has a right to share in the profits that come from the operation of the business which the partnership is formed to carry on. If the partnership contract is in writing (that is, if articles of partnership exist), the ratio in which the partners are to share profits will usually be clearly stated. If they are not spelled out, partners share the profits in equal proportions. Whether the terms are explicitly stated or not, the ratio in which they share profits is not necessarily connected to or dependent on the ratio of each partner's capital contribution to total partnership capital.

   b. A partner has the right to participate in the overall management of the partnership's business operations. He may choose not to participate at all (to be a silent partner), or he may choose to concentrate on managing only one aspect of the business. Nevertheless, he has the right to know what is going on in all areas.

   c. A partner or his authorized representative has the right to inspect the books of the partnership whenever he wants to, and to demand a full accounting regarding ways in which partnership capital is being used and profits are being distributed. A partner may enforce these rights — as well as the more tangible rights — in court.

   d. A partner has a right to receive the balance of his capital contribution upon liquidation of the partnership. The balance is what remains after all the partnership creditors have been satisfied. He has no right to receive any interest on that capital contribution, however, unless there is a delay in transferring it back to the contributor. In case of such a delay, the partner has a right to interest earned on the capital from the day it should have been distributed to the day it actually is.

2. *Obligations:*

a.   A partner has an obligation to share in the losses of the partnership. If this ratio is not stated in the articles of partnership, each partner is obliged to bear the burden of losses in the same proportion in which they share profits. If the ratio of profit sharing is also not stated, they will all bear the burden of losses equally. Again, the ratio in which partners share losses is not necessarily connected to and not dependent upon the amounts their initial capital contribution bears to total partnership capital.

b.   Partners owe very high fiduciary duties to one another. In an effort to insure that each partner will be loyal to the others, it has been established that partners are not allowed to make secret profits from the partnership, to compete with other partners, and so forth. They are on their good faith to disclose all information which they possess to the other partners and to subordinate their personal interests to those of the partnership. A partner's fiduciary duty to the partnership is identical to an agent's fiduciary duty to his principal.

Notice that nowhere has a partner's right to a salary been mentioned. This is because a partner has no right to receive a salary unless it is specifically allowed for in the partnership contract.

**EXAMPLE (Multiple Choice):**

Webster, Davis, and Polk were general partners in the antique business. Webster contributed his illustrious name, Davis managed the partnership, and Polk contributed the capital. Absent an agreement to the contrary, which of the provisions would automatically prevail?
   a. Polk has the majority vote in respect to new business.
   b. Polk has assumed the responsibility of paying Webster's personal debts upon insolvency of the partnership.
   c. Webster, Davis, and Polk share profits and losses equally.
   d. Davis is entitled to a reasonable salary for his services.

**Solution:** (c)

## The principal-agent relationship:

Each partner in a partnership is both an agent and a principal with respect to the other partners. Accordingly, much of partnership law regarding the duties each partner owes the other partners and third parties is nothing more than agency law. (See Chapter 7.) In fact, partnership law is basically a subset of agency law. Accordingly, the act of each partner is the act of the partnership (that is of every partner). The ability of one partner to bind all the others, of course, is only possible within the boundaries of activities clearly connected with the business of the partnership. If an individual partner buys a pleasure boat for his personal enjoyment, the other partners are not bound to contribute a share of the purchase price. But if the same partner buys the same boat for use in the normal course of the partnership business, all the other partners must share in its cost.

As in ordinary agency law, a partner's authority to act as an agent for the partnership may be express, implied, apparent, or it may exist by virtue of partnership by estoppel. In certain particular instances, one partner's actions do not automatically bind the partnership unless they are authorized and/or ratified by all the partners. Such actions include:

- Disposing of the goodwill of the business.

- Assigning partnership property in trust for creditors or on the assignee's promise to pay partnership debts.

- Doing anything that would make it impossible to carry on the ordinary business of the partnership.

- Confessing a judgment.

- Submitting a partnership claim or liability to arbitration or reference respectively.

- Admitting a new partner.

- Any other action which is clearly outside the ordinary scope of the partnership business.

A partnership is liable to third parties for the acts of a nonlegal partner who holds himself out as one with the partnership's knowledge, and a nonpartner who allows himself to be held out as a partner is liable to a third party along with the members of the partnership. The basis of liability in both cases, as noted earlier, is partnership by estoppel. To restate: Partnership by estoppel does not create a legal partnership where none exists; the doctrine of *delectus personae* allows people to choose their own partners. Partnership by estoppel merely imposes partnership liability on a nonpartner, or on a partnership, to a third party when that third party, in reasonably relying on the false representation, materially changes his position accordingly. A third party who knows that a person holding himself out to be a partner is not a partner, cannot, of course, claim partnership by estoppel. A partner who does not consent to allow a nonpartner to be represented as a partner is not liable for the nonpartner's actions if he goes on record that he does not acquiesce to the representation.

Partners are always *jointly liable* on all contractual obligations of the partnership. If a suit is brought against all the partners as joint obligors, each one must be made a defendent in the one suit. A judgment must be against all the joint obligors or none of them. A judgment against one or release of one joint obligor is automatically a judgment against all or release of all of them.

Some jurisdictions differentiate between joint obligations of partners and *joint and several obligations.* In those jurisdictions, joint and several obligors may be sued in one action or in as many different actions as there are joint and several obligors. The option is with the plaintiff. If they are all defendents in one action, the above rules of joint obligation apply. If each is a defendent in a separate action, a judgment may be made against one joint and several obligors without being made against the others. Similarly, the release of one joint obligor in one action does not automatically release the others. Each action is separate and independent of the others and each case will be tried on its own merits. It is up to the plaintiff to choose the course of action which he believes will result in the greatest relief.

The liability for torts committed by one of the partners or by an employee of the partnership is always joint and several and the appropriate rules apply. As in the case of general agency law, the liability can be imposed only if the tortfeasor was acting while carrying on the business of the partnership.

**EXAMPLE:**

Arms, Balk, and Clee formed a partnership to operate a retail drug and sundries store under the name Drug Shop. Arms and Balk each contributed $25,000, and Clee contributed the store building in which the business was to be carried on. Clee was credited with a contribution of $50,000, the fair value of the property. Clee retained title in his own name. It was agreed that Arms whould have the sole right to purchase merchandise on credit. The partners agreed that Balk was to act as manager of the store. The firm hired Dell, a pharmacist, for a five-year term and agreed to pay him a fixed annual salary plus 10 percent of the profits.

Following are events which occurred subsequent to the formation of the partnership.

- Fricke, a supplier of fixtures, indicates to the partners that he would sell fixtures to the firm on credit only if Dell, the pharmacist and a wealthy man, was a partner. Dell, who was present, said that he was a partner, and the sale on credit was made. Dell, however, later notified all others dealing with the firm that he was not a partner.

- Balk ordered merchandise, for resale by the store, on credit from a wholesaler in the firm name.

- Else was admitted as a partner with a 1/5 interest in the partnership and in profits and losses upon payment of $40,000.

- Clee, who was generally known to be a partner in the firm, (a) guaranteed in writing and in the firm name a note executed by a customer in purchasing a car for the customer's own use, and (b) conveyed in his own name the store building to Sweeney.

**Required:**

1. Prior to admitting Else as a partner, if the partnership agreement was silent about sharing profits and losses, how should the partners share a remaining profit of $30,000 after all payments to Dell? Explain.

2. If the partnership becomes insolvent, may creditors hold Dell liable as a partner? Explain.

3. Can the wholesaler hold the firm to the contract? Explain.

4. Will Else have any liability to creditors of the firm for obligations which arose prior to his admission? Explain.

**Solution:**

1. The three partners would share the profit equally in the absence of an agreement to the contrary despite the fact that capital contributions were unequal.

2. As a partner by estoppel, Dell would be held liable to Fricke on the obligation because Dell actively held himself out as a partner. He cannot be so held by others who knew that he was not a partner. In spite of the fact that he shared in profits and absent a finding of partnership by estoppel, Dell would not incur partnership laibility by virtue of his sharing in profits. While a sharing in profits is evidence of partnership, the Uniform Partnership Act provides that no such inference of partnership shall be drawn if such profits were received in payment as wages of an employee.

3. The wholesaler can hold the firm to the contract unless the wholesaler knew of the restriction on Balk's authority. Balk was acting within his apparent authority as an agent of the partnership in carrying on a normal activity. If the wholesaler knew of the restriction, the firm would not be bound.

4. Under the Uniform Partnership Act, a person admitted as a partner into an existing partnership is liable for all the obligations of the partnership arising before his admission as though he had been a partner when such obligations were incurred, but this liability may only be satisfied out of partnership property, and his liability is limited, therefore, to his share of the partnership property.

## Extinguishing the partnership:

Prior to final extinction or termination, the partnership goes through two distinct and separate stages: dissolution and liquidation. Actual termination can be seen as the third stage. The liquidation and termination stages are very closely connected, and the latter almost invariably follows the former. However, a partnership can be dissolved (that is, go through the dissolution stage) without necessarily eventually terminating, although termination begins with dissolution.

*Dissolution* is a change in the members of the partnership. Dissolution of a partnership is automatically caused by the death of a partner, by the admission of a new partner, or by the retirement of an existing partner. However, these changes do not automatically lead to the termination of the partnership — just to its dissolution. The liquidation of partnership assets and satisfaction of outstanding debts must occur before termination results and is complete.

**EXAMPLE:**

Braudy and Jones are partners and wish to admit Halsey to the partnership. If Halsey is admitted
   a. He is liable for preexisting obligations of the partnership to the same extent as Braudy and Jones.
   b. Only Braudy and Jones are liable for preexisting obligations of the partnership.
   c. The old partnership is dissolved.
   d. The old partnership must be wound up and liquidated.

**Solution:** (c)

Given this definition of dissolution as established by the UPA, it becomes clear that any partner has the power to dissolve the partnership by simply leaving it. The partnership agreement determines whether he has the legal right to do so, however, and if that right does not exist, the partner causing the dissolution can be sued by the remaining partners for breach of contract. He cannot be forced to rejoin the partnership, however. (In other words, the remedy of specific performance is not available for the remaining partners.)

Besides the three ways already noted, a partnership can be dissolved:

- If the partners mutually agree to dissolve, either by express or implied language or conduct.

- If the partnership was a joint venture and its purpose has been completed or the time for which it was supposed to exist has elapsed.

- If the partnership becomes illegal subsequent to its formation.

- If the partnership or a partner goes bankrupt. If the partnership becomes insolvent, each individual partner must contribute from his own personal funds sufficient money to satisfy any of the partnership's outstanding debts which exceed total partnership capital. If any of the partners are personally insolvent as well, the solvent partners must personally contribute that much more. Contributions to an insolvent partnership are considered losses, and the solvent partners contribute funds in the same ratio that they share losses in the normal course of operations.

If the partnership or an individual partner is bankrupt and assets must be liquidated to pay partnership or individual debts, a *marshalling of assets* takes place. In marshalling the assets, the bankruptcy court segregates the property of the partnership from the property of the individual partners. Partnership creditors go against the partnership assets first. In the event they are insufficient to satisfy all the outstanding debts, partnership creditors may then go against the assets of the individual partners. The fact that this possibility exists is at the heart of a general partner's unlimited liability. Nonpartnership creditors (personal creditors of the individual partners) go against the assets of the individual partners first. In the event they are insufficient, the creditors can go against the assets of the partnership. The order of claims on a partnership's assets is:

- Partnership creditors.

- Nonpartnership creditors.

- Partner creditors. (That is, partners who have loaned money to the partnership. These loans are distinguished from a partner's initial capital contribution upon admission to the partnership.)

- Return of initial capital contributions to the partnership in the same proportion that the assets were initially contributed.

- Distribution of any remaining surplus among the partners according to their profit-sharing ratios, or equally.

**EXAMPLE (Multiple Choice):**

Kimball, Thompson, and Darby formed a partnership. Kimball contributed $25,000 in capital and loaned the partnership $20,000; he performed no services. Thompson contributed $15,000 in capital and part-time services, and Darby contributed only his full-time services. The partnership agreement provided that all profits and losses would be shared equally. Three years after the formation of the partnership, the three partners agreed to dissolve and liquidate the partnership. Firm creditors, other than Kimball, have bona fide claims of $65,000. After all profits and losses have been recorded there are $176,000 of assets to be distributed to creditors and partners. When the assets are distributed
  a. Darby receives nothing since he did *not* contribute any property.
  b. Thompson receives $45,333 in total.
  c. Kimball receives $62,000 in total.
  d. Each partner receives one-third of the remaining assets after all the firm creditors, including Kimball, have been paid.

**Solution: (c)**

The order of claims on an individual partner's personal assets are:

- Nonpartnership creditors.

- Partnership creditors.

- Partners who have contributed an insolvent partner's portion of funds necessary to satisfy any outstanding debts owed to partnership creditors.

In addition to all the above-mentioned ways in which a partnership may be dissolved, a partner or a third party may petition a court to dissolve a partnership. A partner may petition a court to dissolve the partnership, and the court may agree to do so, if:

- The business can only continue at a loss.

- One of the partners becomes insane or otherwise incapacitated.

- One of the partners wilfully breaches the partnership contract.

- One of the partners acts in a way which is detrimental to the partnership.

A third party may petition a court to dissolve a partnership, and the court may agree to do so, if:

- The third party is a judgment creditor of a partner and is applying to the court for the appointment of a receiver. This action does not always have to lead to dissolution of the partnership.

- The third party is an assignee whose rights to receive the profits ordinarily due the assignor/partner have been denied. The mere assignment of a partner's right to partnership profits does not automatically dissolve the partnership, but an assignee may choose to petition the court for dissolution if he feels there is no other way for him to get relief. An assignee's rights are limited to receiving the assignor's share of the profits; he cannot participate in managing the partnership's business affairs, and cannot demand an accounting or the right to inspect the books — unless he is subsequently admitted as a partner to the partnership by the mutual agreement of all the partners. If and when admitted, of course, his rights are those of a partner, not of an assignee. Again, a petition by an assignee does not automatically dissolve the partnership.

Once the partnership is dissolved — regardless of how — a partner ceases to be the authorized agent of the other partners. Accordingly, he can no longer bind them by his actions.

If the partnership is dissolved because a partner withdrew, it is incumbent upon the remaining partners to personally notify creditors with whom they have dealt regularly of the partnership's dissolution. (Constructive notice is sufficient for the general public.) Otherwise the partnership may be held liable for that partner's actions. Similarly, a withdrawing or retiring partner can protect himself from incurring liability as a result of the actions of the remaining partners by personally notifying creditors (and constructively notifying the public) that he is no longer a partner. If a creditor knows of the dissolution, he cannot go against the partnership or partner regardless of whether he has been properly notified or not.

Other points to remember about dissolution are:

- If a partnership dissolves because a partner withdrew, died, or because a new partner was admitted, it is legally possible — and highly likely — that the new partnership will continue the business of the old partnership as if the dissolution did not occur. In such cases, the creditors of the dissolved partnership become creditors of the new partnership.

- If a partnership dissolves as a result of the admission of a new partner to the partnership, the new partner's liability for partnership debts incurred before his admission is limited to the value of his capital contribution. He has unlimited liability, however, for all partnerhsip debts incurred from the day of his admission on.

● A retiring partner may enter into an agreement with the remaining partners such that those remaining will not hold him responsible for any debts which were incurred while he was a partner but which have not been paid at the time of his withdrawal. Regardless of any such agreement, a creditor of the predissolved partnership can go against the retiring partner's personal assets if the partnership assets at the time of collection are insufficient to satisfy the outstanding debts of the partnership. The retiring partner cannot disclaim his liability to the creditor by pointing to his agreement with the remaining partners. His only recourse, after paying the creditor, is to bring an action against the partners for breach of contract.

**EXAMPLE (Multiple Choice):**

Grand, a general partner, retired, and the partnership held a testimonial dinner for him and invited ten of the partnership's largest customers to attend. A week later a notice was placed in various trade journals indicating that Grand had retired and was no longer associated with the partnership in any capacity. After the appropriate public notice of Grand's retirement, which of the following *best* describes his legal status?

    a. The release of Grand by the remaining partners and the assumption of all past and future debts of the partnership by them via a "hold harmless" clause constitutes a novation.

    b. Grand has the apparent authority to bind the partnership in contracts he makes with persons who have previously dealt with the partnership and are unaware of his retirement.

    c. Grand has *no* liability to past creditors upon his retirement from the partnership if they all have been informed of his withdrawal and his release from liability, and if they do *not* object within 60 days.

    d. Grand has the legal status of a limited partner for the three years it takes to pay him the balance of the purchase price of his partnership interest.

**Solution:** (b)

If the partners intend to terminate the partnership, liquidation follows dissolution, and termination follows liquidation. *Liquidation* occurs by the partnership's satisfying all outstanding debts owed to its creditors from cash on hand and from any cash received by liquidating its assets if the cash on hand is not sufficient. (Remember that creditors include any partners who may have extended a loan to the partnership.) Following the satisfaction of all creditors, the partners' initial capital contributions are returned to them to the extent that they are still intact. Finally, if there is any surplus left — usually in the form of undistributed profits — it is distributed among the partners according to their profit sharing ratios. Again, if no ratios are stipulated, it is distributed equally.

# 9 Corporations

As noted at the beginning of the last chapter, most nonsole proprietorships are some kind of partnership or corporation. Corporations differ from partnerships in many ways:

1. A corporation can only exist in a jurisdiction that authorizes its formation by statute and then only by the incorporators' complying with the statute. A partnership (except a limited partnership) can exist anywhere and can be created by the partners' simple oral agreement to form the partnership.

2. A corporation is a legal entity which exists separate and apart from its shareholders. Even if all the stock is owned by one person, there is a legal differentiation made between the corporation and the stockholder. Because it is a legal entity, a corporation is taxed directly for the income it realizes each period; the personal assets of its stockholders — beyond their investment in the corporation — cannot be attached if the corporation defaults on any of its obligations or commits any torts. A partnership is not a legal entity existing apart from the individual partners. A partnership is not taxed on its income; the partners are personally taxed as the partnership income flows through to them. Also, a general partner's liability is not limited to his capital investment in the partnership; he is subject to unlimited liability (that is, all his personal assets can be attached) for the contracts, debts, and torts of the partnership and other partners acting within the scope of the partnership business. Because it is a legal entity, a corporation can bring suit and have a suit brought against it in the corporation's name. Not being a legal entity, a partnership cannot bring suit or have a suit brought against it in the partnership name.

3. Ownership of a corporation is evidenced by shares of stock which can be freely transferred from one shareholder to another without a transferor or transferee getting the approval of any other shareholder. Ownership of a partnership is evidenced by having an interest in the partnership; this interest cannot be transferred to a nonpartner without the approval of all the existing partners.

4. While the outstanding stock of a corporation is usually owned by more than one person, it can be owned by only one person; the assets of a partnership, by definition, are owned by at least two people.

5. A corporate stockholder is not a principal or an agent of the other stockholders or of the corporation. A partner is both a principal and an agent of the other partners.

6. The stockholders, though owners, are not directly involved in the daily management of the corporation's business affairs, although they do elect the members of the board of directors who, in turn, appoint the corporate officers who directly manage the business affairs day by day. Partners, as owners, can each have an equal and direct voice in the day-to-day management of the partnership's business.

7. A corporation has an unending life; it continues to exist in perpetuity, regardless of the fact that a shareholder dies, sells his stock, or a new shareholder purchases stock. A partnership dissolves (though it does not necessarily terminate) as soon as a partner dies, retires, sells his interest to a new partner, etc. — that is, as soon as the membership of the partnership changes.

## The incorporation process:

A corporation is a creature of the state in which it is incorporated, and whatever rights it may have are given to it by the state. A corporation cannot be created in a jurisdiction which does not have a general incorporation statute. There is no necessary uniformity among state incorporation statutes. Close attention must be paid to the provisions in the relevant state's statute to assure compliance.

A corporation may be incorporated in any state that has such a statute. The choice is usually made by the incorporators according to the statutory provisions which are most beneficial to them. Once incorporated in a given state, a corporation is said to be *domestic* with respect to that state. Corporations are *foreign* with respect to states in which they are not incorporated. Incorporation statutes may differ with respect to fees charged to incorporate, taxes assessed on corporate income, voting rights which must be given to shareholders, restrictions on shareholder voting rights, powers which directors may exercise, powers which shareholders may exercise, ways in which a corporation's articles of incorporation may be changed, and so forth.

The procedures which must be followed to incorporate are determined primarily by the appropriate statutes and also by the Model Business Corporation Act. As with the UCC, the Model Act's provisions do not become law in a state until they have been adopted by its legislature. Again, as with the UCC, adoption of the Act's provisions is voluntary, each provision may be adopted in its entirety or in part, as written or amended.

In general, incorporation is complete and a corporation comes into existence in the following way:

1.  Organizers of a proposed corporation start the ball rolling. Pre-incorporation organizers are called promoters, because it is their job to promote the "corporation" to the public. (Note: To distinguish a proposed, not yet incorporated "corporation" from a fully incorporated corporation, the former will be written within quotation marks.) The promoter tries to interest the public in subscribing to the stock of the "corporation." Although it often appears as though the promoter is offering the stock to the subscriber, in fact it is the subscriber who is legally offering to purchase the stock of the "corporation." Accordingly, as in the case of an ordinary contract, acceptance of the subscription offer binds him, and he becomes a shareholder immediately upon acceptance.

A subscriber of a "corporation" is not the same thing as a person who purchases stock on an installment basis (often called a subscription) from an already existing corporation. The subscriber becomes a shareholder as soon as his offer to purchase stock is accepted, whether he has possession of a stock certificate or not. A purchaser (that is, one who purchases stock on the installment plan), however, is not a bona fide shareholder until he receives his certificates of ownership. Accordingly, up until the time the purchaser receives his certificate, he neither enjoys the rights nor owes the obligations of a shareholder and, in fact, can revoke his offer and renege on the unpaid balance of the purchase price. A subscriber to a "corporation's" stock, on the other hand, enjoys all the rights and owes the duties of a shareholder, and must pay the entire purchase price due (though not necessarily immediately) once his offer has been accepted, whether he has possession of the stock certificates or not. The Model Act stipulates that, unless otherwise agreed to by the other subscribers, or unless a provision is made in the subscription agreement, a subscriber cannot revoke his offer to purchase shares in the "corporation" for six months.

Besides promoting the "corporation's" stock, promoters may also enter into contracts for the benefit of the "corporation." Promoters have a fiduciary duty to both the subscribers and the "corporation" to disclose all relevant information, to account for all monies taken in and paid out for the benefit of the "corporation" and its shareholders, and to act in the best interest of the "corporation" and its owners. Often, in acting in the "corporation's" best interests, a promoter will sign a contract in his own name, believing he is acting as an agent for the "corporation." Any contract on which he signs his own name binds only the promoter; it neither binds a pre-incorporated "corporation" — which has no legal existence and so cannot be bound — nor a corporation after it is incorporated. Nor is a "corporation" or a corporation bound if the promoter signs a contract in its name as opposed to in his own. A "corporation" can only be bound by a promoter's pre-incorporation contract if it expressly or impliedly ratifies the contract after it becomes legally incorporated.

**EXAMPLE (Multiple Choice):**

Smith, a promoter, entered into a contract with Ace Equipment, Inc., for the purchase of equipment for $23,500. Smith contracted for the equipment on behalf of a yet-to-be-formed corporation, Eastern Machinery Co. No mention of Smith's intent or the planned incorporation appeared in the contract. The incorporation has been complete. Smith is
    a. *Not* liable for the $23,500 because of his role as agent for the corporation.
    b. Jointly liable with the corporation for the $23,500.
    c. Primarily liable for the $23,500.
    d. Relieved of liability on the contract when it is ratified by Eastern.

**Solution:** (c)

2. The articles of incorporation are prepared and signed by the "corporation's" incorporators, and submitted to the appropriate state official. The articles of incorporation set forth the name and address of the "corporation"; the names and addresses of the incorporators; the purpose for which the "corporation" is being organized; the number, classes, rights associated with and par value of stock they want authorized; the names and addresses of the provisional directors; any other provisions which the incorporators wish to include; any other provisions which must be included, as required by the state statute.

**EXAMPLE (Multiple Choice):**

A corporation has the power to create and issue the number of shares of stock stated in its
    a. Articles of incorporation.
    b. By-laws.
    c. Minutes of shareholders' meetings.
    d. Minutes of directors' meetings.

**Solution:** (a)

3. When the articles of incorporation are approved by the appropriate state authority, they are allowed to be filed by the "corporation," and the state issues a *charter* or *certificate of incorporation,* which includes a duplicate of the articles of incorporation. Once the articles are filed and the charter is issued, the "corporation" becomes a fully and legally incorporated entity. At this point the business of the promoters and incorporators is finished — unless they happen to be directors or officers of the corporation — and subscribers become shareholders.

Any legal business except banking and insurance can be organized under a state's general incorporation statutes. Banking and insurance companies can only be incorporated under special acts of the state legislature.

There are many perfectly legal advantages to incorporating a business:

- Great amounts of capital can be gathered by selling stock.

- There is limited liability of shareholders.

- Shares (ownership) can be easily transferred.

- Perpetual existence, etc.

To some people, the greatest advantage is that an individual shareholder can escape personal liability for the contracts entered into, debts incurred by, and torts committed by the corporation. In cases where shareholders use the corporation as a shield to protect them from incurring personal liability for fraudulent or criminal actions, or activities which go against public policies, the courts will nevertheless hold the shareholders personally liable for acts performed in the corporation's name. In such circumstances, the courts are said to be *piercing the corporate veil.*

**EXAMPLE (Multiple Choice):**

The separate corporate entity will be disregarded if
    a. One man owns all the shares of stock.
    b. It was used to effect a fraud.
    c. There is a parent-subsidiary relationship between two corporations.
    d. It is used for the purpose of obtaining limited liability.

**Solution:** (b)

A corporation can exist in law (de jure corporation), in fact (de facto corporation), or by estoppel.

1. *De jure corporation:* This is a corporation whose existence has come about after the incorporators have complied with the relevant incorporation statutes to the letter. Its existence as a corporation cannot be challenged by a private citizen or by the state.

2. *De facto corporation:* If a general incorporation statute exists, and the incorporators have made good faith attempts to comply with it in the process of incorporation but, in fact, have not done so in some respect, a de facto corporation exists if corporate business has been carried on in the belief that the statute had been fully complied with. Its existence cannot be challenged by a private citizen, but it can be challenged by the state, although only in a direct action. A de facto corporation has the same rights and duties as a de jure corporation. Remember, however, that the good faith attempt to comply with the statutory requirements must be substantiated or else no corporation — de facto or otherwise — exists.

**EXAMPLE (True/False):**

You have been engaged to examine the financial statements of the Apex Manufacturing Company. Your examination revealed that the Company is owned equally by Gerald Peters, George Jackson, and Donald Wells, evidenced by 1,000 shares of no-par stock held by each. However, your examination further disclosed that the owners have never filed incorporation papers in any jurisdiction. All three owners are actively engaged in the conduct of the business. The Company borrowed $10,000 from William Wells, Donald's brother, secured by a corporate note signed by "Donald Wells, President." All three owners signed individually as sureties on the note.
    1. Since the owners of Apex intended to create a corporation, they could assert successfully the de facto corporation doctrine in defending suits by the Company's creditors against them personally.
    2. Apex Manufacturing Company is *not* a de jure corporation.
    3. The attorney general of the state in which Apex maintains its home office can obtain a court order prohibiting the Company from doing business as a corporation.
    4. William Wells would be able to proceed successfully against the individuals even if a de jure corporation were created.
    5. Taking the facts as stated, the owners could establish that they created a valid limited partnership.
    6. In fact, the three owners are operating as a general partnership with each having personal liability for the Company's debts.

**Solutions:** (1) F, (2) T, (3) T, (4) T, (5) F, (6) T

3. *Corporation by estoppel:* If a third party has had dealings with a defectively organized corporation and tries to disclaim any liability incurred by him and owing to the corporation, by claiming the corporation lacks legal existence, he will be estopped from so claiming. In such a case, as in all other cases of estoppel, the corporation does not come into existence where it did not exist in the first place. Rather the duties and obligations owed to a nonlegal corporation are imposed upon third parties as if they had been dealing

with the real thing. Notice the difference between a corporation by estoppel and a de jure corporation: In the first instance, no corporation legally exists; in the second one, a corporate entity legally exists.

## Carrying on the corporate business:

Upon incorporation, and unless otherwise exempt, the new corporation must register its stock with the federal and state authorities. The federal law which regulates registration of a newly formed corporation is the Federal Securities Act of 1933 (see Chapter 10); the state laws which regulate securities are generally called *blue sky laws.* There is no uniformity among individual states' blue sky laws, so that careful attention must be paid to the appropriate statutes to insure compliance.

The first order of business upon incorporation is the holding of the first director's meeting. This is usually called by the provisional directors who have managed affairs during the pre-incorporation period. At this initial meeting, the participants usually adopt the corporation's by-laws, elect its board of directors, and begin to carry on the business of the corporation which, among other things, includes the sale of stock.

1.   *The corporation's by-laws:* A corporation's by-laws are the rules and regulations which guide the corporation's day-to-day internal affairs. They are usually ratified by the shareholders, as are subsequent modifications. They may stipulate or require any provisions with which shareholders agree, as long as they do not contradict the corporation's charter/articles of incorporation. The charter/articles, in turn, must be consistent with the statutes of the state of incorporation.

If a corporation engages in any activities which are outside of the limitations placed on it by its charter and/or the incorporation statute, the corporation is said to be engaging in *ultra vires* activities. An activity may be perfectly legal and still be ultra vires. For instance, if a corporation buys and sells real property in the face of a charter which forbids it to do so, the activity is ultra vires with respect to that particular corporation, though it is not illegal to deal in real property per se. The Model Act forbids the defense of ultra vires — that is, a person buying real estate from a corporation not authorized to make such sales cannot renege on his contract by instituting an ultra vires defense. Nevertheless, a corporation can be inhibited from carrying on ultra vires activities if a shareholder goes to court to enjoin the corporation from carrying on such activities; if the corporation goes to court (through a representative) to enjoin directors or officers from engaging in such activities; if the attorney general goes to court to ask for an injunction or even to dissolve the corporation entirely.

2.   *The corporation's board of directors:* The corporation's board of directors is elected by the shareholders to manage its business affairs. The directors are not paid to act as directors. The shareholders may vote to keep the provisional directors on or to elect some or all new ones.

Directors have a high fiduciary duty which they owe to the corporate shareholders. They must put the interests of the corporation and shareholders above their own, they cannot make secret profits, they cannot engage in any competitive business or work for a competing business. Directors owe the strictest or highest fiduciary duty and can be held liable for breach of that duty.

This fiduciary duty does not result from any legal relationship between the directors and shareholders, such as an principal/agent relationship, because the shareholders are not legally principals and the directors are not legally agents. The fiduciary duty arises out of the dominant/subservient relationship which the directors have with the shareholders. The unusual control which a board of directors has over the corporation and its shareholders stems largely from the fact that the board is totally independent of the shareholders. Once they elect its members, the shareholders have no right to try to influence the board as a unit, or any individual director. Any action taken by the board as a result of influence exerted by one or more shareholders is illegal and any contract entered into by a director so pressured is void. Theoretically, a director cannot be removed from office until his elected term has expired. (Terms are usually for one year.) In practice, however, shareholders have been able to vote a director out of office quite easily, whether they have cause for such action or not. Negligent directors are usually not held liable to the corporation and its shareholders for losses incurred as a result of the directors' poor business judgment or honest mistake of judgment. Fraudulent directors, of course, can be held liable.

Members of a board of directors control and direct a corporation's business affairs in a general way. Of the many powers they enjoy, the most important — from the shareholders' point of view — is the power to declare dividends. The members of the board also are empowered to appoint the corporation's officers. The officers' duties are usually spelled out in the corporation's by-laws, from which their express and implied authority emanate. Officers have the same fiduciary duty to the corporation and its shareholders as directors do, but as they are actual agents of the corporation and its shareholders, their duty has a firm foundation in agency law.

There is no maximum number of directors which a corporation can have sitting on its board. Whether it consists of two directors or of 222 members, the board can only act as a unit. Any action which an individual board member takes on behalf of the board is not binding unless he also happens to be an officer authorized to take such actions and in so doing bind the corporation. His ability to bind the corporation in such an instance comes from his position as an authorized officer, however, not from his being a member of the board.

Actions are usually taken by the board's passing — as a unit — formal resolutions. In order to pass formal resolutions, or to transact any business, a majority of the board members must be present at the meeting. Once this majority, or *quorum*, is present, a simple majority vote of that quorum is sufficient to pass a board resolution or to transact any other business which must be voted on.

Directors cannot vote by proxy (though shareholders can). If the deciding vote in any instance is a proxy vote, the action is null and void. However, unless otherwise provided by a corporation's articles of incorporation or by-laws, a board of directors may act without a meeting if written consent setting forth the action so taken is signed by each member.

3. *Selling the corporate stock:* The number of shares which a corporation is authorized to issue is established in the charter. Of those which are authorized, the number of shares which are to be actually issued and outstanding during the pre-incorporation period is determined by the promoters and/or incorporators. After incorporation, the board alone determines whether or not to sell additional shares. If all the shares which are authorized to be issued have not been issued, the board can issue them without amending the charter. If all authorized shares are issued and outstanding, the charter must be amended to authorize new shares. Shareholder approval is needed to amend the charter.

A purchaser can acquire stock by paying for it with cash, property, or services. The cash and/or fair market value of the services or property must equal at least the par value of the stock. If a purchaser pays less than par value for a share of stock, he runs the risk of possibly being held liable to a corporate creditor for the difference between the par value per share and actual value of the consideration per share he remitted to the corporation.

**EXAMPLE:**

Franklin Corporation was incorporated in 1970. At that time 150,000 shares of common stock with a par value of $10 per share were sold. Three of the original subscribers who were also the promoters and first directors of the corporation purchased 50,000 shares at $5 per share. The offering price to the public was $15 per share. The three promoters in question sold their shares for $8 per share after they were defeated for re-election as directors three years later. The corporation is now in bankruptcy. All other creditors with the exception of Mabry, Franklin's major creditor, have settled their claims. Mabry had loaned the corporation $500,000. At the time of the loan, Mabry insisted upon audited financial statements before he would extend credit. This was done and the audited financial statements clearly indicated that par value had not been paid by the promoters upon their purchase of the 50,000 shares.

**Required:**

Answer the following, setting forth reasons for any conclusions stated.

    1. What rights does Mabry have against the three promoters?

    2. What rights does Mabry have against the purchasers who bought from the promoters?

**Solution:**

1. Each of the three promoters in question is liable to Mabry for the amount of the difference between stated par value ($10) and what they actually paid ($5). The Model Business Corporation Act provides that par must be paid without qualification, and Mabry's knowledge of the fact that less than par was paid does not prevent recovery.

2. Under the Model Business Corporation Act, Mabry has no right of recovery against the purchasers who bought from the promoters, assuming the purchases were not fraudulent (i.e., were made in good faith).

A stock purchaser may not offer future values in payment — that is, he cannot pay for stock with a promissory note and, if services are to be performed in exchange for stock, they must be performed in the present. A promise to perform services in the future in exchange for shares to be received in the present is not legal consideration for a share of stock.

**EXAMPLE (Multiple Choice):**

The consideration for the issuance of shares by a corporation may *not* be paid in
    a. Services actually performed for the corporation.
    b. Services to be performed for the corporation.
    c. Tangible property.
    d. Intangible property.

**Solution:** (b)

When a stockholder purchases corporate stock, he invests a certain amount of money (or property or services) in the corporation which is then used to carry on the business of the entity. The return on his investment comes in the form of dividends. A stockholder takes a risk whenever he invests, in that the stock he purchases may become worthless, and he may lose his entire investment (but no more). A stockholder purchases no guarantee that the corporation will operate profitably and, even if it does, that dividends will be declared by the board of directors.

(The purchaser of a corporate bond, on the other hand, who also has invested money in the corporation, has a contract with the corporation which guarantees repayment of that investment at some future date. The bond purchaser's investment in a corporation is a loan to the corporation; as a result, besides the guaranteed repayment of the loan principal, the bondholder is also guaranteed interest — that is, a return — on his investment.)

Upon purchasing corporate stock, the shareholder receives a stock certificate which represents his interest in the corporation. It does not represent partial ownership of the corporation's assets; those are owned by the corporate entity alone. It merely guarantees him the right to participate in the corporation's profits if and when they are made.

## Dividends:

There are two types of stock which a corporation sells — *common* (which is usually the least expensive because the greatest risk attaches to it) and *preferred*. Preferred stockholders are given certain rights or priorities over common stockholders. Different classes of preferred come with different rights. Preferred stockholders' rights can be found in the corporate charter; if they are not stipulated there, the right or priority does not exist.

The most common preferences deal with the preferred shareholder's right to receive corporate assets upon liquidation, before common shareholders do, and their right to receive dividends before common shareholders do. Preferred shareholders also usually buy a right to a minimum dividend if and when dividends are declared, and they often purchase the right to receive dividends in arrears if one or more years pass in which dividends are not declared. These rights which preferred shareholders enjoy regarding dividends do not include the right to receive dividends per se, but just to receive them before corporate profits are distributed to common shareholders, only if and when dividends are declared.

This is an important point to make: Neither preferred nor common shareholders have a right to receive dividends, regardless of how high corporate profits may be, until they are officially declared by and at the discretion of the board of directors. Once a dividend is declared, the shareholders to whom they are owing have the same irrevocable right to receive them as an ordinary corporate creditor has the right to satisfaction of an outstanding debt. The shareholders' right to a declared dividend is, however, subordinate to a nonshareholder creditor's right.

There are only two instances when the board of directors can rescind a declared dividend:

- A *stock dividend* (that is, a dividend payable in the corporate stock, as opposed to one payable in cash) can be rescinded after it has been declared, at any time up until it is actually distributed.

- Any dividend which the board has been pressured into declaring by any stockholder (unless, of course, it is a court-ordered dividend resulting from a suit). Such a dividend, unless court-ordered, can usually be rescinded even after it has been distributed.

**EXAMPLE (Multiple Choice):**

Miller Corporation declared a common stock dividend of 1 common share for every 10 common shares outstanding. The owners' equity accounts of the corporation immediately prior to the declaration of the common stock dividend were as follows:

| | |
|---|---|
| Stated capital (10,000 shares of common stock issued and outstanding, $1 par value per share) | $10,000 |
| Earned surplus (retained earnings) | 4,000 |

*No* other transactions are relevant. Immediately after the issuance of the common stock dividend, stated capital will amount to

    a. $11,000.    b. $10,000.    c. $9,000.    d. $1,000.

**Solution:** (a)

The board of directors can legally declare dividends only when there is sufficient capital available from current or retained earnings from which to pay them. Retained earnings usually come from accumulated surplus profits.

**EXAMPLE (Multiple Choice):**

Surplus of a corporation means
     a. Net assets in excess of stated capital.
     b. Liquid assets in excess of current needs.
     c. Total assets in excess of total liabilities.
     d. Contributed capital.

**Solution:** (a)

When dividends are paid out of these accumulated profits or out of current profits, they are taxed as income to the shareholder. Sometimes, however, the dividend is paid out of surplus which derives from a reevaluation upward of corporate assets or from paid-in surplus (that is, the difference between the price the stock was sold at and its par or stated value). When dividends are paid out of this latter kind of surplus, the dividends are called *dividends in partial liquidation.* (If the business is terminating and all assets are being liquidated and returned to shareholders, such dividends are called *full liquidating dividends.*) Dividends in partial liquidation (or full liquidating dividends) constitute a partial (or full) return of the shareholder's original investment. As such, they are not taxable as income; the directors must inform shareholders that they are receiving dividends in partial liquidation. The board of directors needs no approval to declare and pay an ordinary profit-based dividend; the board does need shareholder authorization to declare any dividends that constitute a return of capital.

In no case, however, can a dividend in partial liquidation be declared if the corporation is insolvent or if accrued cumulative dividends on preferred stock are in arrears. In no case can profit-based dividends be declared if the corporation is insolvent or would be rendered insolvent were the dividends to be distributed. In no case can the board declare dividends in such a way as to discriminate among shareholders of the same class of stock. If any of these prohibited dividends are declared, the dividend is illegal.

If a shareholder receives an illegal dividend, whether he knows it is illegal or not, he is bound to return the amount received to the corporation if the corporation is insolvent or is rendered so by the distribution. If the corporation is solvent, a shareholder who receives illegal dividends must return them if he knows they are illegal and/or if he receives them as a result of some fraudulent act on his part. A shareholder who accepts an illegal dividend without knowing that it is illegal is not bound to return it to the corporation if the corporation is solvent at the time of the actual payment. If the corporation is solvent when the dividend is declared, but insolvent when it is distributed, the dividend must be returned in all cases.

If the board of directors declares a dividend illegally, the members who voted affirmatively for the declaration are jointly and severally liable to the corporation for damages for, at the least, breach of trust or negligence. However, if, in declaring dividends, they relied in good faith on audited financial statements or information given to them by responsible corporate officials attesting to the corporation's sound financial position, they will escape liability. The courts often hold similar views when suits are brought against directors by individual shareholders, or by the corporation for reasons other than illegally declared dividends. These plaintiffs often look to the courts for relief when they feel the directors have not acted in the shareholders' or corporation's best interests. If fraud is established, directors will always be held liable for their actions. However, directors will usually not be held liable for simply exercising poor business judgment, no matter how damaging the results of that exercise may be. The only thing the majority of courts usually offer in such instances is advice to the shareholders to either elect new directors at their next opportunity or, if they are in a minority position and lack sufficient voting power to effect such a change, to sell their stock. Many observers believe that there is a coming trend to hold corporate directors responsible and, therefore liable for the harmful effects their poor business judgment has on the corporation. However, to date, directors have escaped liability in these instances.

**EXAMPLE (Multiple Choice):**

Seymore was recently invited to become a director of Buckley Industries, Inc. If Seymore accepts and becomes a director, he along with the other directors will *not* be personally liable for
    a. Lack of reasonable care.
    b. Honest errors of judgment.
    c. Declaration of a dividend which the directors know will impair legal capital.
    d. Diversion of corporate opportunities to themselves.

**Solution:** (b)

Some general rights which shareholders have aside from that of being able to sue directors for fraudulent behavior are that:

1. All shareholders have a right to a stock certificate, which represents the interest the shareholder has purchased. A certificate is usually not necessary for the shareholder to receive dividends or receive communications from the corporation, but it is necessary to possess if the shareholder wants to sell or pledge his shares.

2. Though some state incorporation statutes permit nonvoting stock to be issued by a corporation, those cases are very rare. In the main, each shareholder is entitled to exercise one vote for each share of stock that he owns.

3. Each shareholder — or his authorized representative — has the right to inspect the corporation's books and records. The right is abridged, however, if it can be shown that the shareholder intends to use the information contained therein improperly or illegally.

4. As noted, a corporation does not always sell all the stock which it has the authorization to issue. If the corporation issues stock in stages, it usually must offer existing shareholders the right to purchase enough stock to maintain their proportionate interest in the corporation, before stock is sold to the general public. These rights are called *preemptive rights* and they are taken advantage of by exercising *stock warrants* which have been issued by the corporation to existing shareholders. Stock warrants can be transferred just as shares can. Their value derives from the fact that those in possession of them can purchase the shares at a price less than the going market price. As such, if the market price of a share of stock is $100, and the stock warrants allow a current shareholder to purchase a share for $90, each warrant is worth $10 to the shareholder or to whomever he may sell or give the warrants.

5. Each shareholder has a right to receive dividends. As already explained, the right does not theoretically exist until the board of directors actually declares a dividend. However, if, in the face of very large current and accumulated profits, the directors refuse to declare dividends for other than bona fide business reasons such as planned expansion or proposed research and development — that is, if directors refuse to declare dividends for purely arbitrary, personal, non-business-related reasons — a court might very well force the directors to declare a dividend.

**EXAMPLE:**

Maximum Corporation is a medium-sized manufacturing company whose shares are publicly traded. Maximum's capital structure consists of 500,000 shares of common stock and 200,000 shares of 8 percent non-cumulative preferred. During each of the past five years, Maximum has earned an amount well in excess of the $16,000 which the preferred shareholders would be entitled to if any dividends were declared. The board has stated that it has refrained from declaring any dividends because of the need to expand its operations by construction of new facilities or the acquisition of another corporation. In fact, the real motivation behind the board's dividend policy is to depress the market value of the preferred shares which the board members have been quietly accumulating over the past two years. As a consequence of the foregoing the accumulated earnings and profits of Maximum are now $130,000.

**Required:**

What are the legal implications of the above facts? Set forth reasons for any conclusions stated.

**Solution:**

Although corporate law is quite liberal on the subject of boards of directors' discretion on declaration of dividends, the facts in this circumstance indicate an abuse of discretion. Thus, the preferred shareholders have a valid cause of action against the board. This may take the form of a suit by an individual preferred shareholder or a class action to compel the payment of current and past dividends. Despite the fact that the preferred shares are noncumulative, when the motivation is clearly an abuse of discretion, the courts will act to protect the preferred shareholders for dividends not declared in the past.

Furthermore, Section 10(b) of the 1934 Securities Exchange Act and Rule 10b-5 promulgated thereunder have undoubtedly been violated. One objective of the act is to protect the investing public against market manipulation and other fraudulent acts and practices. Rule 10b-5 provides that "it shall be unlawful for any person, directly or indirectly, by use of any means or instrumentality of interstate commerce or of the mails, or of any facility of any national securities exchange, (1) to employ any device, scheme or artifice to defraud. . . . " Clearly the facts reveal such a "scheme." Finally, the common shareholders could resort to their common-law rights to bring a shareholder derivative action for any damages to the corporation and could seek to have the directors removed for breach of their fiduciary duty to the corporation.

6. Upon dissolution of the corporation, each shareholder has a right to receive a pro rata share of corporate assets, but only after all the creditors' claims have been satisfied. Holders of preferred stock will be given preference over holders of common stock only if the charter allows for it.

It should be pointed out that most of these rights are guaranteed by the provisions of each state's incorporation statutes. However, when a particular statute specifies that a certain right does not exist (for example, the one-share-one-vote right may be abridged) or when a corporate charter does not specifically grant certain rights (for example, pre-emptive rights and priorities upon dissolution must be specifically granted), the statute and/or charter controls.

## Treasury stock:

When a purchaser buys newly issued shares of stock from a corporation, corporate assets are increased by the amount paid for each share (the selling or market price) multiplied by the number of newly issued shares bought. If the market price is greater than the stock's par or stated value, the difference is credited to a surplus account. The name given to such an account is usually "paid-in surplus in excess of par," or some such title.

After this initial purchase, the stock can continue to be traded. When it is so traded it is said to be *publicly traded* or *traded on the open market*. If publicly traded stock is purchased by another individual, the corporation's stockholder's equity accounts remain unaffected.

Publicly traded stock can be repurchased by the corporation itself. Such repurchased stock is called *treasury stock,* and its purchase serves to reduce the stockholder's equity accounts and, as such, the net assets of the corporation, by the amount the corporation paid to repurchase the shares. As long as shareholders are willing to sell their shares back to the corporation, there are no restrictions qualifying the corporation's ability or right to repurchase except one: A corporation may not repurchase its own shares as treasury stock if, in so doing, the rights of corporate creditors will be impaired. Accordingly, a corporation may only repurchase its own shares out of its surplus capital.

**EXAMPLES (Multiple Choice):**

1. Treasury shares of a corporation are its shares which are
    a. Issued and outstanding.
    b. Issued but *not* outstanding.
    c. Outstanding but *not* issued.
    d. Neither outstanding nor issued.

2. A corporation may *not* redeem its own shares when it
    a. Is currently solvent but has been insolvent within the past five years.
    b. Is insolvent or would be rendered insolvent if the redemption were made.
    c. Has convertible debt that is publicly traded.
    d. Has mortgages and other secured obligations equal to 50 percent of its stated capital.

**Solutions:** 1 (b), 2 (b)

As already noted, a corporation cannot issue stock for less than par or stated value. It can, however, reissue treasury stock for any amount.

### Change in the legal existence of a corporation:

The legal form which a corporation initially takes can be changed in any one of the following ways:

1. *Consolidation:* To effect a consolidation, two or more independent corporations combine their total assets to form a brand new corporation. This new consolidated corporation has title to the once separately owned assets, and takes over the debts and liabilities which the now nonexistent constituent corporations owed prior to consolidation. In order to participate in the consolidation, each corporation's board of directors and majority of the shareholders who have appropriate voting rights must assent to the plan. Any dissenting shareholder may demand the fair market value of his preconsolidation stock from the new consolidated entity. The assenting shareholders, on the other hand, exchange their old stock for shares issued by the new corporation.

2. *Merger:* A merger involves combining the assets of two or more corporations also, but one of the merging entities survives and holds title to all combined assets. The non-surviving corporations cease to exist as independent entities upon merging. All the debts and liabilities of the merging entities are assumed by the surviving corporation. The same approval is required to merge as to consolidate by the involved corporations' respective boards and shareholders, and the same rights and relief are available to assenting and dissenting shareholders when the merger is complete.

**EXAMPLE:**

Rex Corporation, one of your clients, has engaged you to examine its financial statements in connection with a prospective merger or a consolidation with King Corporation. Both methods of acquisition are being considered under applicable corporate statutory law. Rex is the larger of the two corporations and is in reality acquiring King Corporation.

**Required:**

Answer the following, setting forth reasons for any conclusions stated.

    1. Discuss the meaning of the terms merger and consolidation as used in corporate law with particular emphasis on the legal difference between the two.

    2. What are the major legal procedures which must be met in order to accomplish either a merger or consolidation?

**Solution:**

1. The major legal difference between a merger and a consolidation relates to the continued existence of the corporations involved. In the case of a merger of two corporations, one corporation, the acquiring corporation, survives. The acquired corporation, on the other hand, transfers all its assets to the acquiring corporation. Consequently, it is absorbed by the survivor and dissolves. The surviving corporation takes all the assets and assumes all the liabilities of the acquired corporation. When two corporations consolidate, however, both corporate parties to the consolidation transfer their assets to a new corporation and then both dissolve. Liabilities of each of the two consolidating corporations are valid against the new consolidated corporation.

2. The major legal procedures that must be followed in order to accomplish a merger or consolidation under applicable corporate statutory law are essentially these:

    a. Approval of the plan of merger or consolidation must be given by the boards of directors of the two corporations who are parties to the merger or consolidation.

    b. Timely written notice must be given to all shareholders of record. A copy of summary of the plan must accompany the notice to shareholders.

    c. Approval must be given by a majority of the shareholders of each corporation who are entitled to vote on the proposed plan of merger or consolidation. Some states require a higher percentage for approval.

    d. The articles of merger or consolidation must be properly filed by an appropriate officer of each corporation.

3. *Bankruptcy:* Federal bankruptcy laws allow a bankrupt corporation to reorganize without terminating. State bankruptcy laws usually view a bankrupt corporation which wants to carry on business as first having terminated and then having reorganized as a brand new corporation.

A corporation's life may be terminated in any of the following ways:

- If all the shareholders voluntarily agree to termination.

- If the board of directors passes a resolution to terminate and this resolution is voluntarily approved of by a majority of shareholders with the appropriate voting rights.

- If the time period for which the corporation was formed expires.

- If the legislature of the state of incorporation acts to terminate the corporation. A corporate charter is basically a contract between the state of incorporation and the corporation. While federal law does not allow a state to revoke, modify, or amend the contract, almost all incorporation statutes contain a provision which reserves for the legislature the right to alter the charter.

**EXAMPLE (Multiple Choice):**

Under which of the following circumstances would a corporation's existence terminate?
    a. The death of its sole owner-shareholder.
    b. Its becoming insolvent.
    c. Its legal consolidation with another corporation.
    d. Its reorganization under the federal bankruptcy laws.

**Solution:** (c)

# *10* Insurance

An insurance policy is basically a contract which involves three parties: the *insured* (usually the person buying the policy), the *insurer* (the person who will pay the insurance benefits), and the *beneficiary* (the person who will receive the benefits and who may be the insured or an independent third party). In general, the terms of the contract provide for the insurer to pay a certain amount of money, or give something of value, to a beneficiary on the happening of a certain event (a death, a fire, a collision, a robbery, or the like). The consideration which the insurer receives to bind this promise is in the form of *premium payments*. A key concept in insurance contracts is that the occurrence of the contingent event upon which payments will be made is beyond the control of any of the parties to the contract.

Insurance, as an industry, falls under state regulation. Insurance companies which conduct business within a particular state must comply with the appropriate statutes which regulate the industry there. Such companies are said to be *domestic* with reference to the home state. Other insurance companies, whose primary place of business is not within the borders of a particular state, are said to be *foreign* companies. While foreign insurance companies do not have to strictly comply with the regulating statutes in the same way that domestic insurance companies do, they must meet certain state-determined standards in order to carry on insurance business within the state.

In general, insurance can only be written by a company in a state if that company is licensed to do so by that state. However, there are times when none of the licensed insurance companies provide the kind of insurance that a potential policy purchaser wants or needs. If such is the case, an unlicensed foreign insurance company may write the policy, provided that it meets the state standards which regulate foreign companies. This kind of insurance is called *surplus-line insurance*.

### Life insurance:

The most common type of insurance is life insurance. The terms of a life insurance contract call for the insurer to pay a prearranged amount of money to a prenamed beneficiary when or soon after the insured person dies. The insured party has the right to choose the beneficiary and can name a creditor, his estate, a charity, a relative, etc., as the beneficiary of the policy. However, once named, the beneficiary cannot be changed unless a provision for change is incorporated into the policy or unless the beneficiary consents to the change.

**EXAMPLE (Multiple Choice):**

Abner purchased a life insurance policy on his life and named Barbara as beneficiary. Later he borrowed from Charles and assigned the policy to Charles as security for the debt. Abner died while the debt was unpaid. Under these circumstances
- a. Barbara will be entitled to the entire proceeds if she had an insurable interest and did *not* consent to the assignment even if Abner had retained the right to change the beneficiary.
- b. If, prior to the loan, Barbara had been named irrevocably as beneficiary without consideration, she will be entitled to the entire proceeds absent her consent to any change in her rights.
- c. The assignment operates to change the beneficiary of the policy from Barbara to Charles, but he is liable to Abner's estate for proceeds in excess of amounts due him.
- d. Normally assignment is *not* permitted to become effective if the value of the policy at the time exceeds the debt.

**Solution:** (b)

In order to take out any life insurance policy, the purchaser (insured party) must have an *insurable interest* in the relevant person's life at the time the policy is taken out. The same insurable interest need not necessarily exist at the time the insured person dies, however. In general, an insured party has an insurable interest if he will sustain a substantial loss upon the happening of the contingent event.

**EXAMPLE (Multiple Choice):**

Dey purchases a life insurance policy on Adam's life and names Jones as beneficiary. Who must have an insurable interest for this policy to be valid and at what time?
- a. Jones at the inception of the policy.
- b. Jones at the time of death.
- c. Dey at the inception of the policy.
- d. Dey at the time of death.

**Solution:** (c)

In the case of a life insurance policy, the contingent event is the death of a particular person, and the insured party must therefore have an insurable interest in the life of that person. The most obvious insurable interest is that of a person who is taking out a life insurance policy on his own life. Insurable interests can also usually be substantiated by close relatives, partners in a partnership, or a close business associate. Each claim of an insurable interest rests on the facts of the particular case. A named beneficiary need not have an insurable interest in the insured party's life (unless, of course, the beneficiary is also the person buying the policy). Proceeds of a life insurance policy may be voluntarily assigned to a third party who has no insurable interest.

**EXAMPLE (Multiple Choice):**

A typical term life insurance policy
- a. Builds up a cash value during its duration against which the policyholder can borrow.
- b. Is assignable.
- c. Creates a vested interest in the named beneficiary.
- d. Does *not* require an insurable interest in the person taking out the policy as do other types of life insurance policies.

**Solution:** (b)

*Premiums:* As noted, the consideration given in exchange for the insurer's promise to pay a certain amount of money to the beneficiary upon the death of some person is paid in the form of premiums. The premiums are usually paid by the person who has taken out or owns the policy.

Premiums are usually fixed in the amount and are determined on the basis of mortality tables, interest, and the expenses of the insurance company. The insurance company uses mortality tables to calculate approximately when the person whose life is insured will die — that is, approximately how many years will elapse from the time the first premium is paid until the policy matures. The policy matures when the person whose life is insured dies. The *net premium* to be paid each year is then determined by the insurance company's assuming an interest rate which, when added to the principal, will allow it to grow so that it equals the total promised death payment at the time of death, as approximated by the mortality tables. On top of this net premium, the insurer adds costs to cover its administration expenses. The net premium plus this provision for expenses equals the *gross premium,* and it is this gross premium that the owner of the policy pays.

The net premiums plus accrued interest are held in a reserve account by the insurance company, as a liability to be paid out at the appropriate time. These reserves can be invested by the insurance company in long-term bonds, mortgages, loans, and so forth, with high yields, because the company knows well in advance approximately when each policy it has issued will mature. In other words, it can make long-range plans. In order to protect the policyholders, however, most states restrict the type of investments into which an insurance company can place its reserves. Very risky ventures must usually be avoided. While states do not regulate the premiums which a life insurance can charge, they do usually approve the mortality tables used.

There are basically three premium payment plans, and conversion from one plan to another, with the appropriate modifications in premiums or death benefits, is usually allowed.

- *Ordinary life insurance* calls for premiums to be paid annually, in fixed amounts, until death.

- *Term life insurance* is issued for a limited number of years and calls for premiums to be paid only during the period covered.

- *Limited payment life insurance* offers coverage until death but allows for the premiums to be paid over a limited number of years. Obviously, given the same death payment, premiums under this type of policy will be higher than under an ordinary life insurance policy.

### Fire insurance:

Another very common type of insurance is property insurance — that is, the insured takes out a policy to protect him (to reimburse him) if certain property is damaged. The most common type of property insurance is fire insurance. Fire insurance protects the policyholder from damages or loss of real or personal property resulting from fire and related dangers. These policies are usually written for shorter periods than life insurance policies.

Because an insurer selling fire insurance cannot estimate when a fire will occur as accurately as he can measure when a natural death is likely to occur (given a certain age and state of health), fire insurance companies must keep their reserves highly liquid and not tied up in long-term investments. Accordingly, fire insurance premiums (as well as general casualty insurance premiums) tend to be much higher than life insurance premiums for the same benefits. The premiums which a fire insurance or casualty insurance company can charge are regulated by the licensing state.

Again, the person who buys property insurance must have an insurable interest in the property which is insured, but here the insurable interest must exist *at the time the loss occurs,* and not necessarily at the time the policy is taken out. Again, policies are assignable, but they cannot be assigned before the loss.

### EXAMPLE:

Marvel Enterprises, Inc., contracted to buy Jonstone's factory and warehouse. The contract provided that if title did not pass to Marvel prior to October 1, 1974, Marvel would have the right to possession on that date pending conveyance of title upon delivery of the deed. The contract also provided that the purchase price was to be adjusted depending upon the actual acreage conveyed as determined by an independent survey. This provision was subject to a further stipulation: the maximum purchase price would not exceed $450,000 nor be less than $425,000 as long as the survey did not reveal major variances nor render title unmarketable.

All the requisite paperwork was not in order by October 1, 1974, and Marvel exercised its option to take possession on that date. Concurrently, Marvel obtained a fire insurance policy on the factory and warehouse effective October 1, 1974. The closing was finally scheduled for October 17, 1974. The survey confirmed the acreage described in the contract of sale, and Marvel tendered the balance of the purchase price on October 17, 1974. During the interim period, however, the factory and warehouse were totally destroyed by fire and Marvel seeks to recover on its fire insurance policy. The insurance company denies liability.

### Required:

Discuss Marvel's rights to recover from the insurance company.

**Solution:**

Marvel will recover against the insurance company for the value of the insured property destroyed, i.e., the factory and warehouse.

The insurance company is undoubtedly asserting a lack of insurable interest on Marvel's part in that legal title had not been transferred to it at the time of the fire. However where a purchaser, pursuant to a contract of sale of real property, takes possession of the premises prior to the closing, the risk of loss is his. Thus, the insurable interest requirement has been satisfied and Marvel may recover. It may also be argued that a valid insurable interest is created by the contract alone.

Fire insurance is usually taken out in the amount of the property's replacement value less depreciation. Fire insurance companies usually offer the insured the opportunity to share the risk of loss with the company, and thereby reduce his premium rates, by means of a concept called *co-insurance*. Let's assume that a policy holder has taken out a fire insurance with an 80% co-insurance clause. (The insurance company usually determines the percentage.) As such, if the value of the property in question is $50,000, the insured can take out a policy for 80% of 50,000 or for $40,000 and assume 20% of the loss, if and when it occurs. If the policy has an 80% co-insurance clause and the insured under-insures the property, the amount paid by the insurance company, if and when the loss occurs, will be proportionately reduced. Thus, if the insured insures his property up to the co-insurance percentage (say it is 80%), he will receive 80% of the loss — not to exceed the face value of the policy. But if the co-insurance percentage is 80%, and the insured insures his property up to only 60% of its value, he will receive only 75% of the loss ($\frac{.6}{.8}$), again not to exceed the face value of the policy. The insurance company will pay the lower of:

- the face value of the policy, or

- the market value of the actual loss, or

- the amount determined by the co-insurance formula, which is:

$$\text{Recovery} = \frac{\text{face value of policy}}{\text{co-insurance \% } \times \text{ total value of entire property at time of loss}} \times \text{Market value of actual loss}$$

In any event, maximum recovery will always be limited to the face value of the policy.

**EXAMPLE:**

Anderson loaned the Drum Corporation $60,000. The loan was secured by a first mortgage on Drum's land and the plant thereon. Anderson independently procured a fire insurance policy for $60,000 on the mortgaged property from the Victory Insurance Company. Six years later when the mortgage had been amortized down to $52,000, the plant was totally destroyed by a fire caused by faulty electrical wiring in the rear storage area.

**Required:**

Answer the following, setting forth reasons for any conclusions stated.

　　1. Anderson seeks recovery of $60,000 from the Victory Insurance Company. How much will it collect?

　　2. Upon payment by Victory Insurance Company, what rights does Victory have?

**Solution:**

1. Anderson's insurable interest equals the extent of the mortgage debt outstanding. Thus, his recovery is limited to the $52,000 debt outstanding plus accrued interest on the debt, but the total recovery cannot exceed $60,000, the maximum coverage under the policy.

2. Upon payment, Victory is subrogated to the rights of Anderson and will succeed to Anderson's rights to receive payments under the terms of the mortgage and mortgage bond. If Drum Corporation fails to continue the payments, Victory may foreclose on the mortgage.

**Other kinds of insurance:**

If an insurance company believes that the chances of a contingent event's happening are less than ever, it will probably issue a policy for anyone who wants protection in the event of its occurrence. Theoretically, then, there are unlimited types of insurance policies which can be bought to suit almost any need. Some types of insurance are more common than others. Besides life, property, and casualty insurance, the most frequently issued insurance policies are:

- Accident insurance.
- Health insurance.
- Marine insurance.
- Liability insurance.
- Collision insurance.
- Fidelity insurance.
- Endowment contracts.

Insurance companies themselves often take out insurance so that they will be reimbursed by another insurance company for money paid out on claims. This is called *reinsurance.*

**The insurance contract:**

Insurance companies generally deal through agents. The general rules of agency law apply to the company/agent, agent/third party, and company/third party relationships. Accordingly, an agent usually binds an insurance company with respect to a third party (policyholder) when he acts within his express, implied, or apparent authority. An agent usually does not have any kind of authority to bind his principal to a life insurance contract, however.

An insurance policy is a contract between the company and the policyholder, and general contract law applies here. For the most part, the policyholder is seen as the promisor or offeror and the insurance company as the promisee or offeree. The agent, of course, is the go-between.

The potential policyholder submits his offer to the insurer by means of filling out an application. If the insurer writes a policy which differs from the application, the company makes a counteroffer, which the policyholder can accept or reject.

Part of the application is a representation of relevant facts which the applicant makes to the insurance company. The application and the actual contract between the two parties are two separate documents; the contract may or may not refer to the application and the representations contained therein. If it is incorporated into the contract, the representation serves as a warranty in most states. As a warranty, the representation states conditions which must exist before the insurer is obligated to meet his obligation *(conditions precedent)* and/or states events which, when they come to pass, will bring an end to whatever obligations exist *(conditions subsequent)*. Thus if a required condition does not exist or come to pass, the policy is void and the insurance company is relieved of its obligation to perform its part of the bargain.

An insurer cannot expect to be relieved of his contractual obligations because of an untrue statement in the applicant's representation, unless such statement was a material misrepresentation of fact which the insurer relied upon as an inducement to enter into the contract. In a successful action, an insurer will be allowed to *rescind* the insurance contract by returning to the insured all premiums paid to date. (Recision is not the same thing as *cancellation.* In cancelling an insurance contract, the insurer returns only the unearned premiums and must perform only to the extent that the retained premiums represent obligations. In rescinding a contract, the insurer returns all premiums and need not perform at all.) An insurer is usually not allowed to rescind a life insurance policy because of an applicant's material misrepresentation if the policy has been in effect for one or two years before the company takes action. This provision in life insurance policies is called the *incontestability clause.*

**EXAMPLE (Multiple Choice):**

Elder mispresented the state of his health on the application at the time he insured his life for $10,000. He named his friend, Spencer, as beneficiary. Spencer is in *no* way related to Elder. Upon Elder's death six years later, the policy is in force, premiums are fully paid, and Spencer is still the beneficiary. The policy contained a two-year incontestable clause. Upon seeking to collect the insurance proceeds
    a. Spencer has *no* insurable interest in the life of Elder and, therefore, cannot collect.
    b. Spencer must have given some consideration to Elder or the insurance company if he is to collect.
    c. Spencer will *not* be precluded from recovery.
    d. Spencer will be denied recovery in that he is a third party beneficiary under a contract obtained by misrepresentation of a material fact.

**Solution:** (c)

Warranties are usually assumed to be material and a breach of a warranty will usually void the contract. There is one exception to this rule: If an applicant lies about his age in the process of obtaining a life insurance policy, the policy is not voided. Instead the insurance company must pay the amount which would have been owing on a policy bought for the same amount had the correct age been known at the outset.

**EXAMPLE (Multiple Choice):**

The Devon Insurance Company issued a $50,000 whole life insurance policy to Finn. Finn's age was incorrectly stated in the application, and, as a result, she paid a smaller premium than that applicable to her age. Devon denies liability asserting as its defense a material misrepresentation by Finn. Under the circumstances, how much will Finn's beneficiary collect?
    a. The entire amount of the policy if the incontestable clause applies.
    b. Nothing, unless the beneficiary can establish that Finn was unaware of her correct age.
    c. The amount of insurance that the premium would have purchased if the correct age had been stated.
    d. The amount of premium Finn paid during her lifetime with interest at the legal rate.

**Solution:** (c)

**EXAMPLE:**

Balsam was a partner in the firm of Wilkenson, Potter & Parker. The firm had a buy-out arrangement whereby the partnership funded the buy-out agreement with insurance on the lives of the partners payable to the partnership. When the insurance policies were obtained by the partnership, Balsam understated his age by three years. Eight years later, Balsam decided to sell his partnership interest to Gideon. The sale was consummated and the other partners admitted Gideon as a partner in Balsam's place. The partnership nevertheless retained ownership in the policy on the life of Balsam and continued to pay the premiums thereon. Balsam died one year later. The insurance company refuses to pay the face value of the policy claiming that the partnership is only entitled to the amount of the premiums paid. As a basis for this position, the insurance company asserts lack of an insurable interest and material misrepresentation.

**Required:**

Answer the following, setting forth reasons for any conclusions stated.

Will Wilkenson, Potter & Parker prevail in an action against the insurance company? Give specific attention to the assertions of the insurance company.

**Solution:**

Yes. An insurable interest in the life of another is present here since the firm had a substantial economic interest in the life of Balsam at the time the policy was procured. It is well recognized that an entity has the requisite standing to procure insurance on its key participants. Certainly a general partner qualifies as a key participant. In addition, the funding of buy-out agreements is essential in many instances, and insurance law recognizes this economic necessity. The insurable interest required for a life insurance policy need only exist at the inception of the policy. Balsam's subsequent retirement does not invalidate it.

The fact that Balsam misrepresented his age will not cause the loss of the entire insurance proceeds. The general rule provides that such a misrepresentation merely reduces the amount recoverable to that which the premiums would purchase if the correct age had been stated.

An insurance company can modify a policy — and in the process it may eliminate any conditions precedent or subsequent — by means of a *waiver*. If an insurer, either directly or through an authorized agent, waives any condition, he cannot turn around later and try to avoid his legal obligations by claiming that the condition precedent did not exist, that the condition subsequent did not come to pass, or whatever.

As is the case with ordinary contracts, insurance contracts are terminated when all obligations are performed as promised. Insurance contracts can also be terminated if cancelled by the insurer, the insured, or by both mutually agreeing to cancel. Most insurance policies have *nonforfeiture clauses,* which protect the policyholder from losing all the equity he has built up through the payment of premiums.

# 11 Federal Securities Regulations

The federal government's regulation of securities stems from two pieces of legislation which were enacted in the early 1930s in the wake of the Great Depression. This chapter will survey the salient provisions of each: the Securities Act of 1933 (called the "truth in securities" act) and the Securities Exchange Act of 1934. Basically, the former deals with "going public" for the first time, and the latter with the subsequent trading of securities after the initial public offering.

## The Securities Act of 1933:

The '33 Act, as it is commonly called, was enacted to protect the investing public by insuring access to truthful information about the financial condition of the corporation issuing stock. The act's provisions apply to securities which are being issued for the first time, that is, to *primary offerings.* Before the '33 Act, securities were regulated (and still are, to some extent) by state securities laws. These "blue sky laws," as they are called, were and are effective only within the relevant states' borders; federal regulation was and is needed to regulate the traffic in securities which extends across state lines (that is, interstate commerce). The '33 Act is administered by the Securities and Exchange Commission, which was set up by, and which also administers, the '34 Act.

To accomplish its aims, the act provides that every corporation which is issuing securities to the public for the first time must file a registration statement — called Form S-1 — with the SEC, in which it must disclose required financial and other information about the issuing corporation. Theoretically, then, the investor will have a fair basis on which to make his investment decision.

Once the SEC approves the statement, the issuing corporation may then begin to sell its securities to the public, but not before. Publicity that is designed to stimulate interest in a corporation's securities before a registration statement has been approved and filed may be considered an illegal offering.

It must be pointed out that in approving a registration statement, the SEC does not recommend an investment or insure investors of a profit; it merely guarantees an adequate disclosure of required facts about the corporation and the securities it proposes to sell. Nor does the SEC guarantee that the facts presented in the registration statement are necessarily accurate; rather it guarantees fair representation. The SEC cannot reject any registration statement, no matter how risky the investment may be or shaky the corporation's financial standing, if the issuer has fully complied with the registration requirements and has fairly disclosed required information.

The act does prohibit fraudulent and misleading statements. The punishment for those responsible for perpetrating such misrepresentations is a fine and/or imprisonment. Liability may be imposed on the corporation as an entity, as well as on its directors, underwriters (those charged with distributing the securities to the public), signers of the statement (usually corporate officers), and experts involved (usually accountants). The named parties are held jointly and severally liable, with civil liability sometimes going as high as the full sales price of the security in question.

As established in the BarChris case *(Escott v. BarChris Construction Corporation),* the corporation will always assume absolute liability in cases involving deficient or fraudulent registration statements. Directors, underwriters, signers and experts may escape absolute liability, however, if they successfully substantiate what is called a *due diligence defense.* A due diligence defense is basically a good faith defense. Judge McLean quoted Section 11(b) of the '33 Act in setting down the elements of due diligence:

97

> As regards any part of the registration statement not purporting to be made on the authority of an expert . . . [the defendant] had, after reasonable investigation, reasonable ground to believe and did believe, at the time such part of the registration statement became effective, that the statements therein were true and that there was no omission to state a material fact required to be stated therein or necessary to make the statements therein not misleading; . . . and as regards any part of the registration statement purporting to be made on the authority of an expert (other than [the defendant]) . . . [the defendant] had no reasonable ground to believe and did not believe, at the time such part of the registration became effective, that the statements therein were untrue, or that there was an omission to state a material fact required to be stated therein or necessary to make the statements therein not misleading.

Consequently, unless the defendant can prove that he did not know or did not have reason to know, as the case may be, of any material misstatements or omissions, he will not succeed in pleading a defense of due diligence and, as such, will not avoid liability.

In general, a registration statement must include:

- A description of the corporation's business.

- A description of the corporation's properties.

- A description of the significant provisions of the security to be offered for sale.

- A description of how the corporation is managed.

- Financial statements which have been certified by an independent public accountant.

The registration statement is divided into two parts. The first part is the *prospectus,* which is distributed to the public as the legal offering document. The entire statement becomes a matter of public record and, once it is filed, is available for inspection at the SEC.

Almost all domestic and foreign corporations issuing securities for the first time must register with the SEC. There are some exceptions, however. The following offerings are exempt from registration:

1.  Offerings for a total of $500,000 or less. In such cases the issuing corporation is allowed to file what is known as a *small registration statement.* Such offerings are called *Regulation A offerings* and the required financial statements are simpler and need not be certified. Also the filing expenses are usually less. As such, Regulation A is helpful to many small businesses.

2.  Private offerings. These are offerings to a maximum of 35 purchasers. To be exempt, the corporation must show that the purchasers are financially sophisticated themselves, or have been provided with sophisticated advice by someone who is independent of the issuing corporation. Also, to be exempt from registration, the issuing corporation must show that the purchasers do not plan to redistribute the securities.

**EXAMPLE (Multiple Choice):**

Of the following securities transactions, which is exempt from federal securities regulation?
  a. An offering of $100,000 of corporate bonds.
  b. The sale of $1,000,000 of limited partnership interests.
  c. A secondary offering of stock which had been previously registered.
  d. The sale of $500,000 of common stock to a single sophisticated purchaser for investment purposes.

**Solution:** (d)

3.  Intrastate offerings. Exemption from registration is available — regardless of how large the offering or how many purchasers there may be — provided that all purchasers and the

corporation are residents of (that is, *domiciled* in) the same state. True intrastate offerings are usually very difficult to establish.

**EXAMPLE (Multiple Choice):**

Under which of the following circumstances is a public offering of securities exempt from the registration requirements of the Securities Act of 1933?
    a. There was a prior registration within one year.
    b. The corporation is a public utility subject to regulation by the Federal Power Commission.
    c. The corporation was closely held prior to the offering.
    d. The issuing corporation and all prospective security owners are located within one state, and the entire offering, sale, and distribution is made within that state.

**Solution:** (d)

4. Offerings by banks.

5. Offerings by municipal, state, and federal governments.

6. Offerings by charitable organizations.

7. Offerings by carriers already subject to the Interstate Commerce Act.

While exempt issuers do not have to comply with the act's registration provisions, they still must comply with the act's antifraud provisions. Consequently, though the act's provisions are usually thought to apply solely to interstate commerce, they can also be applied to intrastate commerce.

**EXAMPLE:**

Boswell Realty Corporation, whose sole business is land development, purchased a large tract of land on which it intended to construct a high-rise apartment-house complex. In order to finance the construction, Boswell offered to sell $3,000,000 worth of shares in Boswell Realty to about 1,000 prospective investors located throughout the United States.

**Required:**

1. Discuss the implications of the Securities Act of 1933 to Boswell's offering to sell shares in the corporation.

2. The Securities Act of 1933 is considered a disclosure statute. Briefly describe the means provided and the principal types of information required to accomplish this objective of disclosure.

3. If an investor acquires shares of stock in Boswell Realty Corporation, is his interest real or personal property? Explain.

**Solution:**

1. The offering is subject to registration under the Securities Act of 1933. Despite the fact that the underlying property is real property, the shares represent the ownership in the corporation which in turn owns the real property. When these shares are offered for sale in interstate commerce (or by the use of instrumentalities of interstate commerce), the registration requirements of the Securities Act of 1933 must be met. These include filing a registration statement with the Securities and Exchange Commission (SEC) and giving a copy of the prospectus to each prospective purchaser of the registered securities.

2. The means of disclosure are the registration statement and the prospectus. The registration statement is filed with the SEC. The prospectus, which contains much of the information included in the registration statement, must be furnished to prospective investors of the registered securities. Both documents must contain full and accurate disclosure of all relevant information relating to such things as the company's business, its officers and directors, its securities, its financial position and earnings, and details about the underwriting. With rare exception, all information in a registration statement is part of the public record and open to public inspection. Photocopies of part or all of a registration statement may be obtained from the SEC at nominal costs.

3. His interest is personal property, because the property held is the shares in the corporaton. The shares represent ownership in the corporation which owns the underlying real property. The separate entity doctrine applies.

## The Securities Exchange Act of 1934:

While the '33 Act deals with newly issued stock being offered to the public for the first time, the '34 Act deals with securities which are actively traded. It could be said that the '33 Act deals with going public and the '34 Act deals with being public.

As noted, the '34 Act created the Securities and Exchange Commission as an independent administrative agency. Its enactment also provided for registration of securities on the national securities exchanges (for example, the American Stock Exchange, or AMEX; and the New York Stock Exchange, or NYSE), as well as set up a mechanism for regulating brokers and dealers by having the National Association of Securities Dealers (NASD) become, in effect, a quasi-governmental regulatory agency.

Some of the basic provisions of the '34 Act are as follows:

1.  All corporations which have 500 shareholders or more, or $1,000,000 or more in assets must register with the SEC. If a corporation does not meet these tests, but is listed on one of the securities exchanges, it too must register. Registration involves disclosing data similar to that required under the '33 Act, but the detail required under the '34 Act is somewhat less extensive. Corporations must also file certain other reports regularly, in order to keep the data in the original registration statement required by the '33 Act up to date. These reports include:

    • *Form 10-K:* This report is filed by the registered corporation annually with the SEC. Theoretically it is a less detailed statement, but as requirements are amended, it is slowly approaching the complexity of the initial registration statement required under the '33 Act.

    • *Form 10-Q:* These are interim quarterly reports which each corporation must file. The financial statements submitted with Form 10-Q do not have to be audited. Accountants must be associated with these reports, however, although not in the capacity of auditors.

    • *Form 8-K:* If any material developments occur in between the filing of any two quarterly 10-Q reports, a corporation must file this form immediately and not wait to include the information in the next Form 10-Q report.

2.  The '34 Act provides that every registered corporation must solicit proxies to shareholders to enable them to vote on matters, even if they are absent from a shareholder's meeting. These proxy statements cannot contain any material misrepresentations. Before distributing the proxies, corporate management must also send out an annual report to the shareholders — also without containing any material misrepresentations. The material to be included in these proxy statements must be submitted to the SEC for approval (to insure adequate disclosure) before they are sent out to the shareholders.

3.  One section of the '34 Act deals with trading by people who are privy to nonpublic information about the corporation. These people are called *insiders.* Section 16 regulates insider trading.

*Section 16A* requires that every shareholder owning 10% or more of the outstanding corporate stock, every director and every officer of a corporation falling under the control of the SEC must file a statement with the SEC upon becoming a 10% or more shareholder, director, or officer. Anyone falling within these three categories must report how many shares he owns and must report every transaction he makes while a *true insider* (that is, while a 10% or more shareholder, director, or officer).

*Section 16B* requires that every true insider who makes a profit from a transaction that took place within a six month period (that is, securities were bought and subsequently sold at a higher price, or sold and subsequently bought at a lower price within six months) must return that profit to the corporation. The exercise of a stock option is a purchase for the purposes of this section.

The reason for having enacted this section, as is the reason for having enacted Section 16A, is to prevent misuse of inside information by insiders. As a means to accomplish this end, the act forces the appropriate true insider to return to the corporation these so-called *short-swing profits* realized while he was a true insider. Short-swing profits must be returned (in other words, liability will be imposed) even if the trader was an insider at the time of the initial purchase or sale, but not at the time of the subsequent sale or purchase respectively, or vice versa (that is, if he was not an insider at the time of the initial purchase or sale but was an insider at the time of the subsequent sale or purchase). The provision applies when the stock involved is that of a corporation which was registered under the '34 Act during the entire transaction, as well as to stock when the corporation is not registered at one end of the transaction but is registered at the other end.

A claim of good faith is useless in a 16B action; liability will be imposed on an insider who reaped short-swing profits even if he did not intend to violate the law and even if he had no knowledge of any confidential inside information.

An action to recover short-swing profits can be brought by a current shareholder (whether he was a shareholder at the time of the transaction or not) or by the corporation.

4. *Section 10B* of the '34 Act is a general antifraud and antimanipulation provision. Section 10B is part of the '34 Act which was enacted by Congress; however, most references to its provisions point to *Rule 10b-5,* which is the law passed by the SEC pursuant to — or interpretive of — Section 10B of the '34 Act.

The kind of activities which this rule prohibits include trying to make it appear as though a nonactively traded security is actively traded, or engaging in transactions which would temporarily raise or lower the market price of securities in order to induce the investing public to buy or sell shares.

The provisions of Rule 10b-5 make it illegal for anyone to use the mails or any instrumentality of interstate commerce or the facilities of any of the national securities exchanges to try to manipulate or deceive anyone in connection with the selling or buying of securities. A person will be found guilty of violating the law whether he manipulates or deceives either directly or indirectly. The most common cases of deceit and manipulation are found when an insider uses material inside information relating to the activities or financial condition of a corporation to his advantage. Thus, he he is guilty he uses the information himself in his own personal trading activities, or if he passes it on to a third party. According to Rule 10b-5, a tippee (recipient of confidential information) is just as liable for violation of the rule as the tipper is — if the former uses the inside information to his advantage. Of course, if he does not use it, the tippee will not be held liable.

**EXAMPLE**:

Darius Corporation has 1,000,000 shares of common stock outstanding of which 450,000 shares are publicly traded over-the-counter and 550,000 are owned by Lynn, its president. The market price of the stock has ranged from $3 to $4 per share over the past year. Lynn obtained his Darius shares on August 10, 1976, when Darius acquired a company wholly owned by Lynn pursuant to an exchange of 550,000 Darius shares for all of the shares of Lynn's company. The Darius shares received by Lynn were unregistered and contained a legend which restricted transfer except on the opinion of counsel that the shares were transferable. The number of Darius shares held by the public was 450,000 both before and after the August 10 exchange.

On September 22, 1976, Archer & Co., Lynn's broker, purchased from Lynn, for its own account and in ten separate transactions, a total of 10,000 shares of Darius at $4.50 per share. The next day Archer purchased from Lynn in eight separate transactions an additional 8,000 shares in total at $5.50 per share, again for its own account. These were the only transactions on September 22 and 23, and trading in Darius shares over-the-counter had otherwise been light in recent months. On September 24, 1976, Archer circulated a story that there was an active demand for Darius shares. Within a few days, Darius stock was quoted over-the-counter at $9 per share.

On September 30, 1976, Archer sold, as agent for Lynn, 50,000 of Lynn's Darius shares for $9 a share to buyers in several states which Archer had solicited in the open market. Archer also sold for $9 per share the 18,000 Darius shares purchased the prior week for its own account. Soon thereafter, trading activity in Darius stock subsided to its normally light volume which was reflected in the market price retreat to $3 per share.

**Required:**

Answer the following, setting forth reasons for any conclusions stated.

1. Did Archer violate the Securities Exchange Act of 1934 when buying and selling the 18,000 shares of Darius?

2. Is Lynn liable to Darius under the Securities Exchange Act of 1934 because he sold 68,000 shares of Darius?

**Solution:**

1. Yes. Under the Securities Exchange Act of 1934, it is unlawful for any person, directly or indirectly, by the use of any means of interstate commerce or the mails, in connection with the purchase or sale of any security, to employ any manipulative or deceptive device or fraudulent scheme or practice, or to misstate, or omit to state, any material fact. The purchases by Archer from Lynn in multiple transactions and the subsequent circulation of a story that there was active demand for Darius shares would be considered a manipulative or deceptive device to raise the price of the stock for personal gain at the public's expense.

2. Yes. To prevent the unfair use of inside information that may have been obtained by a beneficial owner of more than 10% of any class of equity security of the issuer, the 1934 act provides that any profit realized by the beneficial owner from any purchase and sale of that security within any period of less than six months shall be recoverable by the issuer. Here, Lynn has purchased and sold 68,000 Darius common shares within a six-month period, while owning up to 55% of Darius common stock. Thus, Lynn would be liable under this provision to pay Darius the profits he realized on these transactions.

Many aspects of the '34 Act — particularly those relating to the definition of inside information and fraud — have been clarified by the SEC itself and during the proceedings of a handful of relatively recent keystone cases. Such clarifications, brought out in *SEC v. Texas Gulf Sulphur Co.*; the Merrill, Lynch, Pierce, Fenner & Smith case; *Ernst & Ernst v. Hochfelder; SEC v. Bausch & Lomb, Inc.*, for example include:

1. In order to bring a successful action relating to illegally communicated inside information, a plaintiff must prove that:

- The information was confidential.

- The inside information was material.

- It was a factor in the decision to buy or sell.

- The person who passed on the information and the person who made use of the information knew or had reason to know he was passing it on or receiving it illegally.

2. Anyone who has access to confidential inside information is a potential insider. Accordingly, officers, directors, major shareholders, and even employees or creditors can be insiders.

3. Inside information is considered material if:

- A reasonable stock speculator's or even a sophisticated investor's decision to buy or sell is influenced by the information.

- Immediately after becoming privy to the information, a tippee buys or sells stock.

4.  For previously confidential information to be considered public information, at the very least some sort of appropriately informative press release must be issued by the corporation. Neither the SEC nor the courts have been terribly clear on this point, but it is generally understood that there must be some broad public dissemination of the information (for example, an announcement in the *Wall Street Journal*) with a reasonable digestion period allowed.

5.  In order to bring a successful action for fraud, the plaintiff must establish intent — that is, *scienter* — on the defendant's part to engage in fraudulent activities.

**EXAMPLE:**

Taylor Corporation, incorporated and doing business in Delaware, is a manufacturing company whose securities are registered on a national securities exchange. On February 6, 1975, one of Taylor's engineers disclosed to management that he had discovered a new product which he believed would be quite profitable to the corporation. Messrs. Jackson and Wilson, the corporation's president and treasurer and members of its board of directors, were very impressed with the prospects of the new product's profitability. Because the corporation would need additional capital to finance the development, production, and marketing of the new product, the board of directors proposed that the corporation issue an additional 100,000 shares of common stock.

Wilson was imbued with such confidence in the corporation's prospects that on February 12, 1975, he purchased on the open market 1,000 shares of the corporation's common stock at $10 per share. This was before news of the new product reached the public in late February and caused a rise in the market price to $30 per share. Jackson did not purchase any shares in February because he had already purchased 600 shares of the corporation's common stock on January 15, 1975, for $10 per share.

In late February, when the market price of the corporation's common stock was $30 per share, Wilson approached two insurance companies to discuss the proposed issuance of an additional 100,000 shares of common stock. In March, Wilson reported to the board of directors that negotiations had been successful and one of the insurance companies had agreed to purchase the entire 100,000 shares for $3,000,000. The insurance company signed an investment letter, and a legend restricting transfers was imprinted on the face of each certificate issued to it. Moreover, the appropriate stop-transfer instructions were given to the corporation's stock-transfer agent.

Due to unexpected expenses arising from a fire in his home, on April 16, 1975, Jackson sold at $35 per share on the open market the 600 shares of stock he purchased in January. Wilson continues to hold his 1,000 shares.

**Required:**

What questions arising out of the federal securities laws are suggested by these facts? Discuss.

**Solution:**

The facts raise three questions relating to the federal securities laws:

1.  Must the 100,000 additional shares of common stock be registered under the Securities Act of 1933?

No. The offering of the 100,000 additional shares of common stock must be registered under the 1933 Act unless the offering is exempt under one or more of the various exemptions from registration provided by that Act. The exemption which would seem to warrant consideration and discussion is the so-called private placement ("transactions by an issuer not involving any public offering").

The private placement exemption has developed over the years and requires the consideration of various judicial and administrative criteria in determining its availability.

Traditionally, the main consideration has been whether the offerees have needed the protection afforded by the 1933 Act, as evidenced by whether the offerees have access to the same kind of information that registration would disclose and whether they are able to fend for themselves. A number of factors are evaluated in determining whether this objective has been satisfied. They include, among others, the following: (a) offering to a limited number of persons, (b) offering to sophisticated investors such as wealthy persons, lawyers, accountants, or businessmen, and (c) the nature, scope, and size of the offering including the number of units into which the offering is divided and the manner in which the offering is effected.

Limiting an offer to a few people (such as 25) is not determinative. The courts have held and it is the SEC's view that "the statute would seem to apply to a 'public offering' whether to few or many." Further, a sophisticated investor is generally viewed as one who has either sufficient economic bargaining power or such a family or employment relationship that enables him to obtain information from the issuer to evaluate the merits and risks of the investment.

Based on the facts presented, it would seem that Taylor Corporation would have little difficulty establishing an exemption that its offering was a private placement. Although the limited number of offerees is, of itself, not determinative, the offering was made only to two offerees, both of whom would appear to possess the requisite sophistication to make an informed investment decision and the ability to bear the economic risks.

2. Did Wilson violate the antifraud provisions of the Securities Exchange Act of 1934 when he purchased 1,000 shares of common stock based on information available to him but not to the general public?

Yes. Under the 1934 Act, it is unlawful for any person, directly or indirectly, by use of any means of interstate commerce or the mails, in connection with the purchase or sale of any security, to employ any deceptive or fraudulent practice or to misstate, or omit to state, any material fact. Here, Mr. Wilson, an officer and director of Taylor Corporation, knew that the prospects for the corporation were especially bright as of February 12, 1975, when he purchased 1,000 shares at $10 per share. This information was not yet disclosed to the public; thus, he was trading on so-called inside information in violation of the antifraud provision of the 1934 Act. The courts have held that insiders are not permitted to trade on material information until that information has been disseminated to the public.

3. Did Mr. Jackson violate the 1934 Act by profiting on the sale of 600 shares of common stock, and, if so, to whom is he responsible for the profit?

Yes. The 1934 Act prohibits certain insiders, which includes officers and directors, from, generally, realizing any profit from any purchase and sale, or sale and purchase, within any period of less than 6 months. Here, Mr. Jackson's purchase of 600 shares on January 15, 1975, at $10 per share and their subsequent sale on April 16, 1975, at $35 per share constitutes a violation of the 1934 Act. Jackson realized a profit of $25 per share or $15,000 total profit. The 1934 Act provides that a suit to recover such profit may be instituted by the issuer, or by any holder of any security of the issuer in behalf of the issuer, within 2 years after the date such profit was realized. Thus, Jackson is liable to the corporation for the $15,000 short-swing profit inasmuch as he has violated the law prohibiting certain insiders from realizing short-swing profits by trading in their corporation's securities.

Violators of Section 10B and Rule 10b-5 may have civil and/or criminal proceedings brought against them. The plaintiff in a civil suit may recover profits which the insider made or profits which the plaintiff lost by dealing with the insiders. The plaintiff can be either a shareholder who was directly involved in the transaction or any holder of corporate stock — whether directly involved in the transaction or not — for the purpose of returning to the corporation any profits realized by the insider. Of course, in order to bring a successful action, a plaintiff must prove that specific damages were actually suffered.

The steps which the SEC can take with regard to violators of any of the provisions of the '33 Act or '34 Act include the following:

• The SEC can bring a *civil action* in federal court to get an injunction in order to bring a stop to those violating the federal law or the commission's rules.

• The SEC, like every other independent agency, has quasi-judicial powers and, as such, can bring *administrative proceedings*. Consequently, it can prohibit someone from being involved in the securities business or bar someone from being involved with a registered public corporation.

● The SEC can *refer cases to the Justice Department* for criminal action, but it cannot bring criminal action itself.

**EXAMPLE (Multiple Choice):**

The Securities and Exchange Commission is *not* empowered to
   a. Obtain an injunction which will suspend trading in a given security.
   b. Sue for treble damages.
   c. Institute criminal proceedings against accountants.
   d. Suspend a broker-dealer.

**Solution:** (c)

# 12 Accountant's Legal Responsibility

**The negligent accountant . . .**

1. *. . . and his client.*

The relationship between an accountant and the client for whom he works is contractual. Accordingly, the ordinary rules of contract law determine the accountant's rights and the obligations he owes to his client. The latter point will be the focus of this chapter.

Naturally, if an accountant does not meet his obligations or does not perform according to the terms of the contract, he can be sued by the client for breach of contract, just as anybody else can be sued for breach of contract. In particular, because an accountant performs a personal service, he cannot delegate the duties he has contracted to perform to another person, no matter how competent that other person may be, without the knowledge and consent of the client.

As a skilled professional, the accountant is contractually obligated to perform his duties with reasonable care and as skillfully and prudently as an average professional with a similar background and education would. The accountant does not promise that he will be unusually creative or perform his duties any more skillfully or prudently than can be reasonably expected from an average accountant. Thus, the accountant does not promise perfection or infallible judgment. He is allowed to make errors, but only those errors that any skillful, prudent accountant might make.

**EXAMPLE (Multiple Choice):**

Martin Corporation orally engaged Humm & Dawson to audit its year-end financial statements. The engagement was to be completed within two months after the close of Martin's fiscal year for a fixed fee of $2,500. Under these circumstances what obligation is assumed by Humm & Dawson?
   a. None, because the contract is unenforceable since it is *not* in writing.
   b. An implied promise to exercise reasonable standards of competence and care.
   c. An implied obligation to take extraordinary steps to discover all defalcations.
   d. The obligation of an insurer of its work which is liable without fault.

**Solution:** (b)

If an accountant does not exercise this reasonable care in performing his duties, he is liable to the client for breach of contract because of *negligence*. In such a suit, the burden to prove that the accountant has been negligent is on the client. If the client brings a successful action, the accountant will most likely be directed to reimburse the client for all losses which have been proximately caused by the breach — that is, by the negligence.

An accountant will most probably be found negligent if he does not perform an audit in accordance with generally accepted auditing principles (GAAP) — that is, if the auditor does not comply with the standards of performance as set forth by the AICPA Committee on Auditing Procedure. There are basically ten standards or principles to which an auditor must adhere. These are broken down into three groups, as follows:

   a. *General Standards:*

   • The examination is to be performed by a person or persons having adequate technical training and proficiency as an auditor.

   • In all matters relating to the assignment an independence in mental attitude is to be maintained by the auditor or auditors.

   • Due professional care is to be exercised in the performance of the examination and preparation of the report.

b.  *Standards of Field Work:*

- The work is to be adequately planned and assistants, if any, are to be properly supervised.

- There is to be a proper study and evaluation of the existing internal control as a basis for reliance thereon and for the determination of the resultant extent of the tests to which auditing procedures are to be restricted.

- Sufficient competent evidential matter is to be obtained through inspection, observation, inquiries and confirmations to afford a reasonable basis for an opinion regarding the financial statements under examination.

c.  *Standards of Reporting:*

- The report shall state whether the financial statements are presented in accordance with generally accepted principles of accounting.

- The report shall state whether such principles have been consistently observed in the current period in relation to the preceding period.

- Informative disclosures in the financial statements are to be regarded as reasonably adequate unless otherwise stated in the report.

- The report shall either contain an expression of opinion regarding the financial statements taken as a whole, or an assertion to the effect that an opinion cannot be expressed. When an overall opinion cannot be expressed reasons therefor should be stated. In all cases where the auditor's name is associated with financial statements the report should contain a clear-cut indication of the character of the auditor's examination, if any, and the degree of responsibility he is taking.

An accountant is not required to uncover fraud unless he would have uncovered it in the normal course of a reasonably skillful and prudently conducted audit. Accordingly, if an accountant's suspicions are aroused during his investigation, he is expected to follow them through. This means that he is expected to personally investigate those suspicions, and not rely on hearsay or on the opinions of either the client's employees or the accountant's own colleagues. If irregularities do come to light, and the accountant does not follow them through, he will be found negligent if, in having investigated them properly, he would have uncovered or detected defalcations. On the other hand, he will not be found negligent if he does perform his investigation according to GAAP and yet fails to uncover any defalcations which do exist.

2.  *. . . and third parties.*

In general, an accountant is not liable to third parties for any losses they may have suffered as a result of his negligence. The reason behind this concept is that the accountant is generally not bound by contract (that is, there is no *privity of contract*) to third parties, but only to his client. Consequently, third parties have no rights under the accountant-client contract.

Recalling from contract law, you will remember that a third party has contractual rights and duties under contracts to which he is not a direct party only if he is a *third-party beneficiary* of a contract. If a client uses the services of an accountant primarily for the benefit of a third party, that third party is a third party beneficiary. For example, when someone applies to a bank for a loan, the bank usually requires a complete set of financial statements to use as a basis for its decision. If a client contracts the services of an accountant to prepare those statements, the bank is said to be the third party beneficiary of the accountant-client contract. In such a situation, when the accountant knows the use to which the statements will be put — that is, he is aware that a third party or third parties will be relying on the statements — the accountant owes the same duty of care to the third party as he owes to his client. As such, in contrast to the general rule, an accountant can be liable to a third party beneficiary for negligence under these circumstances.

## The fraudulent accountant . . .

1.    . . . *and his client.*

A *negligent* action is one that has been committed unintentionally; a *fraudulent* action is one that has been committed intentionally. A client can charge an accountant with actual fraud or with constructive fraud.

     a.    *Actual fraud* exists when the accountant is conscious of his wrongdoings; that is, he intends to commit a wrong, he intends to deceive.

     b.    *Constructive fraud* is actually *gross negligence.* Although a constructively fraudulent accountant does not manifest intent, he is just as liable to his client as an actually fraudulent accountant. Examples of constructive fraud include:

         • An accountant who prepares financial statements without verifying the figures on them.

         • An accountant who certifies an audit without verifying whether the financial statements' figures are reasonably accurate.

         • An accountant who refuses (as opposed to innocently neglects) to follow through on his aroused suspicions or, if he does follow through, refuses to report his findings.

A client charging fraud has the burden of proving his allegations.

**EXAMPLE:**

Charles Worthington, the founding and senior partner of a successful and respected CPA firm, was a highly competent practitioner who always emphasized high professional standards. One of the policies of the Firm was that all reports by members or staff be submitted to Worthington for review.

Recently, Arthur Craft, a junior partner in the Firm, received a phone call from Herbert Flack, a close personal friend. Flack informed Craft that he, his family and some friends were planning to create a corporation to engage in various land development ventures; that various members of the family are presently in a partnership (Flack Ventures) which holds some land and other assets; and that the partnership would contribute all of its assets to the new corporation, and the corporation would assume the liabilities of the partnership.

Flack asked Craft to prepare a balance sheet of the partnership that he could show to members of his family, who were in the partnership, and friends to determine whether they might have an interest in joining in the formation and financing of the new corporation. Flack said he had the partnership general ledger in front of him and proceeded to read to Craft the names of the accounts and their balances at the end of the latest month. Craft took the notes he made during the telephone conversation with Flack, classified and organized the data into a conventional balance sheet and had his secretary type the balance sheet and an accompanying letter on Firm stationery. He did not consult Worthington on this matter or submit his work to him for review.

The transmittal letter stated: "We have reviewed the books and records of Flack Ventures, a partnership, and have prepared the attached balance sheet at March 31, 1972. We did not perform an examination in conformity with generally accepted auditing standards, and therefore do not express an opinion on the accompanying balance sheet." The balance sheet was prominently marked "unaudited." Craft signed the letter and instructed his secretary to send it to Flack.

**Required:**

What legal problems are suggested by these facts? Explain.

**Solution:**

The main legal problem and implication of Craft's action is the potential liability to which Craft has exposed himself and the Firm by falsely stating that the books and records of Flack Ventures had been reviewed by the Firm in preparing the balance sheet.

Such a statement was fraudulent in that it was made with the requisite knowledge of falsity. Craft, having examined nothing, could not honestly make such a statement. Thus, if the balance sheet contains a material misrepresentation of fact and third party investors lose money in reliance upon the balance sheet, they can recover from the accountants. Privity is not required in order to prevail against an accountant where fraud is present.

The fact that the balance sheet was marked "unaudited" and that the transmittal letter contained qualifying language will not save Craft or the Firm. Nor will the fact that Craft did not follow the Firm's procedures, in that he failed to submit the report for review, free the Firm from liability. As a partner and agent of the firm, he has the legal power to subject the Firm to such liability.

2.   *. . . and third parties.*

An accountant is liable to all third parties for actual fraud and/or constructive fraud if such third parties both relied upon the false information and suffered a loss as a result of this reliance. In cases involving fraud, the third party need not necessarily be a third party beneficiary, nor must the accountant be aware of the use to which his work will be put.

In cases involving negligence, then, an accountant is liable to a limited number of third parties (that is, only to third party beneficiaries who the accountant knew would be relying on the statements he prepared). In cases of fraud, however, the accountant is liable to a potentially unlimited number of third parties (that is, to any third party who relied on the statements and suffered a loss) for an indeterminate, but theoretically unlimited, sum of money.

## Other elements of the accountant-client relationship:

1. *Privileged communications:*

   Privileged communications are defined as those which cannot be disclosed. The basis for keeping certain information from becoming public is that the disclosures of privileged communications violate public policy, because such information is communicated between people involved in confidential relationships, and confidantes will hesitate to engage in free and open discussions if they expect their conversations to become public. The status accorded the communications between an accountant and his client is determined by common law, as well as by statutory law.

   a.   *Common law:* At common law today, there is no such thing as a privileged communication between an accountant and his client. Consequently, if an accountant is questioned in court, he cannot refuse to disclose conversations between himself and his client, or refuse to submit any written letters or memos, on the grounds that such conversations or writings are privileged communications. This common law has not been abridged, revised, or modified, by any federal statutes. Therefore, an accountant must disclose the contents of all communications he has had with his client — when asked to, of course, and when under oath — in all federal courts.

   b.   *Statutory law:* Several states have passed legislation which affords accountant-client communications the status of privileged communications. Thus, in those states which have changed the common law, an accountant cannot be compelled to disclose any confidential conversations or writings between himself and his client. To the extent that such information can be "possessed," privileged communications are the client's property. As such, if the client waives his rights, an accountant can disclose privileged communications. It is the client's choice or right alone to disclose, not the accountant's. The privileged communication status can only be claimed in apropriate state courts; the common law rule still controls, however, in all federal courts — including those located in these several states.

2.  *The accountant's working papers:*

An independent accountant is an independent contractor with respect to his clients. As such, according to common law, the accountant — not his client — is the sole owner of his working papers, unless the contract between the two parties states otherwise. In several states, this common law rule has been incorporated into statutes.

Although his working papers are technically his own, an accountant is nevertheless obligated to his client — with whom he has a confidential relationship — to keep the contents of those papers undisclosed unless the client gives him specific instructions to do otherwise. Similarly an accountant may not sell, trade, lend, or bequeath those working papers — again, unless the client gives him specific instructions to do otherwise. In other words, while the working papers are the property of the accountant, the information within them is confidential.

Working papers are considered privileged communications in those states which have enacted statutes recognizing the existence of privileged communications. As the federal government does not recognize the existence of privileged communications between an accountant and his client, working papers can be subpoenaed and an accountant must produce them in all federal courts.

**EXAMPLES (True/False):**

James Sack, a partner in the firm of Walters, Jones, & Sack, CPAs, prepared tax returns for Ominus, a closely held family corporation. The Corporation's books were kept by a family member. While preparing the tax returns, Sack realized that the books and records were poorly kept and contained several inaccuracies. However, he relied upon them and based his tax computations exclusively upon them. As a result, Sack erroneously included in taxable income some items which did not actually represent income. The errors subsequently were discovered, but, by that time, it was too late to file an amended return or claim for refund to recover the excess taxes paid.

1. James Sack was negligent in preparing the tax return.
2. The Internal Revenue Service would be unable to subpoena Walters, Jones, & Sack's working papers becasue they are privileged communications.
3. Walters, Jones, & Sack will be liable for the excess amount of taxes paid by Ominus.
4. Only Sack, and not the CPA firm, would be liable under the circumstances described.
5. Sack's firm could defend successfully a suit brought by Ominus to recover the excess amount of tax by establishing the contributory negligence of Ominus.
6. The fact that Sack had not been informed of the inadequacy of the records totally exonerates him from liability.
7. Sack has committed a fraud.

**Solutions:** (1) T, (2) F, (3) T, (4) F, (5) F, (6) F, (7) F

## The accountant and the Securities Act of 1933:

The Securities Act of 1933 specifies an accountant's statutory liability to third parties when he is associated with the registration of a corporation involved in an initial issue of its securities.

An accountant's liability to a third party is expanded from common law under the '33 Act. For example, an accountant is liable to all third parties for losses they have suffered as a result of his negligence, whether the plaintiff is a third party beneficiary or not, and whether the accountant expected the plaintiff to rely on his work or not.

**EXAMPLE (Multiple Choice):**

The traditional common-law rules regarding accountants' liability to third parties for negligence
   a. Remain substantially unchanged since their inception.

b. Were more stringent than the rules currently applicable.

c. Are of relatively minor importance to the accountant.

d. Have been substantially changed at both the federal and state levels.

**Solution:** (d)

An accountant is liable to a third party if a registration statement with which he is connected, and/or the financial statements included therein which he has certified, contain a material misstatement or omit a material fact (that is, a material omission). The liability attaches if the accountant is negligent or fraudulent and, if fraudulent, whether the case is one of actual or constructive fraud. The third party does not have to prove reliance on the financial statements or that the loss incurred was the proximate result of the material misstatement or the material omission. All that must be substantiated is that the third party who suffered a loss purchased securities that were described in a registration statement which included certified financial statements that contained a material misstatement and/or a material omission.

**EXAMPLE (Multiple Choice):**

An investor seeking to recover stock market losses from a CPA firm, based upon an unqualified opinion on financial statements which accompanied a registration statement, must establish that

a. There was a false statement or omission of material fact contained in the audited financial statements.

b. He relied upon the financial statements.

c. The CPA firm did *not* act in good faith.

d. The CPA firm would have discovered the false statement or omission if it had exercised due care in its examination.

**Solution:** (a)

In these cases, the burden of proof is on the accountant/defendant as opposed to the third party/plaintiff. As such, the accountant must prove that he was either not negligent or not fraudulent. He can escape liability by proving that he made a reasonable investigation, had a reasonable basis for his beliefs, and did, in fact, believe that the facts included in the financial statements he certified were true. He may reduce his liability (though not necessarily avoid it entirely) if he can prove that the third party's loss was either entirely or partially caused by factors other than the material misrepresentations or material omissions of the certified statements (for example, the losses were caused by mismanagement of the corporation).

Under the '33 Act, an accountant is liable not only for material misrepresentations or omissions as of the date of the financial statements, but also as of the date the registration statement becomes effective. Civil penalties are imposed upon a negligent accountant; civil and criminal penalties are imposed upon a fraudulent accountant.

**EXAMPLE:**

Whitlow and Wyatt, CPAs, have been the independent auditors of Interstate Land Development Corporation for several years. During these years, Interstate prepared and filed its own annual income tax returns.

During 1974, Interstate requested Whitlow and Wyatt to examine all the necessary financial statements of the corporation to be submitted to the Securities and Exchange Commission (SEC) in connection with a multi-state public offering of one-million shares of Interstate common stock. This public offering came under the provisions of the Securities Act of 1933. The examination was performed carefully and the financial statements were fairly presented for the respective periods. These financial statements were included in the registration statement filed with the SEC.

While the registration statement was being processed by the SEC but prior to the effective date, the Internal Revenue Service (IRS) subpoenaed Whitlow and Wyatt to turn over all its working papers relating to Interstate for the years 1971-1973. Whitlow and Wyatt initially refused to comply for two reasons. First, Whitlow and Wyatt did not prepare Interstate's tax returns. Second, Whitlow and Wyatt claimed that the working papers were confidential matters subject to the privileged-communications rule. Subsequently, however, Whitlow and Wyatt did relinquish the subpoenaed working papers.

Upon receiving the subpoena, Wyatt called Dunkirk, the chairman of Interstate's board of directors and asked him about the IRS investigation. Dunkirk responded, "I'm sure the IRS people are on a fishing expedition and that they will not find any material deficiencies."

A few days later Dunkirk received written confirmation from the IRS that it was contending that Interstate had underpaid its taxes during the period under review. The confirmation revealed that Interstate was being assessed $800,000 including penalties and interest for the three years.

This $800,000 assessment was material relative to the financial statements as of December 31, 1974. The amount for each year individually exclusive of penalty and interest was not material relative to each respective year.

**Required:**

Discuss the additional liability assumed by Whitlow and Wyatt in connection with this SEC registration engagement.

**Solution:**

The Securities Act of 1933 has significantly changed the duty and liability of CPAs who examine financial statements used as a part of a registration statement. The CPA has the burden of proving he was neither negligent nor fraudulent in examining the financial statements. The CPA may satisfy his burden of proof by showing that he made a reasonable investigation, had a reasonable basis for his belief, and did believe the financial statements he examined were fairly presented. The above duty is required at the date the registration becomes effective, not at the date of the financial statements.

Thus, Whitlow and Wyatt must continue to examine the financial statements after the date of its report thereon. The fact that the CPA's performance was faultless as of the date of these statements does not excuse the CPA from the continuing obligation to investigate until the time of the effective date of the registration statement in order to determine whether any significant events have occurred subsequently which would materially affect the validity of these financial statements.

Since no privity requirement exists under the Securities Act of 1933, the CPA's potential liability is extremely broad. The CPA firm faces potential liability to the purchasers of the one-million shares to the extent that the omitted disclosure of the tax assessment causes purchasers to lose money on their investment.

## The accountant and the Securities Exchange Act of 1934:

Recall from Chapter 10 that the '34 Act regulates actively traded securities — that is, securities issued by companies that are already being traded as opposed to securities which are being issued for the first time.

The '34 Act requires the filing of annual reports which must include certified financial statements prepared by an accountant. An accountant is liable to third parties for any false or misleading material statements included in those reports which he certifies. A third party — a buyer or a seller — dealing in a security to which any financial statements containing such false or misleading material misstatements refer, may sue an accountant for negligence or fraud. However, as contrasted with the provisions of the '33 Act, the burden of proof falls on the plaintiff. A third party/plaintiff can bring a successful action under the '34 Act only if he can prove all of the following:

- That he relied on the false or misleading statements (that is, that they were material in his decision).

- That he did not know it was false or misleading (that is, that he acted in good faith).

- That the price he paid or received in the transaction was affected by the false or misleading statement.

An accountant can successfully avoid liability if he can prove that he acted in good faith — that is, that he did not know the statements were false or misleading.

Under the '34 Act, an accountant is liable only for false or misleading material statements as of the date of the financial statements. Civil penalties are imposed upon a negligent accountant; civil and criminal penalties are imposed upon a fraudulent accountant.

# 13 Antitrust Laws

Antitrust legislation was enacted to promote free and fair competition by prohibiting anti-competitive business practices. There is no federal common law in this area, only statutory law. However, the statutes that do exist are not as detailed or explicit as one might prefer, and therefore the courts have had many opportunities to interpret them and set precedents.

**The Sherman Antitrust Act:**

This, the first federal antitrust statute, was enacted in 1890. The government's attempt to preserve free and unfettered competition in trade is based on the theory that a truly competitive atmosphere yields the best allocation of economic resources, the lowest prices, the highest quality, and the greatest material progress. As such, the act prohibits any activities which will result in such a concentration of power so as to control prices, which will exclude competition, or which will increase one's share of an existing market.

Section I of the act states that "every contract, combination in the form of trust or otherwise, or conspiracy, in restraint of trade or commerce among the several States, or with foreign nations, is declared to be illegal." Activities which are illegal under this section include:

- Any arrangements entered into to control prices, either directly or by controlling the means of production. It should be emphasized here that it makes no difference what the underlying rationale for price-fixing may be: A businessman who controls prices for the purposes of setting maximum prices is just as guilty of breaking the law as one who tries to set minimum prices.

**EXAMPLE (Multiple Choice):**

One of your CPA firm's clients, Destination Garages, Inc., has entered into an agreement with its principal competitor, Parking Unlimited, Inc., to eliminate cut-throat competition. They have agreed to charge a uniform hourly rate in the different areas in which they compete. The garages are mainly located in Metropolis, but some are located in another state which is just across the state line from Metropolis. It is agreed that the rates to be charged are (1) *always* to be reasonable and (2) to be based upon the rate structure charged by the leading parking lot operator in Central City, the capital of the state in which Metropolis is located. What is the status of the agreement between Destination Garages and Parking Unlimited in regard to federal antitrust law?
   a. Because the garages are real property, antitrust law does *not* apply.
   b. Because the "product" sold is a service, antitrust law does *not* apply.
   c. Regardless of the fact that the prices agreed upon are aimed at avoiding cut-throat competition, are always to be reasonable to the public, and are based upon another company's rates, the prices agreed upon are, nevertheless, in violation of the antitrust law.
   d. If Destination Garages can show that it was in fact merely meeting competition from other parking lots, it would have a complete defense against any alleged antitrust violation.

**Solution:** (c)

- Any arrangements which unduly restrict competition, including anticompetitive mergers, collective refusals to deal with other merchants, reciprocal dealing arrangements, and tying arrangements. A *tying arrangement* is an agreement by a party to sell one product — the tying product — only if the buyer purchases a second product — the tied product.

- Any agreement entered into by competitors to divide the existing market among themselves.

- Arrangements restricting territories or customers.

113

**EXAMPLE (Multiple Choice):**

Inns Corporation operated a major hotel in a metropolitan city. An annual festival week brought many tourists to the city resulting in peak demand for accommodations. The local Tourism Bureau, of which Inns was an active member, embarked on a campaign to increase tourist trade in the area and asked all suppliers of goods to hotels and restaurants to contribute 1 percent of sales revenue to the bureau. Bureau members also were of the opinion that higher prices could be charged during the festival week without hurting the tourist trade. Which of the following actions would most likely violate the antitrust laws?

    a. Rental of Inns' main ballroom on the key day of the festival at a price below that offered by other hotels.

    b. The raising of rates on hotel rooms during festival week when other hotels also raise their rates.

    c. Inns' notification to its purchasing officer to confine its purchases to suppliers contributing to the Tourism Bureau as agreed with other bureau members.

    d. Inns' policy of purchasing soap products from only one manufacturer even though there were offers of lower prices for similar goods from other manufacturers.

**Solution:** (c)

There are two major concepts or doctrines which have been used in interpreting antitrust law: the per se doctrine and the rule of reason doctrine. Curiously, they are virtually diametrically opposed to one another.

1. *The* per se *doctrine:* According to this concept, there are certain anticompetitive practices which are automatic violations of the antitrust laws. Courts will not look to any justification — economic or otherwise — when faced with a *per se* violation. For example, price-fixing of any sort is a *per se* violation and a defendant will not escape liability for having violated the law even if he testifies that he was setting low prices to benefit the public, or even if he testifies that the only way he could enter a market was to fix prices. Other *per se* violations include refusals to deal with certain business people, group boycotts, and territorial allocation of markets.

**EXAMPLE (True/False):**

Four corporations are the largest manufacturers in their industry. Their combined share of the market has constituted over 90% each year for many years. As members of a trade association, certain officers of these corporations meet periodically to discuss topics of mutual interest. Matters discussed include engineering design, production methods, product costs, product pricing, merchandising policy, and inventory levels. The representatives also usually see each other after the association meetings for cocktails where they discuss these and other business matters. These representatives have maintained prices in accordance with an informal oral agreement terminable at will by any company wishing to withdraw. However, they have never reduced their agreement to a written document or memorandum. The four corporations compete with each other in interstate commerce. The states in which these corporations do business have typical "fair trade" laws.

    1. The members of the trade association validly may appoint the trade association as their representative to allocate manufacturing quotas.

    2. An arrangement relating to price fixing would be illegal *per se* if the government merely proved the existence of the oral agreement.

    3. The distributors of the four corporations legally could enter into price maintenance agreements among themselves to prescribe the minimum prices at which they would resell the products bearing the brand name, trademark, or trade name of any of the four corporations.

**Solution:** (1) F, (2) T, (3) F

2. *The rule of reason doctrine:* If the violation is not a per se violation, the courts will read and apply the antitrust laws in a way such that if the alleged violation is proven to be a reasonable restraint of trade, the defendant will not be found guilty. In these cases, courts will listen to pleas claiming economic justification. If, however, the violation is found to be an unreasonable restraint of trade, the defendant will be found guilty of violating the antitrust laws, even if he has not engaged in a per se violation.

Section II of the Sherman Antitrust Act reads, in part, that "every person who shall monopolize, or combine or conspire with any other person or persons, to monopolize any part of the trade or commerce among the several States, or with foreign nations, shall be deemed guilty of a misdemeanor." It has become clear, as a result of several landmark court cases, that monopolistic control that is a result of an historic accident, or that results from growth or development because of a superior product or excellent business judgment, is not a violation of this statute. Monopolies which do violate this statute are those which developed as the result of some willful, intentional, deliberate attempt to take over a huge share of the market (or to exclude competitors) and to sustain that monopolistic power.

The federal courts may issue injunctions to enjoin those engaged in anticompetitive practices. Plaintiffs who have been victimized by anticompetitive practices may bring a civil action and can sue to recover treble damages. (*Trebel damages* are three times the amount of any damages which the plaintiff can prove he has suffered.) In addition, violators are subject to fine and/or imprisonment.

### The Clayton Act:

The Clayton Act, adopted by Congress in 1914, reinforced some of the provisions of the Sherman Antitrust Act. With its enactment, all monopolistic practices became illegal, whether they resulted in actual monopolies or not. As such, the Clayton Act prohibits tying arrangements and exclusive selling and leasing arrangements which would *tend to* create a monopoly. (Tying arrangements have occasionally been allowed when engaged in by franchisors attempting to maintain a certain quality of goods.)

Section 7 of the Clayton Act deals specifically with anticompetitive or monopolistic mergers or acquisitions. It provides, in part, that

> No corporation engaged in commerce shall acquire, directly or indirectly, the whole or any part of the stock or other share of capital and no corporation subject to the jurisdiction of the Federal Trade Commission shall acquire the whole or any part of the assets of another corporation engaged also in commerce, where in any line of commerce in any section of the country, the effect of such acquisition may be substantially to lessen competition or to tend to create a monopoly.

With the enactment of the Clayton Act, agricultural, horticultural, and labor organizations became exempt from the antitrust laws.

#### EXAMPLE (Multiple Choice):

Snowmobile sales by manufacturers in a relevant market amount to about $10,000,000 annually. Sleekat, a manufacturer who sells its snowmobiles directly to dealers, has sales of about $4,000,000 annually in that market of which about $2,000,000 are to Sport Store. Sport Store has about 40% of the retail market and half of its sales are Sleekat vehicles. Four other manufacturers account for the other 60% of wholesale sales and three other dealers account for the other 60% of retail sales. Under these circumstances
   a. Sleekat would probably commit an antitrust violation by acquiring all of the stock of Sport Store.
   b. Sleekat would probably *not* commit an antitrust violation if it required Sport Store to limit its sales of Sleekat vehicles to persons resident in the defined market and provided that the dealership would be terminated for violation.
   c. Sleekat could require Sport Store to sell only Sleekat vehicles and *no* competing vehicles and probably *not* violate the antitrust laws.
   d. Sleekat could avoid any possible violation of the antitrust laws by acquiring the assets of Sport Store.

**Solution:** (a)

### The Robinson-Patman Act:

This piece of legislation, adopted by Congress in 1936, is basically a modification or amendment of Section 2 of the Clayton Act. Its provisions prohibit price discrimination by businesses dealing in interstate commerce of goods which are of like grade and quality, if such discrimination would tend to be anticompetitive. The rule of reason is applied when alleged violations occur.

Discriminatory practices include a seller's offering reduced prices or other "fringe benefits" to only one or perhaps a handful of customers, in order to encourage patronage or to reduce or eliminate competition, without offering the same price reductions or "fringe benefits" to all customers purchasing merchandise of like grade or quality.

**EXAMPLE (Multiple Choice):**

Harvey Enterprises, Inc., sells furniture to the trade in interstate commerce. It can avoid violation of the Robinson-Patman Act if
    a. Its volume of sales is less than $500,000 per year.
    b. It pays rebates to selected large-volume customers.
    c. It provides free advertising to its customers based on their relative volume of purchases.
    d. It pays brokerage commissions to favored customers.

**Solution:** (c)


A buyer who knowingly induces price discrimination or knowingly engages in such practices by benefitting from a seller's discriminatory terms, is also in violation of the law. The buyer's customer who is aware of the illegal practices and, in buying from the merchant, benefits from the discrimination as well, is also in violation of the law.

As noted, such practices violate this law only if they tend to be anticompetitive and are without economic justification. Accordingly, if a seller can prove that he reduced his prices in order to meet the competition, or a buyer can show that he accepted reduced prices in order to promote economies of scale, neither one will be found guilty of violating the Robinson-Patman Act.

It appears, then, that it is possible to engage in an activity which is a per se violation of the Sherman Antitrust Act (such as price fixing), but which, if economically justified, may not be a violation of the Robinson-Patman Act.

**EXAMPLE (Multiple Choice):**

Marvel Toys, Inc., manufactures and sells toys to Gem Stores, a large department store chain, and to Fantastic Discounts, a major toy retailer, at prices below its sales price of similar toys to other retailers in the market area. Its pricing policy vis-a-vis Gem is based solely upon the fact that Gem is a new customer and the low prices were quoted in order to obtain its business and thereby eliminate Marvel's unused production capacity. For Fantastic, the lower prices are charged in order to meet the identical prices legally charged by a competitor. In assessing the potential violation of antitrust laws against price discrimination, it would appear that Marvel Toys
    a. Has *not* violated the antitrust laws as long as none of its competitors can show damages.
    b. Has a valid defense with respect to its sales to Gem.
    c. Has *not* violated the antitrust laws with respect to its sales to Fantastic.
    d. Will *not* have committed any violation if it was operating at a loss at the time of the sales.

**Solution:** (c)

# *14* Employees' Rights

This chapter deals with the relationship between an employer and employee as defined by the Fair Labor Standards Act, the Federal Insurance Contribution Act, the Federal Unemployment Tax Act, and typical state Workmen's Compensation laws.

**The Fair Labor Standards Act:**

This act is also known as the "wages and hours law" because its provisions prescribe minimum hourly wages which must be paid by companies which produce goods for interstate commerce, receive goods in interstate commerce, and must be paid to employees who work in interstate commerce. The act applies to wages paid according to time worked as opposed to wages based on piecework or commissions. The act is also antidiscriminatory in that it requires equal pay for equal work, regardless of an employee's sex.

According to the Fair Labor Standards Act, covered employees must be paid one and one-half times their hourly wage ("time and a half") for each overtime hour worked per week. Overtime begins running after 40 hours per week for employees in stabilized industries, and after 50 hours per week for employees in seasonal industries. Employers may not average hours: If an employee in a stabilized industry works 50 hours in week #1 and 38 hours in week #2, he is entitled to time and a half for the ten hours extra worked in the first week. An employer cannot average the two weeks and pay the employee overtime rates for only 8 hours. (Of course, it is possible — and probable — that the employee will be docked two hours' pay in week #2, but he will be docked at regular rates.)

Executives, administrative and professional employees, agricultural employees, employees who work in retail and service establishments or amusement and recreational establishments, handicapped employees and apprentices, students, and messengers are not covered by these wage and hour provisions.

The provisions in the act relating to children include the prohibition of employing children under 16 years old in any kind of work which could be hazardous to their health or well being and the prohibition of employing children under 14 years old in any kind of work at all, except for child actors, children employed by their parents in nonhazardous positions, or newspaper delivery boys.

Violators of the Fair Labor Standards Act include those employers who directly violate its provisions, as well as people who do not directly violate the provisions as employers, but who buy or sell via interstate commerce goods which they know or have reason to know are produced in violation of the act.

**EXAMPLE (Multiple Choice):**

The federal Fair Labor Standards Act
   a. Prohibits any employment of a person under 16 years of age.
   b. Requires payment of time-and-one-half for overtime to actors engaged in making television productions.
   c. Contains an exemption from the minimum-wage provisions for manufacturing plants located in areas of high unemployment.
   d. Prohibits the delivery by a wholesaler to a dealer in another state of any goods where the wholesaler knew that oppressive child labor was used in the manufacture of the goods.

**Solution:** (d)

Both civil and criminal suits can be brought against violators. Remedies include injunctions to restrain future violation, and the reimbursement of lost wages resulting from sex discrimination. A wage suit may be brought by the victimized employee or by the federal government.

**The Federal Insurance Contribution Act:**

The basic provisions of this act are those terms which allow qualified workers in covered industries to receive monthly retirement payments and Medicare benefits upon retirement at a specified age. The family of a worker who dies before or after reaching this specified age receives the benefits in the deceased employee's stead.

The money to support this program comes from taxes levied under the Federal Insurance Contributions Act. Such taxes are often referred to as FICA taxes or, more commonly, as social security taxes. The act requires employers to withhold a certain percentage of each employee's compensation (compensation includes whatever salary, bonuses, commissions, vacation pay, etc., the employee might receive) and to remit that amount to the government in order to support the program. In addition, each employer must match this amount so that 50% of the total contribution comes from the employee and 50% from the employer. The two factors involved in computing each employee's FICA tax (and, consequently, each employer's contribution per employee) is the *base* — or amount of earnings subject to tax — and the *rate* which is applied to that base.

**EXAMPLE (Multiple Choice):**

The Federal Social Security Act
    a. Applies to self-employed businessmen.
    b. Excludes professionals such as accountants, lawyers, and doctors.
    c. Provides for a deduction by the employee against his federal income tax.
    d. Applies to professionals at their option.

**Solution:** (a)

**The Federal Unemployment Tax Act:**

Unemployment insurance is another element in the federal social security program. It is designed to offer relief to people who are temporarily out of work. The unemployment insurance taxes — commonly called FUTA taxes — are levied only on employers. Accordingly, unlike FICA taxes, they are not deducted from an employee's gross pay. An employer must pay FUTA taxes if he employes one or more employees and is in a covered industry. Unemployment taxes are also paid into state funds, and employers may take credits against the FUTA taxes payable to the federal government for amounts paid into state unemployment funds.

**Workmen's Compensation Laws:**

Workmen's compensation laws are designed to give financial assistance to employees who are injured while on the job. Each state has and administers its own workmen's compensation laws, but there are certain general characteristics which are common to all state statutes, and which this section will cover.

Workmen's compensation is available to all employees injured on the job, whether or not the injury results from the employee's own negligence.

**EXAMPLE (Multiple Choice):**

Workmen's compensation laws are
    a. Governed by federal regulation.
    b. Applicable to all types of employment.
    c. Designed to eliminate the employer's defense of contributory negligence when an employee is injured on the job.
    d. *Not* applicable if the employee signs a waiver and consents to his noncoverage under workmen's compensation at the time he is hired.

**Solution:** (c)

The burden is on the employee to prove he was injured in the regular course of his employment. An employee never receives benefits, however, if he willfully causes his own injury, or if he is injured while substantially drunk or while engaging in activities which are outside the scope of his employment. In addition, independent contractors, employees who work for charities, and agricultural and domestic employees are not covered by workmen's compensation laws.

**EXAMPLE (Multiple Choice):**

Markum was grossly negligent in the operation of a forklift. As a result he suffered permanent disability. His claim for workmen's compensation will be
  a. Denied.
  b. Limited to medical benefits.
  c. Reduced by the percentage share attributable to his own fault.
  d. Paid in full.

**Solution:** (d)

The actual benefits paid out can come from an insurance company, an employer's own fund created for just such a purpose, or from a state fund. Regardless of the source of the benefits, once a claim has been settled, the injured employee cannot then sue his employer personally for additional damages. Nor can he sue any other third party who might have caused the injury. Accordingly, the benefits received in settlement of a claim are said to constitute an *exclusive remedy*. If an injured party does somehow succeed in recovering additional damages from a third party, the insurance company or state board which paid out the original benefits has a lien on any such subsequent recovery, to the extent of the initial benefits paid. As such, the company or board is said to be *subrogated* against the third party to the extent of the benefits it paid the injured employee.

Benefits under workmen's compensation laws also include death benefits for a deceased employee's family or his estate, which are payable as the result of an accidental death. In order for the decedent's family or estate to receive death benefits, the employee's death must have been due to, or must have arisen in the course of, employment. Death benefits are payable even if the death was caused by the employee's own gross negligence. Workmen's compensation usually includes lump sum benefits — in addition to all other benefits — when an employee loses an arm or leg.

# 15  Real Property

Real property is, quite simply, land. If the real property has trees or crops growing on it or oil underneath it, or any other natural resources on or underneath it, those elements are considered part of the real property along with the bare land. (Once extracted or separated from the land, however, these natural elements become personal property.)

On or underneath this real property there may be man-made property, which may or may not be considered part of the parcel. If the man-made additions were added with the intention of permanently improving the land, if removal of the additions would materially destroy the land, or if the intent of the owner who added the additions was to affix them to the land permanently, then such additions will be considered part of the parcel of land. Such permanent man-made additions are called *fixtures*, and they are the property of anyone who holds title to the land. Otherwise, the additions are considered personal property and, unless separately transferred to a subsequent owner of the land, remain the personal property of the person who constructed them.

**Title to Real Property:**

1. *The title transfer:*

    Transferring title to real property from one owner to another usually takes place in two separate stages: First the contract of sale is entered into by the buyer and seller, and then the deed to the land is delivered by the seller to the buyer. During the time between these two dates (which normally is a few months at most) the buyer assumes any risk of loss or destruction of the property, unless otherwise stipulated in the contract.

    A contract for the sale of real property is within the Statute of Frauds and therefore must be in writing to be enforceable. If the contract is enforceable, the seller always has the implied duty to convey *marketable title* to the buyer. Failure to do so, for whatever reason, causes him to be liable to the buyer should the latter choose to sue for breach of contract. If the seller cannot deliver marketable title, the buyer may revoke the contract, whether he chooses to sue the seller or not. A wise buyer makes a title search in between the time the contract is entered into and the deed is delivered, despite this implied duty.

    **EXAMPLE (Multiple Choice):**

    A contract for the purchase and sale of real property
      a. Must be signed by both parties in order to be binding on either.
      b. Must be contained in a formalized, signed, and notarized document if the contract is to be enforceable.
      c. Is *not* assignable unless specifically authorized in the contract.
      d. Contains an implied promise that the title to the property to be conveyed is marketable.

    **Solution:** (d)

    A marketable title is one which:

    • Is free from all encumbrances. An *encumbrance* can be a mortgage, easement, lease, or any such restriction. (See below for definitions and implications of these types of encumbrances.)

    • Is free from defects in the chain of title.

    • Is free from defects which would require the buyer to defend his title in court.

2.  *The deed:*

The deed is the actual instrument by which the ownership of title is transferred from one owner to another; however, it does not actually transfer title unless and until the grantor (present owner/seller) actually has a present intent to convey title to the grantee (future owner/buyer), and the deed is unconditionally delivered to the grantee during the grantor's lifetime. If the grantee is to take title after the grantor dies, then the deed is to be conditionally transferred (that is, upon the grantor's death) and, as such, title can only be transferred by will.

Though there are several different types of deeds, there is certain general information which they all include:

- The names of both parties involved in the transfer. The omission of the grantor's name in the body of the deed is not too serious, as long as his signature appears at the bottom. The omission of the grantee's name is more serious, and may void the deed. However, an omitted grantee's name can be legally filled in as long as it is done before the actual delivery of the deed, and with the grantor's oral or written permission to do so.

- The consideration. Because consideration has already been exchanged to bind the contract (unless a gift is being given), additional consideration is not usually necessary to validate the deed. Nevertheless, nominal consideration is often exchanged, and in those cases the amount exchanged is stated in the deed.

- Certain statutory words of conveyance, depending on the type of deed in question, are stated in the deed to establish the grantor's present intent to transfer title.

- A clear and definite description of the land being transferred.

- Any exceptions which the grantor does not intend to transfer, or elements he wants to reserve for himself.

- Any promises or assurances made by the grantor to the grantee, the most common of which are covenants of title, covenants against encumbrances and covenants of warranty.

- The signature of the grantor or his authorized agent which, along with notarization, is said to *execute* the deed.

When the deed is received, the grantee should record it. If he fails to, his agreement with the grantor is not impaired, but his rights against third parties who attempt to acquire title to the same land will be affected. When a grantee records his deed, he is giving constructive notice to the public that he has title to the land. Actual notice, then, need not be given in order for the grantee to protect his interest. If the deed is not recorded, a subsequent purchaser who buys the land in question from the same original seller for value, and acts in good faith (in other words, without knowing about the first unrecorded deed), and records his deed, will obtain legal title to the land. If the subsequent buyer either does not give value, or does not buy in good faith, or both, he will not take legal title to the land even if he records his deed before the prior buyer does.

**EXAMPLES (Multiple Choice):**

1. In 1960, Octane, Inc., a Delaware corporation, purchased certain land in Montana from the Dillingers but neglected to record the deed. In 1970, the Dillingers sold the same property to Bently, a domiciliary of Montana, who purchased in good faith and recorded his deed. In a suit by Octane against Bently to resolve the title question, Octane will lose because
   a. Octane had no reasonable excuse for its failure to record the deed.
   b. Most recording acts provide a statutory preference for individuals over corporations.

    c. Most recording acts provide a statutory preference for domiciliaries over nondomiciliaries.

    d. A good faith purchaser from the record owner has paramount title over an unrecorded claim of which he has no knowledge.

2. The failure to record a deed will

    a. *Not* affect the rights between the parties to the deed.

    b. Constitute a fraud upon the creditors of the seller.

    c. Defeat the rights of the buyer if the seller subsequently conveys the property to a third party who has actual knowledge of the prior conveyance.

    d. Be disregarded in respect to the rights of subsequent third parties if the deed is a mere quitclaim.

**Solutions:** 1 (d), 2 (a)

The most common types of deeds are warranty deeds, special warranty deeds (or bargain and sale deeds), and quitclaim deeds. Their differences stem from what the transferor guarantees the transferee in terms of title.

    a. In delivering a *warranty deed,* the grantor expressly or impliedly guarantees the grantee absolute title to the land. Thus, the grantor is liable for any and all defects in title, whether he knew about them before the transfer or not, and whether he himself caused them or they were caused by a prior owner.

    b. In delivering a *special warranty deed* or *bargain and sale deed,* the grantor warrants only that there are no defects to title caused by the grantor himself. If the grantee subsequently uncovers a title defect which was not caused by the grantor, he will have no cause for action as against the grantor.

### EXAMPLE:

While vouching additions to the land and buildings accounts during your examination of the financial statements of Dandy Manufacturing, Inc., you learn that Dandy had purchased a factory building from Howard Luff for $247,500. Dandy had engaged the Bigelow Title Insurance Company, Inc., to do the title search and to issue a $247,500 title policy insuring Dandy's fee interest in the real property. Bigelow issued the title policy without exception. Howard Luff gave a typical bargain and sale deed with a covenant against the grantor's acts; or, as it is sometimes referred to, a special warranty deed. It was subsequently discovered that the executor of Luff's father's estate had failed to pay the estate taxes due on the property.

### Required:

What are Dandy's rights against Luff on the deed? Explain.

### Solution:

None. When a seller-grantor gives a bargain and sale deed with only a covenant against his acts, he has no liability for prior defects in title. Since the failure to pay estate taxes was not the responsibility of the grantor, Dandy cannot recover against Luff on the deed.

    c. In delivering a *quitclaim deed,* the grantor makes no promises whatever to the grantor with respect to title defects.

### EXAMPLES (Multiple Choice):

1. Harrison purchased Bigacre from Whitmore. The deed described the real property conveyed and the granting clause read: "Seller hereby releases, surrenders, and relinquishes to buyer any right, title, or interest that he may have in Bigacre." The deed contained no covenants. What is Harrison's legal status concerning title to Bigacre?

    a. Harrison has obtained a quitclaim deed.

    b. If an adverse claimant ousts Harrison from Bigacre, Harrison will have recourse against Whitmore.

    c. The only warranty contained in the deed is an implied warranty of marketability of title.

    d. Harrison's deed is neither insurable nor recordable.

2. Your client, Albert Fall, purchased a prominent industrial park from Josh Barton. At the closing, Barton offered a quitclaim deed. The contract of sale called for a warranty deed with full covenants.

    a. Fall should accept the quitclaim deed since there is *no* important difference between a quitclaim deed and a warranty deed.

    b. An undisclosed mortgage which was subsequently discovered would violate one of the covenants of a warranty deed.

    c. Fall *cannot* validly refuse to accept Barton's quitclaim deed.

    d. The only difference between a warranty deed with full covenants and a quitclaim deed is that the grantor of a quitclaim does not warrant against defects post his assumption of title.

**Solutions:** 1 (a), 2 (b)

### Rights in land without having actual title:

A person may have the right to use land as if it were his own, without actually owning it or having title to the portion he is using. Two such kinds of rights are called *licenses* and *easements*.

1. *Licenses:* When somebody has a license, he has the right to go onto property which is owned by somebody else, for a particular purpose, for a given time period, subject to good behavior. The person granting the license is the *licensor,* and the person being licensed is the *licensee*. The duration of the license depends on their own particular agreement. A licensee has absolutely no legal interest in the property he is licensed to use. He has no right to possess the land or any part of it. He only has the right to use it temporarily in the agreed upon manner for the agreed upon period of time. A license is granted at the option of the licensor and, as it creates no interest, is revocable. Of course, a licensor who revokes a license without justification may be breaching a contract.

A license is neither assignable nor inheritable. If the licensor transfers his title in the land to someone else, the license is automatically terminated, although it may be subsequently renegotiated with the new title holder. Because a license does not create an interest in the property for the licensee (that is, because there is no transfer of property), a license may be granted orally, as well as in writing, and be equally enforceable. In other words, licenses do not fall within the Statute of Frauds.

A typical example of a license being granted is when a hotel guest is given the right to use a hotel room for a certain amount of time.

2. *Easements:* An easement also grants a nonowner a limited right to use someone else's land in a particular way but, unlike a license, it does create an interest in the property. Consequently, easements — for the most part — fall within the Statute of Frauds and must be in writing to be enforceable. Easements can be created in four different ways:

- *Express easements:* A binding express easement is one that is in writing and has been recorded the way a deed is. If the easement is not in writing, it cannot bind the current owner or any subsequent owners; if it is in writing but is not recorded, it can bind the current owner who granted the easement, but not any subsequent owner who purchases the property for value and in good faith.

- *Implied easement by necessity:* This is an easement created or implied by operation of law. It is granted to a person whose situation is such that he cannot function without having the right to use another's property. For instance, if Mr. X owns a parcel of land and sells off all but a central portion to Mr. Y, such that X cannot leave the portion he has retained without crossing over Y's parcel, X will be granted an easement by necessity.

● *Implied easement by implication:* Consider the following: Mr. X owns two lots which are adjacent to each other. On each lot is a carport and between the two lots and carports is a driveway with half of it running on one lot and half on the other. If X sells one of the adjacent lots to Y, he impliedly grants an easement to Y over the portion of the driveway on the lot he has retained, and he has impliedly reserved as easement over the portion of the driveway on the lot he has sold.

● *Easement by prescription:* An easement by prescription arises when a person uses land owned by another on a continuous and uninterrupted basis for a prescribed period of time — that prescribed period varying from one jurisdiction to another but usually covering 10 to 20 years — in a way that is adverse to the rightful owner, and in an open way. However, if the rightful owner gives permission to use the land, no easement by prescription arises or is acquired, because the use is not adverse.

**EXAMPLE:**

Your client, Abe Starr, owns 100 acres of undeveloped land on the outskirts of New City. He bought the land several years ago to build an industrial park in the event New City grew and prospered. The land was formerly used for grazing and truck gardening. A subsequent inspection revealed that several adjacent landowners recently had been using a shortcut across his land in order to reach a newly constructed highway.

**Required:**

What are the legal implications of the above facts? Explain.

**Solution:**

Starr is in danger of having an easement by prescription created against his land by the continued use of the shortcut by the adjacent landowners. If an easement is created, it will represent a defect in his title in that the adjacent landowners will have the legal right to continue to use his land as an access route to the highway. In order to create an easement by prescription, the use must normally be for 15 or 20 years and must be —

1. Wrongful, which it apparently is.
2. Open and notorious, which it apparently is.
3. Continuous and without intervention, which it apparently is.

However, since it is unlikely that the prerequisite 15 to 20 years of continued use has elapsed, Starr should take active and immediate measures to prevent a prescription easement from coming into existence. His best course of action is to institute an action against the adjacent landowners for trespass if they refuse to obey his order to discontinue the unlawful entry upon his land.

Another concept to be familiar with is that of *eminent domain.* By exercising its rights of eminent domain, the government may acquire title to real property belonging to a private citizen — even if the private citizen objects and does not want to give the property up. However, in order to exercise this right, the government must acquire the real property for public use — for example, to build a highway — and must pay *fair* compensation for it.

**Types of ownership interests:**

Real property may be owned forever or for a limited period of time, by one person or by more than one, with or without implications for the future.

Rights of ownership in real property are called *estates.* There are basically two kinds of estates: *freehold estates* (those which last for a lifetime) and *nonfreehold estates* (those which last for a limited period of time).

1. *Freehold estates:* There are two types of freehold estates: a life estate and a fee simple estate.

a.  A *life estate* is one in which its owner — called a *life tenant* — has an interest which terminates at his death. Accordingly, a life tenant cannot direct the way in which the life estate will be disposed of after his death, because he has no interest in it at that time. In other words, a life estate cannot be inherited from a life tenant. The person to get the property after the death of the life tenant — the *remainderman* — is usually designated by the original owner.

b.  A *fee simple estate* is one in which the owner has an ownership interest in the property during his lifetime and holds title to the property, as well. Consequently, the owner of an estate in fee simple can leave or devise it to someone at his death; it is an estate of inheritance.

2.  *Nonfreehold estates:* A nonfreehold estate is any estate (in other words, any interest in real property) which is not a freehold estate — which is not a life estate or a fee simple estate. The length of time for which the party in question will possess the real property is limited in some way. Types of nonfreehold estates include: estates for a predetermined number of years, tenancy at will, tenancy by sufferance, and periodic tenancy.

When two or more people have an interest in the same real property, they are said to have an interest in a *concurrent estate*. The kinds of joint ownership or concurrent interests include:

a.  *Tenancy in common:* When two or more people are tenants in common, they each hold an undivided interest in the same property, with each having the right to possess, but neither having a specific claim on any particular portion of, the property. There is no requirement that either tenant acquire his interest from the same person (they could each acquire an interest from a different prior co-tenant), at the same time, or in the same manner (one could buy his interest, another could be given his as a gift, and so forth). There is no right of survivorship with respect to tenancy in common; when one tenant dies, his interest passes to whomever he designates and not to the surviving co-tenant(s).

Each co-tenant is entitled to a pro rata share of any profits which the property may yield, and each co-tenant is required to contribute his proportionate share of the operating expenses, and bear his proportionate share of losses. A creditor of any co-tenant may compel, at any time, judicial partition of the property so that he can satisfy a valid claim.

Tenancy in common can be terminated by the transfer of all co-interests to a single person, or by partitioning the property among the existing co-tenants such that each one becomes the exclusive owner of one clearly defined portion of the entire property.

b.  *Joint tenancy:* Joint tenants are co-owners of the same piece of property wherein the right of survivorship exists. Thus, if one joint tenant dies, he cannot will title to his interest to a beneficiary; rather, title to the deceased tenant's interest passes directly to the surviving joint tenant(s).

**EXAMPLE (Multiple Choice):**

A joint tenant's interest in real property
   a.  Can only be created by deed.
   b.  Need *not* be created at the same time *nor* pursuant to the same instrument.
   c.  Will *not* pass under the laws of intestate succession.
   d.  *Cannot* be sold or severed during the life of the joint tenancy.

**Solution:** (c)

Again, all joint tenants must share the expenses and losses, and have a right to share in the property's profits. The personal creditor of a joint tenant can compel judicial partition of the debtor's interest only during the joint tenant/debtor's lifetime.

A joint tenancy can be severed by any joint tenant during his lifetime. He can do this by either selling his interest or mortgaging his interest to a third party who, in turn, becomes a joint tenant. Joint tenants are not necessarily partners; when they are not partners, approval of all current joint tenants is not necessary to "admit" a new joint tenant.

c. *Tenancy by the entirety:* This is a special type of joint ownership which is enjoyed only by husbands and wives, each of whom is a tenant by the entirety. The couple must be married (engaged couples cannot own real property as tenants by the entirety) at the time they enter into this type of ownership relationship. Tenancy by the entirety is similar to joint tenancy in that the right of survivorship exists and title automatically vests in either surviving spouse. However, it is different from joint tenancy in that neither spouse alone can sell any interest in the property — they must sell their interests together or not at all.

Tenancy by the entirety is dissolved by either so selling the property or upon divorce of the tenants. In the case of divorce, if the property is not given up, the two ex-spouses then hold title to it as tenants in common. Personal creditors of either spouse may not go against any portion of property held by the debtor as a tenant by the entirety.

Very often one has a definite interest in land and absolute title, but he will come to enjoy both at some later time. Such interests are called *future interests*. There are two types of future interests:

1. *Remainder interests:* The remainderman referred to above in the section on life estates has a future or remainder interest in that life estate. A remainder estate, then, is the balance or remainder of an estate that a third party will enjoy only after the previous party's interest in that property terminates. That previous party's estate may terminate at his death, or when he reaches a certain age, or after a specific number of years, or when the remainderman reaches a certain age, or whenever the original owner determines. The remainderman's estate may be either a freehold or a nonfreehold estate.

2. *Reversionary interests:* When the terms of an instrument of transfer are such that the estate will definitely, or can conceivably, return to the grantor or his estate at some point in the future, the grantor is said to have a reversionary interest in the property in question.

### Real estate mortgages:

A real estate mortgage is security for a debt or other obligation. The security itself is real property which most often takes the form of a lien on that property. The agreement, or security interest, is represented by an instrument which transfers the interest in the property to the creditor. The creditor or obligee is called the *mortgagee,* and the debtor or obligor is called the *mortgagor.* A *purchase money-mortgage* exists when a seller conveys real property to a purchaser and the real property which was the subject of the transaction is the property which secures payment of the unpaid balance of the purchase price. (Refer to the review of the concepts presented in Chapter 3 — Secured Transactions.) Because a real estate mortgage creates an interest in real property, it is within the Statute of Frauds and must be in writing to be enforced.

The mortgagor continues to own the property (actually the interest or equity he has in the property increases with each payment he makes to the mortgagee) until he defaults on his obligation. Accordingly, it is incumbent upon the mortgagor — unless otherwise provided for in the mortgage — to pay all the real estate taxes on the property. The mortgagor is entitled to use the property in any way he wants to and is entitled to all the profits which it yields — again, unless the mortgage states otherwise.

A mortgagor has the right to sell and transfer title of any mortgaged property. In so doing, the mortgagor may sell it such that the new purchaser buys the property and assumes the mortgage, or buys the property subject to the mortgage. In the first case, the new owner is personally liable to the mortgagee for the unpaid balance of the purchase price which the seller still owes. In the second case, he is not personally liable for it, though in practice he usually does pay off the unpaid balance. The original owner/debtor remains personally liable to the mortgagee for the unpaid balance, whether the new owner assumes the mortgage or buys the property subject to the mortgage. The only time the seller can legally disclaim his liability is if the mortgagee expressly releases him from his obligation. Such an express release is called a *novation*.

**EXAMPLE (Multiple Choice):**

Farber sold his house to Ronald. Ronald agreed among other things to pay the existing mortgage on the house. The Safety Bank, which held the mortgage, released Farber from liability on the debt. The above described transaction (relating to the mortgage debt) is
   a. Invalid in that the bank did *not* receive any additional consideration from Farber.
   b. *Not* a release of Farber if Ronald defaults, and the proceeds from the sale of the mortgaged house are insufficient to satisfy the debt.
   c. A novation.
   d. A delegation.

**Solution:** (c)

In the case of a default, the mortgagee usually forecloses on the mortgage and takes possession of the mortgaged property. If the value of the property at the time of default is less than the unpaid balance, the mortgagee may demand the balance from the original mortgagor or, if the property has been resold, from a subsequent owner if he has assumed the mortgage. The original mortgagor is a *surety,* and the party assuming the mortgage is the *primary debtor* (see Chapter 4). The mortgagee is a third party creditor beneficiary of the primary debtor (person assuming the mortgage) and, consequently, can enforce his promise.

The mortgagee should record his mortgage, thereby giving the public constructive notice of its existence, in order to protect his interests as to third parties.

**EXAMPLE (Multiple Choice):**

A real estate mortgage
   a. Need *not* be in writing.
   b. Creates an intangible personal property right for the mortgagee.
   c. If properly recorded, gives constructive notice to subsequent purchasers and mortgagees of the recording mortgagee's interest.
   d. Is *not* assignable by the mortgagee.

**Solution:** (c)

### Real estate leases:

A real property lease is a grant of an estate in real property and a contract at one and the same time. It is a grant of an estate in real property because the owner or landlord gives a nonowner or tenant an exclusive right to use and possess the real property for a specified period of time.

(When the definite term in exceptionally long, the tenant's interest or estate is that of a *leasehold*.) It is a contract because it creates enforceable rights and duties, the most glaring of which is the landlord's right to receive rent and the tenant's duty to pay rent.

A lease does not create an interest in the property for the tenant. However, if, by its terms, it cannot be performed within one year (that is, if the lease is for more than one year), it must be in writing to be enforceable, as per the Statute of Frauds. Most states also require that the lease be signed by the tenant in order to be enforceable.

Though the terms of any one lease are very often unique, there are certain concepts which most leases deal with and, when the lease is silent as to a particular point, which jurisdictional statutes provide for:

1. *Subleasing:* In subleasing the tenant or sublessor transfers part of his interest to a third party or sublessee. For instance, a tenant with a three year lease may sublease the property to a sublessee for one year. Any one lease will state a tenant's rights regarding his ability to sublease. If a tenant can and does sublease the property, the sublessee is liable only to the sublessor and the sublessor remains liable to the landlord.

2. *Assignment:* An assignment of a lease is a transfer by the tenant/assignor of his entire interest to a third party/assignee. An assignment, therefore, is not the same thing as a sublet, and a lease may permit one without necessarily permitting the other. An assignee may either assume the lease or not. If he assumes it by means of an *assumption agreement* the assignee is personally liable to the landlord — not to the assignor — for the entire term of the lease, whether he is in the possession of the premises or not. If the assignee does not assume the lease, he is liable to the landlord only when he is in possession of the property. The original tenant/assignor remains liable on the lease if the assignee defaults, whether the assignee assumes the lease or not. Again, an assignor's liability can be disclaimed only if he is expressly released from his obligation by the landlord by means of a novation.

**EXAMPLE:**

Unlimited Fashions, Inc., leased a store in the Suburban Styles Shopping Center for five years at $1,500 a month. The lease contained a provision which prohibited assignment of the lease. After occupying the premises for two years, Unlimited sublet the premises to Fantastic Frocks for the balance of its term, less one day, at $2,000 per month. Unlimited moved out on a Sunday and removed all its personal property and trade fixtures such as portable clothing racks, cash registers, detachable counters, etc. Which of the following *best* describes the legal status of the parties involved?
   a. Unlimited has *not* breached its contract with Suburban.
   b. Suburban is entitled to the additional $500 rental paid each month by Fantastic to Unlimited.
   c. Removal of the trade fixtures in question by Unlimited was improper and it can be held liable to Suburban for their fair value.
   d. Fantastic is a tenant of Suburban.

**Solution:** (a)

3. *Wrongful abandonment:* This occurs when a tenant abandons the premises and stops paying rent before the term of the lease ends. When the premises are wrongfully abandoned, a landlord may:

   • Not rerent the premises and legally demand future rent payments from the tenant as the payments become due; or

   • Rerent the premises, give the tenant notice that he is doing so, and hold the tenant liable for any loss in rent the landlord may suffer; or

   • Rerent the premises without notifying the tenant that he is doing so. In such a case, the tenant will not be held liable to the landlord for any loss suffered.

4. *Wrongful eviction:* This occurs when a landlord evicts a tenant before the lease expires. Upon being wrongfully evicted, a tenant may either sue the landlord for breach of contract and recover money damages, or regain possession of the premises. Eviction may be either *actual* (the landlord actually locks the tenant out of the premises) or constructive (the landlord makes life so uncomfortable for the tenant by, say, cutting off his water, that the tenant is forced out). In order for a tenant to bring a successful suit based on constructive eviction, he must actually vacate the premises first.

**EXAMPLE:**

Reynolds leased a manufacturing building from Philip under a written lease for a period of five years at a specified rental and with a provision that the lessor would keep the structure in repair.

Reynolds subleased a portion of the lower floor to Signor giving him access through a hallway from the main entrance. Philip subsequently mortgaged the building, and Central Savings, the mortgagee, ultimately foreclosed and acquired good title to the property. Reynolds was unable to get Central Savings to make certain minor repairs and had withheld rent in an amount equal to the repairs he was forced to make. Central Savings meanwhile notified both Reynolds and Signor that the lease was terminated and that both were to pay rent directly to it for one month and then vacate.

**Required:**

1. Discuss Reynolds' right to withhold rent in the amount of repairs.

2. Absent a breach by the tenants, discuss Central Savings' right to:

    a. Evict the tenants.

    b. Require Signor to pay the rent directly to it.

**Solution:**

1. Reynolds had no right to withhold rent in the amount of repairs. Covenants by lessor and lessee are deemed independent unless it is clear that the parties intended the contrary. However, if the breach were sufficiently serious, it might furnish the basis for a claim of constructive eviction. This does not seem to be the case on the facts.

2a. Central Savings has no right to evict the tenants. When the lease preceded the mortgage, the tenant's term is not affected by the later mortgage absent an agreement by the tenant to the contrary.

2b. Signor is a sublessee and, as such, a tenant of Reynolds. Absent a provision in the lease prohibiting the sublease, Reynolds committed no breach by the subletting, and the sublessee, as a tenant of the sublessor, has no direct obligations to the lessor.

5. *Tenancy by sufferance:* This occurs when a tenant wrongfully continues to occupy the premises after his lease has expired. In such a situation, a landlord may either treat the tenant as a trespasser; or treat the tenant as if he has renewed the lease for the same amount of time and, as such, demand payment of rent; or remove the tenant by some legal process and then sue him for damages.

6. *Death of a tenant:* A lease does not terminate on the death of a tenant – or on the death of a landlord. The rights therein and the obligation to pay rent falls to his estate. If the estate does not pay the rent, the landlord has the same options for relief as are available in the case of wrongful abandonment by a tenant.

**EXAMPLE (Multiple Choice):**

Vance obtained a 25-year leasehold interest in an office building from the owner, Stanfield.
    a. Vance's interest is non-assignable.
    b. The conveyance of the ownership of the building by Stanfield to Wax will terminate Vance's leasehold interest.
    c. Stanfield's death will *not* terminate Vance's leasehold interest.
    d. Vance's death will terminate the leasehold interest.

**Solution:** (c)

# 16 Wills, Estates, and Trusts

**Wills:**

A will is the legal means by which a person disposes of his property at his death. There is no legal requirement that one draw up a will, but a will is an invaluable aid in settling a decedent's estate. If a person dies leaving a will, he is said to have died *testate*; otherwise he is said to have died *intestate*.

A will is unique among documents in that it can be revoked at any time and as often as is desired before the testator's death. No will is irrevocable. A testator cannot be bound to the terms of any will until death, at which point the person or persons administering the will is bound by its terms. In other words, the will takes effect at — and not before — the testator's death.

In order to be valid and enforceable, a will must contain the following characteristics:

1.  A will must be *written.* However, it can be informally written, either in pencil or pen or on a typewriter, and on any kind of paper. A memorandum — that is, a document which proposes terms of disposal but is not, for one reason or another, a properly executed will — may be incorporated into a will by reference. However, in order to be validly incorporated, the memorandum must be in writing, must exist at the time the actual will is executed, must be clearly described in the actual will, and must be described in the actual will as existing. A memorandum can only clarify or expand on terms stated in the actual will; it cannot add new terms or contradict existing terms. Thus, if a will names X, Y, and Z as beneficiaries, a valid memorandum can give the address to where their respective inheritances should be delivered, but a memorandum cannot validly add W to the roster of heirs. On rare occasions an oral will may be valid, as in the case of soldiers and sailors dying in combat, or death bed dispositions of personal property.

2.  The *testator's signature* must appear on the will. Although some jurisdictions allow the signature to appear anywhere on the document, usually it must appear at the end of the will. Without this requirement, it would be very difficult to establish whether a testator had or had not meant to include in his will any portions following a signature.

3.  A will must be *attested to* by witnesses whose function is to acknowledge that the testator intended to and did execute the will, and that he was capable of doing so. Witnesses need not necessarily know the contents of the will, but they must know they are attesting to a will and they must attest in each other's presence. The number of witnesses required to attest and their qualifications are usually included in the applicable statute, but the minimum amount of witnesses required is usually two. The most common qualification referred to is that none of the qualified witnesses may have an interest in (that is, be a beneficiary of) the will he has been asked to witness. If a witness does have an interest in the will, he will either have to disqualify himself as a witness or relinquish his interest. An executor who does not have an interest in the will may be a qualified witness, while a spouse of someone with an interest may not.

4.  The last characteristic of a valid will is that it must be *publicized.* That means that the testator must publicly declare in front of the witnesses that the executed document is intended to be his Last Will and Testatment. Nowadays, however, this formality may be dispensed with without risking an invalid will.

*The testator:*

The testator must have intended to execute the will or else it will not be valid. Accordingly, a testator who operates under duress, undue influence, or mistake, or who is a victim of fraud has not executed a valid will; the terms of such a will will not be enforced. In practice, it is very difficult to prove undue influence and/or fraud when a will has been properly executed, signed, and attested to. In any event, the burden to do so rests with those making the charge.

In order to be valid, a will must have been drawn up by a testator with the *capacity* and *power* to execute the document. Though these two terms appear to have similar connotations, there are differences between their meanings. Power to execute a will refers to the testator's general ability, by virtue of his intelligence, to handle his own affairs independently. In many jurisdictions, wills executed by children are not valid because children are not considered to have the power to execute a will. Capacity is a narrower concept and refers to the testator's mental ability at the particular time he executes a will. If a person is insane, he will usually not have the capacity to draw up a will; however, he may have the requisite capacity in more lucid moments and a will executed during such periods will generally not be invalid because of the testator's lack of capacity.

A testator may only dispose of the following in his will:

1. Property which he owns when he draws up his will.

2. Property which he does not own when he executes his will but which will eventually revert to him or to his estate.

3. Property which he owns as a tenant in common.

He may not dispose of by will:

1. Property which he owns as a joint tenant.

2. Property which he owns (with his spouse) as a tenant by the entirety.

*Types of wills:*

Types of wills are usually defined according to the form they take or the contents within. Aside from the most common type of will — that is, one which is properly executed, signed, attested to, and written by a single testator — there are:

1. *Holographic wills:* These are wills which are handwritten by the testator and not attested to by any qualified witnesses. They are usually written by testators finding themselves in unusual circumstances, without the means or the time to execute a valid will. In certain jurisdictions, holographic wills are valid and enforceable as long as the statutory requirements for such wills are complied with. A holograpic will is usually unenforceable if the paper on which it is written contains any printing of any sort, such as a letterhead or even just a printed address or date.

2. *Nuncupative wills:* These are wills which are oral declarations made by the testator in front of qualified (disinterested) witnesses. Thus, nuncupative wills are those which are not written, but are attested to. Again, these will be declared valid in jurisdictions which enforce nuncupative wills, as long as the appropriate statutory requirements have been adhered to. In most jurisdictions which declare nuncupative wills as valid, the testator must have been on his death bed; soldiers and sailors usually execute nuncupative wills. Real property generally cannot be disposed of in nuncupative wills.

3. *Joint wills:* Such wills are those wherein the same instrument is executed as the will for two or more testators, each of whom must sign the document.

4. *Mutual or reciprocal wills:* In the case of a mutual or reciprocal will, each testator executes a separate document, but the terms of each one are reciprocal in that each mutual testator disposes of his estate in favor of the other.

5. *Conditional wills:* These are wills which take effect only when a conditional event takes place.

6. *Codicils:* Codicils are not wills as such, but are separately documented additions to or modifications of an already existing will. In order to be enforceable, a codicil must specifically refer to the will which it is amending or modifying, as well as be properly executed (written, signed, attested to) as the original will must be.

## Beneficiaries' rights:

A testator can name any person or organization or whatever as a beneficiary of his estate. Beneficiaries can include the testator's family, his estate, a charity, his company, or a pet. The terms of his will can include provisions for the legal custody of his children, as well as for the manner in which his estate is to be administered. Barring an improperly executed will, all terms of disposition must be adhered to, and beneficiaries satisfied, except in the case of ademption or abatement.

Ademption and abatement occur when a testator who owned property at the time the will was executed no longer owned it at his death, or else still owned it, but its value had declined, and he had not amended the will accordingly.

If the legacy is specific property, the beneficiary's interest is cancelled. To illustrate: If the testator owned a boat at the time he executed his will, willed that boat to a beneficiary, but no longer owned it at the time of his death, yet did not amend the will accordingly, the beneficiary's interest in the boat is cancelled. The boat is said to be *adeemed property*.

If the legacy was general property which reduced in value in between the time the will was originally executed and the testator died, the property is *abated*, and each beneficiary gets a proportionate share of its remaining value. To illustrate: If the testator willed a total of $75,000 to A, B, and C — with A to get $50,000 or 2/3; and B and C each to get $12,500 or 1/6 — but, at the time of his death there remains only $60,000 for distribution, A will get 2/3 of the $60,000, or $40,000, and B and C will each get 1/6 of the $60,000, or $10,000 each.

If a legatee dies before the testator does, and the testator fails to modify his will accordingly, the legacy is said to *lapse*. Neither the legatee's surviving family nor his estate has any right to the lapsed legacy. However, if the legatee was a child or grandchild of the testator he predeceased, then the legacy does not lapse, but rather the original legatee's children divide the legacy equally among them. This type of distribution among the deceased legatee's children is called a *distribution per stirpes*.

A spouse cannot be disinherited by the testator. Each state has enacted legislation which entitles a surviving spouse to a minimum percentage of the decedent spouse's estate. If the testator did not bequeath anything to the surviving spouse, the latter can assert his or her rights under the statute. If the testator leaves a small amount, and the statute entitles a surviving spouse to a greater proportion of the estate than he or she has been left, the surviving spouse may elect to *go against the will* (that is, renounce it) and *take under the statute* if it would be more beneficial to do so. A surviving spouse is entitled to take under the statute whether the decedent dies testate or intestate.

A will can be contested when the following circumstances exist:

1. A will may be contested by a legally interested party claiming fraud, duress, undue influence, lack of testator's capacity or improper execution.

2. If a testator conditioned a beneficiary's receipt of a legacy — for example, if the legatee will realize the legacy only if he survives the testator, or does not marry the surviving spouse, or does not contest the will, or has children — the condition

must exist before the property can pass to the beneficiary. However, if the conditions are illegal, the beneficiary can contest the will. In such cases the contesting beneficiary will usually be allowed to receive his legacy without first complying with the testator's conditions.

*Revocation:*

As noted, a will is never irrevocable; it can be amended, modified, or completely revoked up until the time of the testator's death. A will may be considered revoked by the testator himself or by operation of law, under any of the following circumstances:

1. If the testator signals that he intends to revoke the will by intentionally destroying it in some way — tearing it, crossing it out, burning it — it will be considered revoked.

2. If a testator properly executes a subsequent will whose terms are inconsistent with those of the prior document, that prior document will be considered revoked. If the terms of the subsequent will are not entirely inconsistent with the first, but there is a statement in it expressly revoking the first, the first will be considered revoked.

3. A will is revoked by operation of law when:

● The testator marries for the first time after its execution. If a testator divorces or separates from a spouse after execution of his will, the will or any of its provisions which benefit the divorced or separated spouse, are not necessarily revoked. This holds true even if the testator remarries.

● If the testator becomes a parent (whether for the first time or not) by natural birth or adoption after execution of a will, the will may be revoked as to that child if there are no appropriate provisions in it for the child.

*Intestate succession:*

A person who dies without having executed a valid will is said to die *intestate.* In such circumstances, the relevant jurisdiction distributes the decedent's estate according to its Statute of Descent. In distributing the estate, the state attempts to comply with the regulating statute and to comply with what it believes would have been the decedent's wishes, at one and the same time. Statutes differ in many respects, but there are some elements that appear in almost all of them:

● Only those who were blood relatives of the decedent may inherit property from a decedent who dies intestate.

● Debts of a decedent are satisfied out of his personal property before being satisfied out of his real property.

● Surviving spouses are entitled, by statute, to a share of the estate.

● After satisfying creditors and distributing to the surviving spouse, the decedent's children share equally — that is, per capita — in the remaining estate. The decedent's grandchildren will share per stirpes any amount which would have gone to their parents, if the parent (that is the decedent's child) predeceased the decedent whose estate is being distributed.

**Estates and their administration:**

A decedent's estate must be distributed and looked after whether he dies testate or intestate. It is the purpose of estate administration, then, to carry out the decedent's wishes if he dies testate, or to comply with the Statute of Descent if he dies intestate. Though the wishes of a testator may be apparent according to the terms of his will, there are statutory rules determining how an estate is to be managed. Naturally, as with all statutory regulations, rules will vary from jurisdiction to jurisdiction. Nevertheless, there are again some generalities which determine how an estate will be administered in almost all jurisdictions.

The procedure of estate management is called *probate,* and all estates are managed and their assets disbursed under the supervision of a probate court. The more clearly defined and all-encompassing the will (in the case of testate succession), the less confusing and costly the probate procedure.

*The executor/administrator:*

If the decedent states in his will the name of the person to administer the affairs of his estate, that named person becomes the *executor* of the estate. If the decedent dies intestate, or dies testate but does not name an executor, or has named an executor but has not executed a valid will, the court appoints an *administrator* to do what an executor would. (The feminine forms are *executrix* and *administratrix.*) The court will first attempt to name as administrator some qualified adult relative or friend of the decedent; if none is available, a public administrator will be named.

The estate becomes the responsibility of the executor or administrator, who — upon taking on his duties — legally holds title to all the estate property. The executor/administrator is charged with satisfying all the estate's and decedent's creditors and distributing the remaining estate to the beneficiaries according to the terms of the will or Statute of Descent, whatever the case may be.

Executors or administrators are expected to:

● Perform their duties as skillfully as possible.

● Make every attempt to preserve the estate's assets.

● Pay all the valid debts of the estate, including funeral expenses and any last illness expenses.

● Post a bond with the court for the benefit of the beneficiaries, to insure faithful performance of his duties — unless the testator specifically exempted the executor from this duty.

An executor/administrator acts in a fiduciary capacity and, as such, cannot secretly purchase or sell off any of the estate assets. As a fiduciary, he must make full disclosure to the beneficiaries of all transactions, at the risk of having such transactions rendered void. The executor/administrator owes his undivided loyalty to the estate at all times and is expected to act in good faith.

If an executor/administrator breaches any of these duties, he will be held personally liable to the estate for any loss caused by the breach, and may be subject to removal by the court upon the request of any or all the beneficiaries. In addition, if a bond has been posted, the bonding company will be liable to the estate for any loss resulting from a breach of the executor's duties.

**EXAMPLE (Multiple Choice):**

Madison died 15 years after executing a valid will. He named his son, Walker, as the executor of his will. He left two-thirds of his estate to his wife and the balance equally to his children. Which of the following is a right or duty of Walker as executor?

    a. Walker must post a surety bond even if a provision in the will attempts to exempt him from this responsibility.

    b. Walker has an affirmative duty to discover, collect, and distribute all the decedent's assets.

c. If the will is silent on the point, Walker has complete discretion insofar as investing the estate's assets during the term of his administration.

d. Walker can sell real property without a court order, even though he has *not* been expressly authorized to do so.

**Solution:** (b)

## Probate:

If the decedent dies testate, the will must be proved in court by the attesting witnesses. Once the court is satisfied that the testator intended to execute the existing will, and that he had the power and capacity to do so, the document will be admitted to probate. After the will is admitted to probate, the executor/administrator must take an inventory of all the estate assets, value them, and file the information according to prescribed procedure. The estate representative then collects the assets, liquidates them when necessary, pays the creditors who have proven their claims to be valid, pays the federal and state estate and inheritance taxes, and distributes the balance of the estate to the beneficiaries.

Heirs must prove their status (that is, their right to inherit) whether the decedent executed a will or died intestate. This is usually done by having a relative or close friend of the decedent testify as to an heir's relationship to the decedent.

Certain assets are not part of the probate estate — that is, they do not come into the possession of the executor/administrator to be inventoried and distributed. The most common such asset is insurance on the life of the decedent. These death payments pass directly to a named beneficiary. The payments on life insurance policies which name the estate as beneficiary do pass directly into the estate and come under the representative's control.

### EXAMPLE (Multiple Choice):

Which of the following problems are within the competency of a CPA?
a. The validity of a will to be admitted to probate.
b. The parties who would have the standing in court to contest the validity of the will.
c. The validity of a trust created under the terms of the will.
d. The value of a decedent's gross estate at the time of death and alternate valuation date.

**Solution:** (d)

## Trusts:

A trust comes into existence when one person (the creator/trustor/settlor/founder) transfers title to property (the trust corpus) to a second person (the trustee) who is to administer it for the benefit of a third party (the beneficiary). The beneficiary is said to have *equitable title* to the trust property. Thus there are three roles to be played in connection with every trust: that of the creator, the trustee, and the beneficiary. Each role may be played by more than one person.

A trust can be created expressly by a creator. The creator may set up the trust either in writing or orally — unless the trust property is real property, in which case the instrument falls within the Statute of Frauds and therefore must be in writing. The creator can set up a trust while he is living (an *inter vivos trust*) or by will (a *testamentary trust*). In the case of a testamentary trust, the will whereby it is created must have been validly executed if the trust is to be enforceable. A trust must be created for legal purposes or else it is void. Whenever a trust is void (whether because it has been created for illegal purposes or because of some other reason), title to the trust property remains with the creator or his estate, and not with the trustee. Similarly, a beneficiary of a void trust does not hold equitable title to its property. A creator need not receive legally sufficient consideration from a beneficiary in order to bind him to the terms of the trust. In fact, a beneficiary need not necessarily be aware of or consent to the creation of the trust in order for the trust to be valid.

*The three parties to a trust:*

1.  *The creator:* The creator must have the capacity (cf. wills) to create a valid trust or else it will be void. Once the trust is created it is irrevocable (unless created by will and the will itself is revoked) unless the creator expressly reserves the right to revoke it. A creator may also be either a sole trustee or a sole beneficiary, although he may not be both. Any violation of these rules renders a trust void.

2.  *The beneficiary:* A beneficiary can be a single individual, several individuals, a corporation, a minor, a charity (whether one that is commonly recognized as such, like the Red Cross, or one composed of any class of people, like the Deaf Lawyers of the Mississippi River Valley). In order for a beneficiary to enforce his rights in the trust, he must be specifically named in the trust instrument or clearly identified in some way. If he is so named or identified, he can sue a trustee who is not administering the trust properly. In most cases, a beneficiary can assign his interest in a trust and a beneficiary's creditors can attach his trust interest. A beneficiary who does not want to benefit from the trust or who does not consent to the creation of a trust may refuse to accept its benefits by properly disclaiming them. However, unless he does so in strict compliance with the prescribed procedure, the beneficiary will be presumed to accept the trust's benefits.

3.  *The trustee:* Any legal entity (a person, a corporation, etc.) with the legal capacity to hold title to an asset can be named as a trustee. A named trustee has the right to refuse the appointment and if he does, he will not be held liable for anything to anybody. If a trustee does accept an appointment, he functions as an independent administrator and is agent for neither the creator nor the beneficiary. Nevertheless, he does act in a fiduciary capacity, and the following duties imposed upon a trustee result from that capacity:

    a.  A trustee must act exclusively for the benefit of the beneficiaries to whom he owes undivided loyalty, and must subordinate his interests to those of the beneficiaries.

    b.  A trustee cannot borrow the assets of a trust, and cannot lend them to anyone with whom he has business dealings or to any corporation of which he is a director or officer, or in which he owns stock.

    c.  A trustee may delegate purely administrative duties to another, but he cannot delegate any duties the performance of which demands discretion.

    d.  A trustee must act honestly and in good faith.

Besides the duties which are imposed upon a trustee as a result of his fiduciary obligations, some duties are imposed upon him by law:

    a.  A trustee must manage the trust assets as skillfully and prudently as possible; he must manage the trust's assets the way a reasonable man would manage his own. He is therefore expected to divest the trust of all nonproductive assets, or of those investments which are losing money, and reinvest the proceeds in prudent investments, or into assets in which the state allows a trustee to invest, if and when such a statute exists. If the trust corpus loses money, the trustee is liable to the beneficiaries to the extent of the loss, only if he does not meet the prudent, reasonable man standard. If the standard is met, he will escape liability.

    b.  A trustee is expected to use the trust *principal* to pay for the trustee's initial fees for opening the trust and his final fees for closing the trust, for the principal payments on loans, for permanent improvements on assets, and, generally, all *extraordinary* items. Similarly, the trust principle is credited with most extraordinary items.

c. A trustee is expected to use the trust *income* to pay for all ordinary taxes, interest payments on loans, repairs of assets, administrative expenses, operating expenses, and so forth. Similarly, trust income is credited with most ordinary income items.

A trustee is granted express powers which are stipulated by the creator in the trust instrument. He also enjoys any implied powers which are necessary for him to administer the trust. Implied powers usually include the trustee's right to engage counsel or accountants (and pay their fees), sell or lease trust property, and the like. He has no implied right to borrow money or mortgage trust property; to engage in such activities a trustee must have express authority.

Other duties conferred upon a trustee include the trustee's obligation to keep accurate records and to render a full accounting to any beneficiary who requests one. His rights include the right to compensation and his right to resign. A trustee may resign if he is discharged according to the trust instrument's terms, if all the beneficiaries consent to his resignation, or if the court consents.

A trustee risks liability in the following situations:

a. A trustee is personally liable for his own torts.

b. A trustee is personally liable to a beneficiary for any loss of value to the trust property if he does not exercise reasonable skill or prudence in administering the trust property. He is also personally liable to a beneficiary if he breaches any of his trustee duties or if he comingles trust assets with his own, whether or not he acts in good faith and/or prudently.

c. A trustee is personally liable on any contracts he makes on behalf of the trust, unless his personal liability has been specifically excluded by the terms of the contract.

d. If a trustee acts illegally (if, for example, he steals) while performing his duties as trustee, he may be criminally prosecuted, removed as trustee by court order, and forced to return to the trust estate any funds which he embezzled or assets of which he illegally took possession.

**EXAMPLES: (True/False):**

Accountant Smathers is Trustee of a testamentary trust established by Parker's will. The corpus of the trust consists of "blue chip" securities and a large office building subject to a mortgage. The will provides that trust income is to be paid to Parker's wife during her lifetime, that the Trust will terminate on her death, and that the corpus is then to be distributed to the Brookdale School for Boys.

1. If Smathers receives a cash dividend on one of the Trust securities, he may not use it to purchase additional securities for the trust corpus without compensating Parker's wife.
2. If Smathers receives a 5 percent stock dividend, he should distribute it to Mrs. Parker.
3. The cost of insurance on the office building should be deducted by Smathers from the income paid to Mrs. Parker.
4. Monthly principal payments to amortize the mortgage are deducted from Mrs. Parker's income.
5. Proceeds from fire insurance on the office building would be a part of the corpus.
6. The cost of exercising stock warrants is chargeable to trust income.
7. The Brookdale School is the residuary beneficiary of the trust created under Parker's will.
8. The beneficiaries of the trust have an equitable interest in the trust income and corpus.
9. The beneficiaries of the trust would have standing in court to proceed against the trustee for waste of the corpus.

10. If Mrs. Parker and the Brookdale School agree to terminate the trust and divide the corpus, Smathers would have to comply with their wishes.

**Solutions:** (1) T, (2) F, (3) T, (4) F, (5) T, (6) F, (7) T, (8) T, (9) T, (10) F

## *Types of trusts:*

1. *Those which the creator sets up himself:*

   There are two types of trusts set up by the creator himself: charitable trusts and private express trusts. Basically, if a trust set up by the creator does not fall into the category of a charitable trust, it is a private express trust.

   A *charitable trust* is one which has a charitable (or social) purpose and whose beneficiaries are classes of people (for example, the nuns living in a particular convent) rather than individuals (Sister A, Sister B, and Sister C). The trust may be *inter vivos* or testamentary, and created orally or by a written instrument. A charitable trust may exist in perpetuity. If the purpose for which the creator set up a testamentary trust cannot be carried out for one reason or another, a court will apply the trust property toward the carrying out of the creator's intent in as similar a way as possible. In so doing, a court will be said to apply the *cy pres doctrine*.

   As noted, a *private express trust* is any trust set up by the creator which is not a charitable trust. A private express trust cannot last longer than the lives of the beneficiaries in existence when the trust is created, plus 21 years. This rule was established to insure that private express trusts would not go on and on for unreasonable periods of time. Violation of the *rule against perpetuities* renders the trust void.

   Unless expressly forbidden in the trust instrument, a beneficiary may borrow against or assign his interest. However, trusts whose instruments do expressly forbid either one or both of these two actions are special kinds of private express trusts called *spendthrift trusts*. As the name of this trust suggests, a creator usually sets up a spendthrift trust to protect the beneficiary from himself. Another prohibition in a spendthrift trust is that a beneficiary's creditors cannot attach his interest in the trust property until it has actually been distributed to him. Because of this last characteristic, spendthrift trusts are illegal in a few states.

2. *Those which are created by operation of law:*

   Trusts which are created by operation of law are also called *implied trusts*. There are two kinds of implied trusts of which to be aware: resulting trusts and constructive trusts.

   a. *Resulting trusts* are created by operation of law when one person transfers property to a second person and it is understood that the transferor/creator had no intention of transfering title to the transferee/trustee. In such instances, a trust will result in favor of the transferor or his estate, regardless of the claims of the transferee. Because resulting trusts are created to prevent injustice being done to the transferor, this kind of trust requires no writing to create it, even if real property is being transferred.

   b. *Constructive trusts* are created to prevent the unjust enrichment of a transferee/trustee who has acquired property through fraud, duress, undue influence, mistake, breaching his fiduciary duty, or any other illegal means. The wrongdoing trustee is bound to return the assets of the constructive trust to their lawful owner — that is, to the unintentional transferee/creator.

*The termination of a trust:*

Trusts which are created by operation of law are terminated when the "trust property" is returned to the transferor/creator by the transferee/trustee. Other trusts terminate if and when:

- The purpose for which the trust was created has been accomplished.

- The purpose for which the trust was created cannot be accomplished, or fails.

- The time period during which the trust was to exist expires.

- None of the above three things happen but the creator and all the beneficiaries agree to terminate the trust.

- The sole trustee and sole beneficiary are one and the same person.

Upon the termination of any trust, it is incumbent upon the trustee to distribute any remaining trust property to the beneficiaries entitled to it or to return it to the creator or his estate.

# Business Law Review Questions — First Examination

1. Unless otherwise provided by a corporation's articles of incorporation or by-laws, a board of directors may act without a meeting if written consent setting forth the action so taken is signed by
   a. A plurality of them.
   b. A majority of them.
   c. Two-thirds of them.
   d. All of them.

2. In attacking a corporation having 15% of the relevant market in a highly concentrated (oligopolistic) industry, the Justice Department will most likely prevail under the Sherman Act's monopoly provisions if it shows that
   a. A significant amount of sales in interstate commerce is involved.
   b. The five leading corporations in the industry controlled 60% of the relevant market.
   c. The corporation through product innovation has improved its percentage share from 12.5% to 15% over the past three years.
   d. The corporation has manifested a specific intent to monopolize.

3. A contract was created by a false representation of a material fact. The fact was known to be false by the person making the representation, and there was an intent to deceive the party who relied on the representation to his detriment. This contract is voidable on the basis of
   a. Undue influence.
   b. Fraud.
   c. Duress.
   d. Negligence.

4. In connection with a contract for the sale of goods, in which of the following ways can the implied warranty of merchantability be excluded by the seller?
   a. By an oral statement which mentions merchantability.
   b. By a written statement without mentioning merchantability.
   c. By an oral statement which does not mention merchantability.
   d. By an inconspicuous written statement which mentions merchantability.

5. Farley Farms, Inc., shipped 100 bales of hops to Burton Brewing Corporation. The agreement specified that the hops were to be of a certain grade. Upon examining the hops, Burton claimed that they were not of that grade. Farley's general sales agent who made the sale to Burton agreed to relieve Burton of liability and to have the hops shipped elsewhere. This was done, and the hops were sold at a price less than Burton was to have paid. Farley refused to accede to the agent's acts and sued Burton for the amount of its loss. Under these circumstances
   a. Farley will prevail only if the action by its agent was expressly authorized.
   b. Even if Farley's agent had authority to make such an adjustment, it would not be enforceable against Farley unless ratified in writing by Farley.
   c. Because the hops were sold at a loss in respect to the price Burton had agreed to pay, Burton would be liable for the loss involved.
   d. Farley is bound because its agent expressly, impliedly, or apparently had the authority to make such an adjustment.

6. Unless specifically excluded, a contract for the sale of goods includes a warranty of
   a. Good title.
   b. Fairness.
   c. Usefulness.
   d. Adequate consideration.

7. The basic distinction between a bilateral contract and a unilateral contract according to common law rules is
   a. That one must be signed, sealed and delivered, whereas the other need not.
   b. There is only one promise involved when the contract is unilateral.
   c. The Statute of Frauds applies to one and not to the other.
   d. One is assignable whereas the other is not.

8. Waldo Carpets, Inc., decided to sell a portion of its two-acre property and the president of Waldo wrote several prospective buyers the following letter:

   Dear Sir:

   We are sending this solicitation to several prospective buyers because we are interested in selling one acre of our property located in downtown Metropolis. If you are interested, please communicate with me at the above address. Under no circumstances, will we consider a price of less than $90,000.

   Cordially,

   *James Waldo*

   James Waldo, President
   Waldo Carpets, Inc.

   In this situation
   a. The Statute of Frauds does not apply because the real property being sold is the division of an existing tract which had been properly recorded.
   b. Markus, a prospective buyer who telegraphed Waldo that he would buy at $90,000 and forwarded a $90,000 surety bond to guarantee his performance, has validly accepted the offer.
   c. Waldo must sell to the highest bidder.
   d. Waldo's communication did not constitute an offer to sell.

9. What fiduciary duty, if any, exists in an agency relationship?
   a. The principal owes a fiduciary duty to his agent.
   b. The agent owes a fiduciary duty to third parties he deals with for and on behalf of his principal.
   c. The agent owes a fiduciary duty to his principal.
   d. There is no fiduciary duty in an agency relationship.

10. A joint tenancy
    a. Cannot be created by deed.
    b. Will be found to exist by judicial preference if it is unclear as to whether a joint tenancy or tenancy in common was intended by the grantor.
    c. Cannot be created in respect to personal property.
    d. Provides a right of survivorship in the surviving joint tenant.

11. The Securities Act of 1933, in general, exempts certain small stock offerings from full registration. What is the maximum dollar amount which would qualify for this exemption?
   a. $300,000.
   b. $500,000.
   c. $750,000.
   d. $1,000,000.

12. Jane Luft, doing business as Luft Enterprises, owned a tract of land upon which she had intended to build an additional retail outlet. There is an existing first mortgage of $70,000 on the property which is held by the First County National Bank. Luft decided not to expand, and a buyer, Johnson, offered $150,000 for the property. Luft accepted and received a certified check for $80,000 plus a signed statement by Johnson promising to pay the existing mortgage. What are the legal rights of the indicated parties?
   a. Luft remains liable to First County despite Johnson's promise to pay.
   b. First County must first proceed against Johnson on the mortgage before it has any rights against Luft.
   c. The delegation of the debt is invalid if Johnson does not have a credit rating roughly comparable to Luft's.
   d. The bank is the incidental beneficiary of Johnson's promise to pay the mortgage.

13. The scope of secured transactions in the Uniform Commercial Code does not include
   a. Pledges.
   b. Transactions where title has not passed.
   c. After-acquired collateral.
   d. Sale of corporate debentures.

14. A surety will not be liable on an undertaking if
   a. The principal is a minor.
   b. The underlying obligation was illegal.
   c. The principal was insolvent at the time of the surety's agreement to act as surety.
   d. The surety was mistaken as to the legal implications of the surety agreement.

15. Which of the following statements best describes the insurable interest requirement?
   a. It is an historical anachronism and has little or no validity in modern times.
   b. It is identical for life and property insurance.
   c. It has been abolished by most modern insurance legislation in respect to fire insurance.
   d. At a minimum, it must exist at the time of the loss in respect to property insurance.

16. The parol evidence rule prohibits contradiction of a written contract through the proof of
   a. A previous oral contract.
   b. A subsequent written contract.
   c. The mearning or clarification of the contract's terms.
   d. A subsequent oral contract.

17. Under what conditions will both the debtor and the surety be able to avoid liability on a debt owed by the debtor to the creditor?
   a. The debt exceeds $500 and the debtor's obligation is not contained in a signed writing.
   b. The debtor lacks the capacity to enter into the contract with the creditor.

   c. There is a tender of payment by the surety.
   d. The debtor is released by the creditor.

18. The federal Social Security Act
   a. Does not apply to self-employed businessmen.
   b. Excludes professionals such as accountants, lawyers, and doctors.
   c. Provides for a deduction by the employee which is available against his federal income tax.
   d. Provides that bonuses and commissions paid as compensation are included as wages in the calculation of employer-employee contributions.

19. Paperbox Company is one of four equal-sized paper-carton container companies whose sales constitute 90% of paper container sales in the relevant market. Competition has been intense. In order to control costs within reasonable limits the chief executive officers of the four companies have agreed that they will set a maximum price, agreed upon by them, to be paid for the pulp they purchase. From an antitrust standpoint
   a. No antitrust violation occurs if the price set is reasonable.
   b. The agreement is a *per se* violation of the antitrust laws.
   c. No antitrust violation occurs if the suppliers of raw pulp agree that the price is reasonable and works in the best interest of all parties.
   d. The agreement will not violate the antitrust laws if it can be shown that it is necessary to prevent insolvency of one of the parties to the agreement who controls 30% of the market.

20. An offer is generally effective when it is
   a. Dispatched.
   b. Signed.
   c. Mailed.
   d. Received.

21. A surety can avoid liability on his surety undertaking if he can show
   a. Death of the creditor.
   b. Bankruptcy of the creditor.
   c. A material alteration by the debtor and creditor of the contract which the surety guaranteed.
   d. Lack of capacity of the debtor.

22. The typical fire insurance policy
   a. Covers all damages caused by fire whatever the source.
   b. Does not cover water damage which results from the fire department extinguishing the blaze.
   c. Will not permit recovery for business interruption unless there is a special indorsement.
   d. Prohibits the assignment of the policy both before and after a loss.

23. Parker owed Charles $100,000 secured by a first mortgage on Parker's plant and land. Simons was the surety on the obligation but his liability was limited to $50,000. Parker defaulted on the debt and Charles demanded and received payment of $50,000 from Simons. Charles subsequently foreclosed the mortgage and upon sale of the mortgaged property netted $75,000. Simons claims a right of subrogation for his loss. Under the right of subrogation Simons should receive
   a. Nothing.
   b. $25,000.
   c. $37,500.
   d. $50,000.

24. Price has in his possession an otherwise negotiable instrument which reads:

> "I, Waldo, hereby promise to pay to the order of Mark or bearer . . ."

Which of the following is true with respect to the above instrument?
    a. Mark's signature is required to negotiate the instrument.
    b. The instrument is non-negotiable.
    c. If Mark indorses the instrument, Mark assumes potentially greater liability to subsequent transferees than if Mark transfers it by mere delivery.
    d. Since the instrument is payable to Mark's order, it is a draft.

25. What pricing agreements among competitors are legal?
    a. An agreement which is aimed at lowering prices.
    b. An agreement which is aimed at eliminating cutthroat competition by stabilizing prices.
    c. An agreement which seeks to fix prices reasonably and fairly for the consumers' benefit.
    d. None because competitors are forbidden to enter into agreements which determine the price of the product they sell.

No. 111

DIANA DAVIDSON
21 West 21st Street
Toronto, Canada

*April 1, 1977*

Pay to the
order of    *Stanley Stark*    $1,000.00

*One thousand & no/100's Canadian Dollars*

*Diana Davidson*
Diana Davidson

FIRST NATIONAL TRUST
Buffalo, New York

*For Finder's Fee*

After examining the above instrument, which of the following conclusions is correct?
    a. It is non-negotiable because it is payable in Canadian money.
    b. It is a demand instrument but does not qualify as a negotiable instrument, because it is drawn in Canada and payable by a bank in the United States.
    c. The instrument is a negotiable foreign check (draft), and in the event of dishonor a formal protest must be made by the party seeking recovery.
    d. Diana Davidson is the maker of the instrument and as such is primarily liable thereon.

27. Under what conditions will the Statute of Frauds be a defense under the Uniform Commercial Code where there is a contract for the sale of goods worth more than $500?
    a. The seller has completed goods specially manufactured for the buyer which are not salable in the ordinary course of the seller's business.
    b. The written memorandum omits several important terms but states the quantity, and it is signed by the party to be charged.
    c. The party asserting the Statute of Frauds admits under oath to having made the contract.
    d. The goods in question are fungible and actively traded by merchants in the business community.

28. Winslow Manufacturing, Inc., sought a $200,000 loan from National Lending Corporation. National Lending insisted that audited financial statements be submitted before it would extend credit. Winslow agreed to this and also agreed to pay the audit fee. An audit was performed by an independent CPA who submitted his report to Winslow to be used solely for the purpose of negotiating a loan from National. National, upon reviewing the audited financial statements, decided in good faith not to extend the credit desired. Certain ratios, which as a matter of policy were used by National in reaching its decision, were deemed too low. Winslow used copies of the audited financial statements to obtain credit elsewhere. It was subsequently learned that the CPA, despite the exercise of reasonable care, had failed to discover a sophisticated embezzlement scheme by Winslow's chief accountant. Under these circumstances, what liability does the CPA have?
    a. The CPA is liable to third parties who extended credit to Winslow based upon the audited financial statements.
    b. The CPA is liable to Winslow to repay the audit fee because credit was not extended by National.
    c. The CPA is liable to Winslow for any losses Winslow suffered as a result of failure to discover the embezzlement.
    d. The CPA is not liable to any of the parties.

29. The purpose of the Statute of Frauds is to render agreements unenforceable unless they are
    a. Legal.
    b. Not fraudulent.
    c. Written.
    d. Supported by consideration.

Items 30 and 31 are based upon the following information:

A petition in bankruptcy was filed against Burt on July 1, 1975. Burt was insolvent during 1975 and owed a large amount of money to various creditors, including Charles. Charles has furnished assorted merchandise to Burt on credit. On February 1, 1975, Burt paid $3,000 to Charles on account with an intent to prefer him over other creditors. On April 1, 1975, Burt paid Charles an additional $2,000 with the same intent. On May 1, 1975, Charles sold goods to Burt, for cash, at the normal price of $1,400; this was his only other transaction with Burt in 1975. On all occasions, Charles had no basis upon which to believe that Burt was bankrupt.

30. In this situation
    a. Neither the February 1 nor the April 1 transfers constituted an act of bankruptcy.
    b. Both the February 1 and the April 1 transfers constituted acts of bankruptcy.
    c. The May 1 sale of goods to Burt is neither an act of bankruptcy nor a voidable preference.
    d. Both the February 1 and the April 1 transfers may be voided by the trustee in bankruptcy.

31. If Charles received his payments with actual knowledge of Burt's insolvency in the bankruptcy sense, the amount which the trustee may recover is
   a. $6,400.
   b. $5,000.
   c. $2,000.
   d. $1,400.

32. The consideration received by a corporation when issuing shares of stock shall constitute stated capital to the extent of the par value of the shares, and any excess shall constitute
   a. Treasury shares.
   b. Earned surplus.
   c. Restricted surplus.
   d. Capital surplus.

33. Which of the following classes of employees is exempt from both the minimum wage and maximum hours provisions of the Federal Fair Labor Standards Act?
   a. Members of a labor union.
   b. Administrative personnel.
   c. Hospital workers.
   d. No class of employees is exempt.

34. The board of directors of a corporation may declare, and the corporation may pay, cash dividends except when the corporation is
   a. Privately owned.
   b. Highly leveraged.
   c. Insolvent.
   d. In a risky growth industry.

35. During the course of your audit you discover a dispute concerning one of your client's checks. The check had been sent to a supplier but without indicating the sum on the face of the instrument. The supplier fraudulently filled in the check for $500 more than the amount indicated in the letter which accompanied the check. A subsequent holder in due course is asserting the right to recover the full amount stated in the completed instrument.
   a. Alteration is a complete defense against all parties.
   b. The holder in due course can only collect an amount equal to the authorized amount.
   c. The holder in due course may enforce the instrument as completed.
   d. The holder in due course must first proceed against the fraudulent supplier.

36. Your client, Robert Rose, has the following instrument in his possession.

March 1, 1976

One month from date, I, Charles Wallace, do hereby promise to pay Edward Carlson seven hundred and fifty dollars ($750.00).

(signed) *Charles Wallace*

Edward Carlson wrote "pay to the order of Robert Rose" on the back and delivered it to Rose.
   a. Robert Rose is a holder in due course.
   b. The instrument is a negotiable promissory note.
   c. Edward Carlson is a holder in due course.
   d. All defenses, real and personal, are assertible by Wallace against Rose.

37. Ted Dolson has filed a voluntary petition in bankruptcy. His assets are listed as $4,200 and his liabilities $18,750. His creditors include (1) three employees who have not been paid wages for six weeks at $100 per week per employee, (2) the United States government for $6,900 in back income and social security taxes, (3) his former wife for back alimony payments of $3,000, and (4) suppliers for goods purchased on open account of $7,050. In this situation
   a. All the debts in question are dischargeable in bankruptcy.
   b. Claims must be filed within three months of the filing of the petition in bankruptcy.
   c. The wage earners have the first priority after administration costs.
   d. The United States government claim will take precedence over the claims of all parties.

38. In order to hold the principal liable under the ratification doctrine for the unauthorized act of a party purporting to act as his agent
   a. The principal need not have been in existence at the time the contract was made.
   b. The purported agent must have been acting for an undisclosed principal.
   c. The principal must have full knowledge of the facts regarding the action taken on his behalf.
   d. The ratification must be in writing and made within a reasonable time after the unauthorized action was taken on his behalf.

39. Under the Securities Act of 1933, subject to some exceptions and limitations, it is unlawful to use the mails or instruments of interstate commerce to sell or offer to sell a security to the public unless
   a. A surety bond sufficient to cover potential liability to investors is obtained and filed with the Securities and Exchange Commission.
   b. The offer is made through underwriters qualified to offer the securities on a nationwide basis.
   c. A registration statement has been properly filed with the Securities and Exchange Commission, has been found to be acceptable, and is in effect.
   d. The Securities and Exchange Commission approves of the financial merit of the offering.

40. The usual fire insurance policy does not
   a. Have to meet the insurable interest test if this requirement is waived by the parties.
   b. Permit assignment of the policy prior to loss without the consent of the insurer.
   c. Provide for subrogation of the insurer to the insured's rights upon payment of the amount of the loss covered by the policy.
   d. Cover losses caused by the negligence of the insured's agent.

41. Which of the following provable debts is not discharged by bankruptcy?
   a. Hospital bills.
   b. Wages earned more than three months prior to commencement of bankruptcy proceedings.
   c. Liability for breach of a fiduciary duty resulting from a fraud committed by the debtor-fiduciary.
   d. Rent payments due which have accrued within three months of the filing of the petition in bankruptcy.

42. One of the major purposes of federal security
regulation is to
   a. Establish the qualifications for accountants
      who are members of the profession.
   b. Eliminate incompetent attorneys and account-
      ants who participate in the registration of
      securities to be offered to the public.
   c. Provide a set of uniform standards and tests for
      accountants, attorneys and others who practice
      before the Securities and Exchange Commission.
   d. Provide sufficient information to the investing
      public who purchases securities in the market-
      place.

43. Maxim Corporation, a wholesaler, was indebted to
the Wilson Manufacturing Corporation in the amount of
$50,000 arising out of the sale of goods delivered to
Maxim on credit. Wilson and Maxim signed a security
agreement creating a security interest in certain collateral
of Maxim. The collateral was described in the security
agreement as "the inventory of Maxim Corporation,
presently existing and thereafter acquired." In general,
this description of the collateral
   a. Applies only to inventory sold by Wilson to
      Maxim.
   b. Is sufficient to cover all inventory.
   c. Is insufficient because it attempts to cover
      after-acquired inventory.
   d. Must be more specific for the security interest
      to be perfected against subsequent creditors.

44. Martinson is a duly licensed CPA. One of his clients
is suing him for negligence alleging that he failed to meet
generally accepted auditing standards in the current year's
audit thereby failing to discover large thefts of inventory.
Under the circumstances
   a. Martinson is not bound by generally accepted
      auditing standards unless he is a member of the
      AICPA.
   b. Martinson's failure to meet generally accepted
      auditing standards would result in liability.
   c. Generally accepted auditing standards do not
      currently cover the procedures which must be
      used in verifying inventory for balance-sheet
      purposes.
   d. If Martinson failed to meet generally accepted
      auditing standards, he would undoubtedly be
      found to have committed the tort of fraud.

45. Caskill Corporation issued 100 shares of its $10 par
value common stock to Mr. Jason, its vice-president, for a
price of $1,000. In consideration he paid $200 cash, gave
a note for $400, cancelled $300 salary owed him for
services rendered to the corporation, and promised to
render $100 worth of future services. His shares are
   a. Paid in full.
   b. 50% paid for.
   c. 90% paid for.
   d. 20% paid for.

46. Walters & Whitlow, CPAs, failed to discover a fraudulent scheme used by Davis Corporation's head cashier to
embezzle corporate funds during the past five years.
Walters & Whitlow would have discovered the embezzle-
ments promptly if they had not been negligent in their
annual audits. Under the circumstances, Walters & Whitlow
will normally not be liable for
   a. Punitive damages.
   b. The fees charged for the years in question.
   c. Losses occurring after the time the fraudulent
      scheme should have been detected.

   d. Losses occurring prior to the time the fraud-
      ulent scheme should have been detected and
      which could have been recovered had it been so
      detected.

47. Jackson was a junior staff member of an accounting
firm. He began the audit of the Bosco Corporation which
manufactured and sold expensive watches. In the middle
of the audit he quit. The accounting firm hired another
person to continue the audit of Bosco. Due to the change-
over and the time pressure to finish the audit, the firm
violated certain generally accepted auditing standards
when they did not follow adequate procedures with
respect to the physical inventory. Had the proper procedures been used during the examination they would have
discovered that watches worth more than $20,000 were
missing. The employee who was stealing the watches was
able to steal an additional $30,000 worth before the thefts
were discovered six months after the completion of the
audit.

**Required:**
   Discuss the legal problems of the accounting firm as
a result of the above facts.

48. You have been assigned by the CPA firm of Stanford,
Cox & Walsh to audit the accounts of Super Appliances,
Inc., a retail discount chain. Super sells almost exclusively
to retail customers in the ordinary course of business. It
typically requires 25% as a down payment and takes a
promissory note and a signed security agreement for the
balance. However, if the purchase price of the appliance
or appliances purchased by the customer exceeds $500,
it arranges with a local financing company, Friendly
Finance, to have credit extended to the customer. In such
cases, Friendly supplies the 75% financing and takes a
promissory note and a signed security agreement. A
financing statement is neither obtained nor recorded by
Super or Friendly.

**Required:** Answer the following, setting forth reasons for
any conclusions stated.

   1. Does Super or Friendly have a "purchase-
money security interest" in respect to the appliances sold
to Super's customers?
   2. What is the legal importance of the distinction
between a "purchase-money security interest" and the
usual nonpossessory security interest?

49. Your client, Williams, Watkins, and Glenn, is a
general partnership engaged primarily in the real estate
brokerage business; however, in addition, it buys and sells
real property for its own account. Williams and Watkins
are almost exclusively responsible for the brokerage part of
the business, and Glenn devotes almost all of his time to
partnership acquisitions and sales of real estate. The firm
letterhead makes no distinction along these functional
lines and all members are listed as licensed real-estate
brokers. Normally acquisitions are made in the firm
name; although for convenience or other reasons, Glenn
occasionally takes title in his own name for and on behalf
of the firm.

   The partnership agreement contains, among other
provisions, the following:
   •   No partner shall reduce the standard real estate
commission charged (6%) without the consent of at least
one other partner.

• No partner shall purchase or sell real property for or on behalf of the partnership without the consent of all other partners. Title to real property so acquired shall be taken exclusively in the partnership name, unless otherwise agreed to by all the partners.

• All checks received which are payable to the partnership and all checks and cash received for or on behalf of the partnership shall be deposited intact in one of the partnership's bank accounts.

Watkins showed a magnificent $350,000 ranch estate, listed for over a year with the firm by John Foster, to numerous prospective purchasers. The firm's exclusive listing had recently expired and Watkins was afraid the firm would lose the sale. Foster's price was firm, and he had repeatedly refused to negotiate with interested parties or accept an offer below $350,000. The most recent prospective buyer offered $340,000 but would not budge from that price. Watkins, fearing that a rival broker might obtain a buyer and cause him to lose the commission, agreed to lower the commission to $11,000 which was acceptable to Foster. Watkins did this without the consent of either of the other partners.

**Required:**
1. Can Williams, Watkins, and Glenn or Williams and Glenn recover from Foster the $10,000 reduction in the commission granted by Watkins to Foster? Explain.
2. What recourse does the partnership or the other partners have against Watkins? Explain.

50. On September 30, 1975, Dayton Blasting Company purchased 25 cases of blasting caps from Whitten Blasting Cap Company. In this connection, it gave Whitten the following instrument:

September 30, 1975

Dayton Blasting Company hereby promises to pay Whitten Blasting Cap Company Six Hundred Fifty Dollars ($650.00) on December 1, 1975, plus interest at 6% per annum from date.

Dayton Blasting Company

By *Malcolm Smalley*
MALCOLM SMALLEY, President

Whitten promptly transferred the above instrument to Vincent Luck for $600. James Whitten, president of Whitten, indorsed the instrument on the back as follows: "Pay to the order of Vincent Luck" signed Whitten Blasting Cap Company per James Whitten, President.

Approximately half of the blasting caps were defective and Dayton refused to pay on the instrument. Dayton returned the defective cases and used the balance.

**Required:**
What are Vincent Luck's rights on the instrument in question? Explain.

51. Sill Corporation operates a retail appliance store. About a year ago, Sill borrowed $3,000 from Castle to supplement its working capital. At that time it granted to Castle a security interest in its present and future inventory pursuant to a written security agreement signed by both parties. Castle duly filed a properly executed financing statement a few days later. In the ordinary course of business, a customer purchased a $500 television set from Sill. The customer knew of the existence of Castle's security interest.

**Required:**
What rights does Castle have against Sill's customer? Explain.

52. Upon examining the books of account of Madison, Bradley, South, & Tilson, a general partnership, you ascertain that South is in financial difficulty. He is not insolvent but has been forced to assign 90% of his partnership interest to his largest creditor in order to forestall legal action by the creditor. The creditor in question is particularly obnoxious and undesirable in the eyes of the other partners.

**Required:**
Discuss the legal implications to the partnership, the partners, and South's creditor resulting from the above-mentioned assignment. In particular, discuss the rights of each and their relationship to one another and the partnership.

53. Davidson was one of Fenner Corporation's chief stock clerks. His net weekly salary was $125. Unfortunately, he lost a substantial sum of money betting on sports events, and he owed $2,000 to the loan sharks. Under these circumstances, he decided to raise the amount of his paychecks to $725 per week. His strategem was to wait until the assistant treasurer, in whose office the paymaster check imprinting machine was located, was away from his desk. He would then go into the office and artfully strike the number 7 over the number 1 and raise the paycheck amount from $125 to $725. The checks were promptly negotiated to Smith, a holder in due course, who cashed them at his own bank, and the checks were subsequently paid by Fenner's bank, Beacon National. The fraudulent scheme was discovered within a week after Beacon returned Fenner's canceled checks for the month. By that time five weekly paychecks had been raised by Davidson and cashed by Smith. Fenner promptly notified Beacon of the fraud.

**Required:** Answer the following, setting forth reasons for any conclusions stated.

1. To whom is Davidson liable?
2. What are the rights and liabilities of Fenner?
3. What are the rights and liabilities of Beacon?
4. What are the rights and liabilities of Smith?

54. The CPA firm of Martinson, Brinks & Sutherland, a partnership, was the auditor for Masco Corporation, a medium-sized wholesaler. Masco leased warehouse facilities and sought financing for leasehold improvements to these facilities. Masco assured its bank that the leasehold improvements would result in a more efficient and profitable operation. Based on these assurances, the bank granted Masco a line of credit.

The loan agreement required annual audited financial statements. Masco submitted its 1975 audited financial statements to the bank which showed an operating profit of $75,000, leasehold improvements of $250,000, and net worth of $350,000. In reliance thereon, the bank loaned Masco $200,000. The audit report which accompanied the financial statements disclaimed an opinion because the cost of the leasehold improvements could not be determined from the company's records. The part of the audit report dealing with leasehold improvements read as follows:

Additions to fixed assets in 1975 were found to include principally warehouse improvements. Practically all of this work was done by company employees and the cost of materials and overhead were paid by Masco. Unfortunately, fully complete detailed cost records were not kept of these leasehold improvements and no exact determination could be made as to the actual cost of said improvements. The total amount capitalized is set forth in note 4.

In late 1976 Masco went out of business, at which time it was learned that the claimed leasehold improvements were totally fictitious. The labor expenses charged as leasehold improvements proved to be operating expenses. No item of building material cost had been recorded. No independent investigation of the existence of the leasehold improvements was made by the auditors.

If the $250,000 had not been capitalized, the income statement would have reflected a substantial loss from operations and the net worth would have been correspondingly decreased.

The bank has sustained a loss on its loan to Masco of $200,000 and now seeks to recover damages from the CPA firm, alleging that the accountants negligently audited the financial statements.

**Required:** Answer the following, setting forth reasons for any conclusions stated.

    a.    Will the disclaimer of opinion absolve the CPA firm from liability?

    b.    Are the individual partners of Martinson, Brinks & Sutherland, who did not take part in the audit, liable?

    c.    Briefly discuss the development of the common law regarding the liability of CPAs to third parties.

55.   You have been assigned by a CPA firm to work with the trustees of a large trust in the preparation of the first annual accounting to the court. The income beneficiaries and the remaindermen are in dispute as to the proper allocation of the following items on which the trust indenture is silent:

    (1)   Costs incurred in expanding the garage facilities of an apartment house owned by the trust and held for rental income.

    (2)   Real estate taxes on the apartment house.

    (3)   Cost of casualty insurance premiums on the apartment house.

    (4)   A two-for-one stock split of common stock held by the trust for investment.

    (5)   Insurance proceeds received as the result of a partial destruction of an office building which the trust owned and held for rental income.

    (6)   Costs incurred by the trust in the sale of a tract of land.

    (7)   Costs incurred to defend title to real property held by the trust.

**Required:**

    1.    Explain briefly the nature of a trust, the underlying concepts in the allocation between principal and income, and the importance of such allocations.

    2.    Indicate the allocations between principal and income to be made for each of the above items.

56.   Pierce Auto Parts, Inc., needed additional working capital for a six-month period. It had a large inventory in its possession consisting of finished products, work in process, and raw materials. Merrill Financing Corporation was contacted regarding a $25,000 loan. Merrill was willing to make a loan, but only if it was secured by collateral. Merrill obviously did not wish to take physical possession of the inventory, and Pierce needed access to the work-in-process inventory in order to finish the auto parts which required minor additional work, packaging, and labeling. Hence, the parties agreed to enter into a field warehousing arrangement covering the finished inventory and the nearly completed work-in-process inventory. The raw materials were not included because they were already subject to the secured interest of another creditor who had duly filed a financing statement.

**Required:** Answer the following, setting forth reasons for any conclusions stated.

    1.    Discuss the procedures used in, and the business and legal aspects of, field warehousing.

    2.    How may Merrill perfect its security interest?

    3.    Suppose the raw materials are subsequently field warehoused by Merrill for an additional $5,000 loan. What rights will Merrill have?

# Business Law Review Answers — First Examination

1. (d) Answering this question correctly is just a matter of having mastered the details in Chapter 9.

2. (d) This question addresses itself to the provisions of the Sherman Act itself — not to any court interpretations. Therefore, even if answers (a), (b), and (c) are factually correct (which is not relevant here), only answer (d) represents an actual provision of the Sherman Antitrust Act.

3. (b) This question is a breeze. The information offers a classic definition of fraud — that is, answer (b). Knowing the definitions of key concepts, then, can put points in your pocket just as the ability to apply those concepts to fact situations can.

4. (a) In order for a seller to exclude the implied warranty of merchantability, the word merchantability must be clearly and/or conspicuously used in the disclaimer. Given this overriding requirement, answers (b), (c), and (d) must be eliminated.

5. (d) A principal is liable for the acts of his agent as long as the agent acted within his actual (that is, his express or implied) or apparent authority. Consequently, answer (a) must be eliminated as a general mistake in definition, regardless of the facts of this particular situation. In like manner, answer (b) is inappropriate, because an agent with actual or apparent authority has the power to bind his principal to a third party without the principal ratifying an adjustment in writing. Finally, because acting through an authorized agent offers the principal no protection from losses on a sale, answer (c) cannot be considered.

6. (a) The UCC imposes upon the seller an obligation to warrant good title. This is neither an express nor an implied warranty, but one which simply exists (unless specifically excluded) because of the fact that the transaction involves the selling of goods.

7. (b) There is no rule that says an exam cannot have a very simple question of definition. The correct answer — (b) — should be second nature to you by now: A bilateral contract is an exchange of a promise for a promise; a unilateral contract is an exchange of a promise for an act. Assignability, the applicability of the Statute of Frauds, and the need for a contract to be signed and delivered (almost nothing has to have a seal these days) have nothing to do with whether the contract is bilateral or unilateral.

8. (d) Even without reading the Waldo letter carefully, the candidate should knock out answer (a); once a contract involves real property or interests therein, it must be in writing to be enforced. A careful reading of the letter will reveal that the contents do not constitute an offer. Rather the letter is an invitation to the recipient to submit an offer to Waldo, with the constraint that no offer can be for less than $90,000. Naturally, once (d) is correct, (b) and (c) cannot be so.

9. (c) This question is almost a give-away. At the very heart of the agent's responsibilities is that of owing his highest fiduciary duty to the principal he represents. Your eye should easily zero in on the only correct answer here — that is, (c).

10. (d) This question is, again, a matter of having the subject matter at your command. It should not take you any longer to answer this question than it takes for you to get to the last period. Even if you have not studied the details of joint tenancy to know whether (a), (b), and (c) are right or wrong, you should most definitely know that (d) is correct, because the right of survivorship is the key to, or at the heart of, the joint tenancy relationship.

11. (b) This question — as do most questions of Federal Securities Regulation (Chapter 11) — just asks for you to give back facts you have memorized. Know the '33 Act and '34 Act cold, and questions like these will be giveaways.

12. (a) In assuming the mortgage, Johnson becomes primarily liable to the bank. Though Luft thus becomes secondarily liable to the bank, she is still liable despite Johnson's assumption of the mortgage. Consequently, before reading any of the other choices, the candidate can stop at (a) and mark that as the correct answer. However, the other choices should be investigated just to be sure. As a result of the transaction described in the question, Luft becomes a surety and, as such, is immediately — although not primarily — liable on the obligation. Answer (b), then, is wrong. Answer (d) is wrong, too; the bank is not an incidental beneficiary but, rather, is a third party creditor beneficiary. Answer (c) appears to have been thrown in from out of left field and is not a viable choice at all.

13. (d) This appears to be a simplistic question, but it does illustrate an important point. Most candidates for this examination learn details without getting an overall feeling for the UCC. While it is not necessary to commit the Code's provisions to memory by section and subsection it is wise to understand what areas are covered — and not covered — in each of the Code's 10 articles.

14. (b) This question tests the candidate's knowledge of what defenses are available to a surety. A surety cannot successfully raise the defense that the principal is a minor (a), was insolvent when the surety entered into the contract (c), or that the surety himself did not understand the legal impli-

147

cations of the contract he entered into (d). A surety can, however, successfully escape liability if, as stated in answer (b), the underlying obligation was illegal.

15. (d) In direct contrast to answers (a) and (c), the concept of an insurable interest has been developed over many years and is an integral part of any life and property insurance policy. Its development has been aimed toward eliminating the possibility of one person's benefiting from the loss of another's life or property, under circumstances in which the former has nothing to lose and everything to gain by such an eventuality. With respect to life insurance policies, the insurable interest must exist at the time the policy is taken out; with property insurance, at the time the loss occurs. Answer (b) is therefore eliminated.

16. (a) This is, again, a question that should require no thought if you know the parol evidence rule cold. Just read the choices carefully — there is room here for a sloppy mistake — and answer (a) will clearly (and logically, if you understand the purpose of the rule) emerge as the correct choice.

17. (d) The debtor and surety are both primarily liable on an obligation. One party can always avoid liability if the other one satisfies the obligation in full. However, the only time both can avoid the obligation entirely is when the debtor is released by the creditor. The surety is obliged to pay the debtor's debts; if the debtor has no debts, neither does the surety.

18. (d) To answer this question correctly, one need not have a detailed knowledge of social security law. A broad understanding of the nature and purpose of social security, a careful reading of the alternative choices, and, of course, a quick recounting of your own experience with the law's provisions should lead you to select (d) as the correct answer.

19. (b) A *per se* violation of antitrust law is one in which the activity engaged in is in and of itself illegal. There are no extenuating circumstances investigated, and the rule of reason cannot be depended upon as a defense. Price-fixing is a *per se* violation, regardless of the rationale behind the action taken. Answers (a), (c), and (d), then, are clearly wrong.

20. (d) Know when an offer, an acceptance, a refusal, and a contract are effective. An offer is generally effective when it is received, so answer (d) is correct.

21. (c) Answers (a), (b), and (d) are obviously not right, because these are three of the most common reasons for a suretyship agreement to be entered into. The correct answer is (c). A surety can almost always avoid liability if the debtor/creditor contract has changed in a material way without the surety's knowledge or consent — unless he is

a compensated surety, and the circumstances are very particular.

22. (c) Answer (a) is not correct; no fire insurance policy will cover damages resulting from a fire caused intentionally by the insured. Answer (b) is not correct either; most fire insurance policies specify that they cover damages caused by fires and related damages (of which such water damage is one). Answer (d) is wrong too; most fire insurance policies prohibit assignment of the policy before a loss, but permit assignment after a loss.

23. (b) The right of subrogation allows the surety (Simons) to step into the shoes of — that is, to assume the rights of — the creditor (Charles) when the former pays the debtor's debt. As such, the amount which would normally have gone to Charles — the $75,000 netted from the sale of the mortgaged property, less Parker's $50,000 equity interest arising from Simon's payment — should go to Simon.

24. (c) This is a good question because it reaffirms the fact that the candidate can and should work only with the information he or she is given. Based on the information given here (that is, without reading anything into it) the instrument appears to be negotiable; consequently, answer (b) cannot be right. As bearer paper (note: pay to the order of Mark or bearer) this note need not be indorsed to be negotiated; mere delivery is sufficient, and so answer (a) is incorrect. Finally, answer (d) is incorrect also. There are only two parties involved here; thus this instrument is a promissory note, not a draft, with Waldo the maker and Mark the payee. Again, almost by a process of elimination, the candidate must conclude that (c) is the correct answer.

25. (d) Price-fixing of any sort is a *per se* violation under the Sherman Antitrust Act. As such, it is absolutely illegal under any and all circumstances, regardless of the defense for it. Answer (d) is the only choice here that is correct. Do not be fooled into thinking that the setting of a maximum price ceiling or that private attempts to stabilize prices is any less of a violation than the setting of minimum price floors is.

26. (c) Answer (c) is correct here. Answers (a) and (b) are incorrect; an instrument is not rendered nonnegotiable because it is payable in non-U.S. currency (a note can be payable in any universally recognized foreign currency) or because it is drawn on a non-U.S. bank. With respect to answer (d), Diana Davidson is the *drawer* of the *draft* (not the maker — this is not a note), and she is not primarily liable. Recall that liability does not arise until the draft is presented for acceptance and accepted; once accepted, the primarily

liable party is the bank/drawee. The maker is secondarily liable.

27. (d) The Statute of Frauds is a very important concept to master and very popular with the examiners. Know it well — exceptions and all — and you will not have any problems with questions of this type.

28. (d) A CPA is not duty-bound to uncover fraud. He is not liable to anyone — client or third party — for losses directly or indirectly resulting from undetected defalcations, unless they could have been discovered during the course of an audit conducted by a reasonably careful accountant. Accordingly, answers (a) and (c) are wrong, and answer (d) is right. Answer (b) is wrong because National's decision not to extend credit to Winslow had nothing to do with the CPA's performance.

29. (c) A contract must be legal, not fraudulent, and supported by valid consideration, in order for it to be enforceable — whether it is within the Statute of Frauds or not. Answers (a), (b), and (d) are therefore wrong. However, only if it falls within the Statute, must it be written to be enforceable.

30. (c) To constitute an act of bankruptcy, a preferential transfer must have been made within four months of the petition. Thus, the February 1 transfer was not an act of bankruptcy, although the April 1 transfer was. Any answer including both or excluding both transfers as acts of bankruptcy [that is, (a) and (b)] is therefore wrong. Answer (d) is inappropriate as well, because the transfers may be voided only if the creditor had reasonable cause to know that the debtor was insolvent.

31. (c) If the preferential transfer is voidable (that is, if the creditor knew of the debtor's insolvency), the trustee in bankruptcy may recover all amounts transferred from the debtor to the creditor, as acts of bankruptcy, except those amounts exchanged in a bona fide sale for value. Accordingly, the February 1 transfer of $3,000 is not recoverable, because it was not an act of bankruptcy (it was not transferred within four months of the petition), and the May 1 transfer of $1,400 is not recoverable (it was for a bona fide sale for value). Only the April 1 transfer of $2,000 (made within four months of the petition) can be recovered.

32. (d) This question highlights the fact that all four parts of the Uniform CPA exam are, to some extent, interrelated. This question tests accounting theory as much, if not more so, than it tests the candidate's knowledge of business law. In any event, the answer is straightforward, and you either know that consideration received in excess of a stock's par or stated value is accounted for as additoinal paid-in capital — that is, answer (d) — or you do not.

33. (b) The minimum wage and maximum hours provisions of the FLSA apply to all employees engaged in interstate commerce and whose wages are not based on commissions or piecework except: those employed by retail and service establishments; executives, administrative, and professional employees; those employed by amusement and recreational establishments; agricultural employees; and apprentices, students, messengers, and handicapped workers. Given the choices, then, the only possible answer here is (b).

34. (c) Your gut reaction should tell you that answer (a) is not correct. It is not illegal for a board of directors to exercise poor business judgment, which they might be doing in the situations described in answers (b) and (d). But it is definitely illegal for a board to declare and/or pay cash dividends when the corporation is insolvent. The correct answer is (c).

35. (c) Only real defenses are good against a holder in due course. Fraud in the inducement — of which this situation is a variation — is a personal defense and therefore is not good against a holder in due course. Thus, as answer (c) states, the holder in due course may enforce the instrument as completed.

36. (d) The first thing that should jump out at you as soon as you read this instrument is the absence of the magic words of negotiability — that is, "pay to the order of" or "pay to bearer." Once you see that, it becomes clear that answers (a), (b), and (c) cannot possibly be correct. Only (d) can be correct.

37. (c) The Federal Bankruptcy Act stipulates which claims have priority when a trustee in bankruptcy attempts to satisfy creditors from the assets of a bankrupt's estate. According to the Bankruptcy Act, answer (c) is correct.

38. (c) Because it involves very detailed subject matter, this question is a good example of one which most candidates will have trouble with. The first thing to do when you hit a fuzzy question like this is to eliminate the obvious wrong answer(s) — in this case, answer (a). (How can you bind something that does not exist?) Give it a little thought and you will realize that (d) is probably wrong too, because an oral contract is as enforceable as a written contract, as long as it is not within the Statute of Frauds. That leaves (b) and (c). More thought will lead you to (c) as the correct answer, because it is precisely when the agent is not authorized to act for the principal — and not when he has been authorized to act for the principal (disclosed or not) — that the ratification doctrine comes into play.

39. (c) The thrust behind this question is to test the candidate's knowledge of exactly when a new issue can be legally offered to the public. That

point in time is when the required registration statement has been duly filed with the SEC and becomes effective, and not before (answer (c) ). The SEC does not require the filing of a surety bond (thus eliminating (a)), and its approval of a registration statement is not tantamount to a positive evaluation or endorsement of the registered securities (thus eliminating (d) ). The choice of whether to use the services of an underwriter or not is strictly that of the issuing corporation; the SEC does not require that an underwriter be involved. Accordingly, answer (b) is also incorrect

40. (b) Even if you are not quite sure of exactly when a fire insurance policy can be assigned, you can back into the correct answer quite easily here. The usual fire insurance policy does provide for subrogation of the insurer to the insured's rights upon payment of the benefits, and does cover losses caused by the insured agent's negligence. As for waiving the necessity of an insurable interest, it is highly unusual if not completely impossible for anyone to have the power to waive the requirement that the insured have an insurable interest in the property in question at the time of the loss.

41. (c) Most questions on bankruptcy are quite easy, because the rules are spelled out fairly clearly in the Federal Bankruptcy Act. There is no interpretation involved in this question; it is a black and white situation. The answer — which is (c) — is right in Section 17, 4 of the act.

42. (d) While federal securities regulation requires those involved with marketing securities (including attorneys and accountants) to provide for complete and honest disclosures to the public, it does not attempt to set standards regarding the ability, competence, and so forth of such professionals. Accordingly, answers (a), (b), and (c) are incorrect. The primary purpose of such regulations, as stated in answer (d), is to provide investors with the facts they need to evaluate the merits of the security being offered for sale.

43. (b) The Code provides that any description of collateral is sufficient if it provides a reasonable identification; it does not have to be specific to be valid. Thus, the description of Maxim Corporation's "presently existing and thereafter acquired" inventory is neither inadequate nor improper; answer (d), then, is wrong. The term inventory refers to all goods held for general sale in the course of business; therefore (a) is eliminated. Via the "floating lien" concept, a security interest can and does attach to new inventory which replaces that which existed at the time of the agreement but which has been subsequently sold; therefore (c) is not right.

44. (b) Answer (a) is not correct because as a duly licensed CPA, and by virtue of contract law,

Martinson is bound to exercise due professional care, whether he is a member of the AICPA or not. Contrary to answer (c), GAAS do cover procedures to be used in verifying inventory for balance sheet purposes; the need for suggested procedures directly resulted from the McKesson and Robbins case. (These procedures can be found in *Statements on Auditing Standards No. 1*.) With regard to (d), rather than having committed a tort, Martinson would probably have been found liable for breach of contract.

45. (b) As stipulated in Section 19 of the Model Business Corporation Act, "neither promissory notes nor future services shall constitute payment or part payment for the issuance of shares of a corporation." At $10 par value per common share of stock, 100 shares will cost $1,000. Because Jason's note for $400 and his promise to render services valued at $100 (a total of $500 of the $1,000 due) represent future payments, his shares are only 50% paid for. (Of course, the cancellation of money owed a creditor, by that creditor, is valid consideration.)

46. (a) The remedies described in (b), (c), and (d) may be available to a client, provided, of course, he can prove negligence (which would be seen as a breach of the contractual duty to exercise due professional care) on the part of the auditor. Punitive damages are usually awarded only in cases involving deliberate conduct, or a conscious attempt to defraud. Intent (which, by definition, is not present in simple negligence cases) is the key concept here. The correct answer is (a).

47. The firm is undoubtedly liable for negligence. The failure to follow generally accepted auditing standards indicates negligence in the conduct of the audit. Although the courts do not always recognize adherence to the custom of the profession (generally accepted auditing standards) as a defense, they invariably hold that the failure to follow customary practice constitutes negligence. The fact that Jackson left in the middle of the audit and caused a problem for the firm is of no consequence. The firm, by reason of the negligence of its agents, will be liable for the actual loss up to at least the $30,000 worth of watches stolen after the completion of the audit. This loss would not have occurred if the audit had been conducted properly. In addition, the firm may also be liable on the initial $20,000 of thefts to the extent that prompt discovery in the course of the audit would have permitted recovery of this loss.

48. 1. Yes. Both Super, the seller, and Friendly, who financed many of the purchases by Super's customers, qualify as "purchase money security" lenders. The Uniform Commercial Code provides

that a security interest is a "purchase money security interest" to the extent that it is —

(a) taken or retained by the seller of the collateral to secure all or part of its price; or

(b) taken by a person who, by making advances or incurring an obligation, gives value to enable the debtor to acquire rights in or the use of collateral if such value is in fact so used.

Those items financed by Super meet the requirements of (a) and those items financed by Friendly meet the requirements of (b).

2. A nonpossessory security interest is one in which the lender or seller does not have posssession of the property subject to the security interest. In such situations, the lender or seller perfects the security interest against third parties by filing a financing statement. An exception is made for the purchase-money security interest relating to consumer goods (for example, installment sales to the consumer) wherein the lender or seller is protected against other creditors of the debtor (but not bona fide consumer purchasers for value from the debtor) without the necessity of filing a financing statement. Hence, bothersome and costly paperwork is eliminated unless the secured party wishes to protect itself from a fraudulent sale by the consumer to a bona fide consumer purchaser for value. The risk is relatively unimportant in relation to the cost of filing, consequently many sellers and commercial lenders assume this risk themselves.

49. 1. No. In the real estate brokerage business, it is customary for a general partner, such as Watkins, to have the apparent authority to reduce the commission charged by the firm. Hence, unless Foster was aware of the express limitation contained in the partnership agreement regarding an individual partner's right to reduce the brokerage commission, he will prevail against any attempt to recoup the $10,000 reduction in commissions. Watkins had the apparent authority to make the reduction, and the firm and the other partners are unfortunately bound by his action.

2. Watkins is liable to the partnership or his fellow partners for the $10,000 reduction in the commission charged because his reduction without the consent of a fellow partner, which he did not have, was in direct violation of the partnership agreement. Furthermore, it would appear that Watkins' wrongful act in reducing the brokerage commission on the sale of the Foster property would be a valid basis for a dissolution of partnership.

50. Vincent Luck is an assignee of the contract rights evidenced by the instrument. He is not a holder in due course because the instrument does not contain the words of negotiability, i.e., pay to order or bearer. The indorsement, "Pay to the order of Vincent Luck" and signed by Whitten, does not cure the defect. Thus, Luck takes the instrument subject to all defenses assertible by Dayton Blasting.

However, Luck does take all of Whitten's rights as a assignee. Because Dayton used approximately 50% of the cases of caps, Luck should be able to recover for them.

51. None. The Uniform Commercial Code provides that a retail customer in the ordinary course of business takes free of a security interest created by his seller even though the security interest is perfected and even though the buyer knows of its existence. A buyer in the ordinary course of business is, generally, a person who, in good faith and without knowledge that the sale to him is in violation of the ownership rights or security interest of a third party in the goods, buys goods from someone in the business of selling them.

By duly filing a financing statement, Castle perfected its security interest in then-existing as well as after-acquired inventory. Even though Castle held a perfected security interest in Sill's inventory, the customer who purchased the television set from Sill in the ordinary course of business took the property free of Castle's security interest.

52. Neither South's financial difficulties nor his assignment of 90% of his partnership interest to his largest creditor alters the legal status of the partnership. There is no dissolution of the partnership, nor any basis for dissolution; it remains viable and unchanged in its membership.

South continues as a full-fledged partner. There is no cause for his removal, and he retains his prior rights. The only difference is that the creditor will receive 90% of the profits that are allocable to South. Furthermore, in the event of default by South, his creditor may obtain a judgment on the underlying debt and an order charging or attaching South's partnership interest.

South's creditor does not become a partner. He has no right to participate in the management or administration of partnership business nor, in the absence of a court order, to examine the books, or demand information of the partnership. His rights are limited to receipt of the appropriate share of profits assigned in accordance with his contract with South.

53. 1. The embezzler, Davidson, is liable to whichever party bears the ultimate loss.

2. Fenner Corporation would normally be able to recover $600 per check from Beacon National because it has a real defense (material alteration), which is valid even against a holder in due course.

However, Beacon National has a possible defense of contributory negligence by Fenner on the basis that Fenner did not exercise proper safeguards to prevent improper use of the check-imprinting machine. The Uniform Commercial Code provides that any person who by his negligence substantially contributes to a material alteration of the instrument is precluded from asserting the alteration against a holder in due course or against a drawee or other payor who pays the instrument in good faith and in accordance with the reasonable commercial standards of the drawee's or payor's business. In any event, Fenner is still liable to the extent of the original amount of $125 per check.

3. Normally, Beacon National must credit Fenner's account for the overpayments. It in turn has an action against the parties endorsing the instruments based upon a breach of their warranty that there were no material alterations. However, as discussed above, the possible defense of contributory negligence would be equally applicable here.

4. Smith, as a holder in due course, has the same rights and liabilities as Beacon National as they are given above.

54. **a.** No. The disclaimer of opinion will not absolve the CPA firm from liability. The auditor was negligent by failing either to take adequate measures to determine whether the leasehold improvements existed or to give notice that their existence had not been verified. As a result of such negligence and the bank's reliance upon the report, the CPA firm would be liable to the bank.

An auditor generally will not be held responsible for limitations on the audit if the auditor's report gives adequate notice of them. A disclaimer of opinion is the means used by the auditor to give adequate notice of limitations. Although the CPA firm attempted to disclaim an opinion on the financial statements, the wording in the auditor's report was sufficiently unclear that it is doubtful a court would find the report accomplished its intended purpose. The disclaimer said only that the "actual cost" of the improvements could not be determined, and the explanation strongly implied that the improvements actually existed and had substantial value (by use of such phrases as "were found" and "work was done") when in fact they did not exist. Consequently, the report was misleading.

**b.** Yes. The individual partners of the CPA firms are liable even though they did not take part in the audit. A partnership is an entity that is an association of two or more persons as co-owners to carry on a business for profit. All partners are jointly and severally liable and therefore personally responsible for the firm's liability to the bank. The individual partners may have to satisfy the bank's claims from their personal assets, even though they did not personally take part in the audit.

**c.** Determination of the liability of a CPA to third parties requires balancing two conflicting recognized interests of the law:

(1) The CPA's reasonable right to self-protection from claims of unknown persons whom the CPA has no reason to suspect would rely on his report, and

(2) The important public policy of protecting third parties who rely upon financial statements from the adverse effects of incompetent performance by professionals.

The *Ultramares* case in 1931 firmly established the doctrine of privity of contract leaving a CPA liable for simple or ordinary negligence only to a client. However, the opinion in that case indicated that a CPA could be liable to third parties if the conduct of the examination or preparation of the auditor's report involved fraud or negligence so gross as to permit an inference of fraud.

An additional basis upon which a third party could recover is as a third-party beneficiary. This relationship would be found in cases where it was clearly indicated that the engagement was undertaken for and was intended to benefit the third party, typically a lender.

The position of courts in upholding the doctrine of privity of contract began to change in the 1950s and 1960s. Court decisions began to reflect the view that CPAs owe a duty of care not only to their own clients but also to those whom they *should* know will rely on their reports in the transactions for which these reports are prepared. The courts began to rule that the CPA is liable for negligence for careless financial misrepresentations relied upon by foreseen and limited classes of persons. This extended the CPA's liability to third parties for simple or ordinary negligence to *reasonably* limited and *reasonably* definable classes of persons whom the CPA might *reasonably* expect would rely upon his report.

55. 1. A trust generally involves a transfer of income-producing property (principal) by will, deed, or indenture to a trustee who takes legal title to the property subject to a fiduciary obligation to manage and conserve the property for the benefit of others who are described as beneficiaries. A trust generally provides that the trustee shall invest the trust principal and pay the income therefrom to the income beneficiary and at the termination of the trust transfer the trust principal to the remainderman. The property that composes the principal of the trust may change

from time to time as the trustee sells and reinvests the proceeds.

The will or trust agreement can provide the rules for allocation of items between principal and income. In the absence of specific trust provisions, the law of the jurisdiction in which the trust is located will govern. For this purpose, most jurisdictions have adopted the Uniform Principal and Income Act or some variation thereof. Income produced by the investment and management of the trust principal is kept separate for distribution to the income beneficiary. However, ordinary operating expenses incurred by the trust in generating earnings are charged against income. Similarly, expenses incurred in acquiring or protecting the trustee's title to principal are charged against principal. Thus, the allocation between principal and income of a trust is of great importance because it affects the respective benefits derived from the trust by the income beneficiary and the remainderman.

2. (1) Principal
   (2) Income
   (3) Income
   (4) Principal
   (5) Principal
   (6) Principal
   (7) Principal

56. 1. Field warehousing is a very practical and useful device used essentially as a financing arrangement rather than a storage operation. The term connotes the use of the debtor's own facilities or premises (his "field") as the place of the warehouse. Thus, the expense in moving and storing the property in an independent warehouse is avoided. An area is normally set aside and fenced in, and signs are posted indicating the creation of such a relationship. Locks are typically changed, and a bonded warehouseman is put in charge of the operation to control the segregated field warehouse. The warehouseman may be an employee of the debtor or an employee of an independent warehouse. Typically, negotiable warehouse receipts are issued covering the property warehoused, and these are retained by the creditor as collateral for a loan or other form of credit. So long as a bona fide field warehousing arrangement is entered into and maintained, its validity is well recognized. The chief elements necessary to validate such an arrangement are the independence of the field warehouseman and his control over the property subject to the arrangement. In fact, this is a type of pledge, and through the warehouseman, the lender must have physical dominion over the property. Temporary relinquishment of the property to the debtor for limited purposes such as labelling or packaging is permitted.

2. The usual method of perfecting the security interest of the lender in such an arrangement is the physical dominion and control over the property, as in a pledge. However, the Uniform Commercial Code also permits filing a financing statement as an additional method of perfecting the security interest of the lender.

3. Merrill's rights are clearly subordinate to the claims of the prior interest of the other creditor who has duly perfected his security interest by filing. Merrill's rights will have value only to the extent that the raw materials are worth more than the prior creditor's claim.

# Weakness Identification Key
# First Examination

After you have corrected your answers from the sample examination, circle the numbers of the answers you had incorrect or found difficulty in answering. A large number of incorrect answers in any subject area indicates a weakness. Go back to the appropriate chapters in this book, consult another text, or check with your course instructor, to understand where your difficulty lies.

**Question Numbers**

|  | 1 - 10 | 11 - 20 | 21 - 30 | 31 - 40 | 41 - 50 | 51 - 60 |
|---|---|---|---|---|---|---|
| Contracts | 3, 7, 8 | 16, 20 | 27, 29 | | | |
| Sales | 4, 6 | | | | | |
| Secured Transactions | | 13 | | | 43, 48 | 51, 56 |
| Suretyship | | 14, 17 | 21, 23 | | | |
| Bankruptcy | | | 30 | 31, 37 | 41 | |
| Commercial Paper | | | 24, 26 | 35, 36 | 50 | 53 |
| Agency Law | 5, 9 | | | 38 | | |
| Partnerships | | | | | 49 | 52 |
| Corporations | 1 | | | 32, 34 | 45 | |
| Insurance | | 15 | 22 | 40 | | |
| Federal Securities Regulations | | 11 | | 39 | 42 | |
| Accountant's Legal Responsibility | | | 28 | | 44, 46, 47 | 54 |
| Antitrust Laws | 2 | 19 | 25 | | | |
| Employees' Rights | | 18 | | 33 | | |
| Real Property | 10 | 12 | | | | |
| Wills, Estates and Trusts | | | | | | 55 |

154

# Business Law Review Questions — Second Examination

1. Unlimited Fashions, Inc., leased a store in the Suburban Styles Shopping Center for five years at $1,500 a month. The lease contained a provision which prohibited assignment of the lease. After occupying the premises for two years, Unlimited sublet the premises to Fantastic Frocks for the balance of its term, less one day, at $2,000 per month. Unlimited moved out on a Sunday and removed all its personal property and trade fixtures such as portable clothing racks, cash registers, detachable counters, etc. Which of the following best describes the legal status of the parties involved?
   a. Unlimited has not breached its contract with Suburban.
   b. Suburban is entitled to the additional $500 rental paid each month by Fantastic to Unlimited.
   c. Removal of the trade fixtures in question by Unlimited was improper and it can be held liable to Suburban for their fair value.
   d. Fantastic is a tenant of Suburban.

2. Digital Sales, Inc., leased office space from Franklin Rentals for a five-year period. The lease did not contain any provisions regarding insurance by the lessee. During the term of the lease the office building was gutted by a fire that started in an adjacent building and spread to Franklin's building. In this situation
   a. Digital has an implied obligation to insure the portion of the building it leased, to protect its interest in the property and that of the lessor.
   b. Digital has an insurable interest in the building, but only to the extent of the value of its leasehold.
   c. If the building is fully occupied and leased on long-term leaseholds, Franklin has no insurable interest.
   d. If Franklin sold the building, it could nevertheless continue the insurance coverage and collect on the policy because its insurable interest in the building runs from its prior ownership.

3. On June 10, Central Corporation sold goods to Bowie Corporation for $5,000. Bowie signed a financial statement containing the names and addresses of the parties and describing the collateral. Central filed the financing statement on June 21, noting the same in its accounting books.
   a. Central need not sign the financing statement to perfect its security interest in the collateral.
   b. Central must file the financing statement prior to the sale if a security interest is to be perfected.
   c. Central must sign the financing statement in order to perfect its security interest.
   d. Central had a perfected security interest in the collateral even before the financing statement was filed.

4. Franklin's will left his ranch "to his wife, Joan, for her life, and upon her death to his sons, George and Harry, as joint tenants." Because of the provisions in Franklin's will
   a. Joan cannot convey her interest in the ranch except to George and Harry.
   b. The ranch must be included in Joan's estate for federal estate tax purposes upon her death.
   c. If George predeceases Harry, Harry will obtain all right, title, and interest in the ranch.

   d. Joan holds the ranch in trust for the benefit of George and Harry.

5. Martinson Services, Inc., agreed to rent two floors of office space in Jason's building for five years. An escalation clause in the lease provided for a $200 per month increase in rental in the fifth year of occupancy by Martinson. Near the end of the fourth year, during a serious economic recession, Martinson's business was doing very poorly. Martinson called upon Jason to inform him that Martinson could not honor the lease if the rent was increased in the fifth year. Jason agreed in a signed writing to allow Martinson to remain at the prior rental, and Martinson did so. At the end of the fifth year Martinson moved to another office building. Then, Jason demanded payment of $2,400 from Martinson.
   What is the legal standing of the parties involved?
   a. A binding accord and satisfaction has resulted between the parties.
   b. The agreed upon rent reduction is valid due to the increased burden of performance as a result of events beyond Martinson's control.
   c. Martinson's relinquishment of the legal right to breach the contract provided the consideration for the reduction in rent.
   d. The writing signed by Jason does not bind him to the agreed reduction in rent.

6. Fox, Harrison, and Dodge are the general partners of Great Expectations, a limited partnership. There are 20 limited partners. The general partners wish to add two more general partners and sell additional limited partnership interests to the public. The limited partnership certificate is silent on these matters. The general partners
   a. Can admit the two additional partners as general partners without the consent of the limited partners if the general partners vote unanimously to do so.
   b. Cannot admit additional limited partners unless there is unanimous written consent or ratification of their action by the limited partners.
   c. Can admit additional limited partners if a majority of the general and limited partners consent to do so.
   d. Cannot admit any general or limited partners without amending the written partnership agreement.

7. Kimball, Thompson, and Darby formed a partnership. Kimball contributed $25,000 in capital and loaned the partnership $20,000; he performed no services. Thompson contributed $15,000 in capital and part-time services, and Darby contributed only his full-time services. The partnership agreement provided that all profits and losses would be shared equally. Three years after the formation of the partnership, the three partners agreed to dissolve and liquidate the partnership. Firm creditors, other than Kimball, have bona fide claims of $65,000. After all profits and losses have been recorded there are $176,000 of assets to be distributed to creditors and partners. When the assets are distributed
   a. Darby receives nothing since he did not contribute any property.
   b. Thompson receives $45,333 in total.
   c. Kimball receives $62,000 in total.
   d. Each partner receives one-third of the remaining assets after all the firm creditors, including Kimball, have been paid.

155

8. Charles Wilson and Donald Black decided to merge their competing business proprietorships. The resulting partnership was established by a mere handshake. The oral partnership agreement did not cover profit sharing or salaries. For this partnership
    a.   The federal antitrust laws do not apply.
    b.   The Statute of Frauds does not require Wilson and Black's agreement to be in writing.
    c.   The partnership is voidable by the creditors of either proprietorship.
    d.   Wilson is entitled to a reasonable salary for his services as managing partner.

9. Gregor paid $100 to Henry for a thirty-day written option to purchase Henry's commercial real property for $75,000. Twenty days later Henry received an offer from Watson to purchase the property for $85,000. Henry promptly notified Gregor that the option price was now $85,000, or the option was revoked. Gregor said he would not pay a penny more than $75,000 and that he still had 10 days remaining on the option. On the 28th day of the option Gregor telephoned Henry that he had decided to exercise the option; he tendered his $75,000 check the next day which was to be held in escrow until delivery of the deed. Henry refused to accept the tender stating that he had decided not to sell and that he was going to retain the property for the present. Which of the following best describes the legal rights of the parties involved?
    a.   Henry effectively revoked his offer to sell because he did this prior to Gregor's acceptance.
    b.   Consideration given for the option is irrelevant because the option was in writing and signed by Henry.
    c.   Because Gregor's acceptance was not in writing and signed, it is invalid according to the Statute of Frauds.
    d.   Gregor's acceptance was valid, and in the event of default he may obtain the equitable remedy of specific performance.

10. Joe Walters was employed by the Metropolitan Department Store as a driver of one of its delivery trucks. Under the terms of his employment he made deliveries daily along a designated route and brought the truck back to the store's garage for overnight storage. One day instead of returning to the garage as required, he drove the truck twenty miles north of the area he covered expecting to attend a social function unrelated to his employment or to his employer's affairs. Through his negligence in operating the truck while enroute, Walters seriously injured Richard Bunt. Walters caused the accident and was solely at fault. Bunt entered suit in tort against the store for damages for personal injuries, alleging that the store, as principal, was responsible for the tortious acts of its agent. Under these circumstances
    a.   Metropolitan is not liable because Walters was an independent contractor.
    b.   Metropolitan is not liable because Walters had abandoned his employment and was engaged in an independent activity of his own.
    c.   Metropolitan is liable based upon the doctrine of *respondant superior*.
    d.   Bunt can recover damages from both Walters and Metropolitan.

**Items 11 and 12** are based on the following information:

On February 1, 1975, Barron Explosives received an order from Super Construction, Inc., for 200 cases of dynamite at $25 per case with terms of 2/10, net/30, for delivery within two months, FOB seller's warehouse. The order was duly accepted in writing by Barron. Super soon discovered that it was already overstocked with dynamite and, therefore, it contacted Chubb Construction Company to see if it would be interested in taking over the contract. Chubb Construction Company indicated it would take over the contract and signed the following agreement on February 10, 1975:

Super Construction, Inc., hereby assigns its contract for the purchase of 200 cases of dynamite at $25 per case ordered from Barron Explosives on February 1, 1976, to Chubb Construction Company. Chubb Construction hereby accepts.

(Signed) Super, President
Super Construction, Inc.

(Signed) Chubb, President
Chubb Construction Company

Since February 1, 1975, the price of dynamite has increased substantially, and as a result, Super wishes to avoid the assignment and obtain the dynamite for itself. Barron wishes to avoid having to deliver to either party.

11. Which of the following statements best describes the legal status of the parties to the contract?
    a.   Barron can avoid its obligation on the contract if it has reasonable grounds for insecurity because Chubb's credit rating is inferior to that of Super's.
    b.   The assignment in question transfers to Chubb both the rights and the duties under the contract.
    c.   Super can avoid the assignment to Chubb based upon the fact that it is lacking in consideration on Chubb's part.
    d.   The contract is not assignable because it would materially vary Barron's duty to perform.

12. Assume that instead of Super Construction assigning the contract Barron Explosives found that it could not perform, and therefore, it assigned the contract to a nearby competitor, Demerest Explosives. Demerest promised Barron it would perform on the Super contract and expressly released Barron from any responsibility. Demerest subsequently defaulted and has refused to deliver.
    a.   Barron's delegation of its duty to perform to Demerest Explosives constitutes an anticipatory breach of contract.
    b.   Super Construction need not perform since the assignment of the contract materially alters its burden of performing.
    c.   Super Construction can immediately proceed against Barron upon default by Demerest.
    d.   Super Construction has recourse only against Barron.

13. Martin Wilson was hired by Gismore Enterprises, Inc., an operator of a drill press. Gismore is fully covered by workmen's compensation insurance. Wilson did not believe in the safety regulations posted by management; hence, he removed the protective shields designed to prevent any possible injury to his hands. In this way he could meet production standards with a minimal effort and collect production bonuses. In the process of his work, Wilson unfortunately caught his hand in the drill press and the operating physician decided that amputation was the only alternative if Wilson's life were to be saved. Wilson seeks to recover. In this situation
    a.   Wilson can recover in negligence against Gismore.
    b.   Wilson will be denied all recovery because of his assumption of the risk.

c. If Wilson was working overtime, workmen's compensation rules would not apply.

d. Even if Wilson is guilty of contributory negligence, workmen's compensation rules provide for recovery.

14. Donald Fisk is a limited partner of Sparta Oil Development. He paid $10,000 for his limited-partnership interest. In addition, he loaned Sparta $7,500. Sparta failed to find oil and is in financial difficulty. Upon dissolution and liquidation,

a. Donald Fisk will receive repayment of his loan only after all outside general creditors have first been satisfied, but prior to any other distributions.

b. Donald Fisk will receive repayment, along with the other limited partners, in respect to his capital and loan after all other creditors have been satisfied.

c. The last item to be distributed, if anything remains, is to the general partners in respect to profits.

d. If Donald Fisk holds partnership property as collateral, he may resort to it to satisfy any deficiency if partnership assets are insufficient to meet creditors' claims.

15. Filmore hired Stillwell as his agent to acquire Dobbs' land at a price not to exceed $50,000; the land is badly needed to provide additional parking space for Filmore's shopping center. In order to prevent Dobbs from asking for an exorbitant price, Filmore told Stillwell not to disclose his principal. Stillwell subsequently purchased the land for $45,000. Under these circumstances

a. Stillwell and Filmore committed fraud when they did not disclose the fact that Stillwell was Filmore's agent.

b. Absent an agreement regarding the compensation to be paid Stillwell, he is entitled to the difference between the $50,000 limitation and the $45,000 he paid for the land; i.e., $5,000 based upon quasi contract.

c. Dobbs may rescind the contract upon his learning the truth as long as the conveyance has not been accomplished.

d. Dobbs may sue either Filmore or Stillwell on the contract in the event of default by Filmore.

16. Williams, Watkins, and Glenn is a limited partnership. At present, there are three general partners and sixteen limited partners. The partnership is engaged in the grain-futures business. The general partners decided to expand the business substantially by offering one million dollars of limited-partner interests to the investing public in several states at $5,000 per limited-partner interest. A majority of the existing limited partners object to the proposition. Under the circumstances, the limited partnership

a. Has been dissolved.

b. Must file a registration statement with the SEC if it is going to offer the one million dollars of limited-partner interests to prospective buyers.

c. Is exempt from federal registration because a limited-partner interest is not a "security."

d. Is recognized as a general partnership as a result of the dispute between the general and limited partners and each is entitled to an equal vote in the management of the partnership.

17. Marvel Toys, Inc., manufactures and sells toys to Gem Stores, a large department store chain, and to Fantastic Discounts, a major toy retailer, at prices below its sales price of similar toys to other retailers in the market area. Its pricing policy vis-a-vis Gem is based solely upon the fact that Gem is a new customer and the low prices were quoted in order to obtain its business and thereby eliminate Marvel's unused production capacity. For Fantastic, the lower prices are charged in order to meet the identical prices legally charged by a competitor. In assessing the potential violation of antitrust laws against price discrimination, it would appear that Marvel Toys

a. Has not violated the antitrust laws as long as none of its competitors can show damages.

b. Has a valid defense with respect to its sales to Gem.

c. Has not violated the antitrust laws with respect to its sales to Fantastic.

d. Will not have committed any violation if it was operating at a loss at the time of the sales.

18. Young, a minor, purchased a car from Ace Auto Sales by making a down payment and signing a note for the balance. The note was guaranteed by Rich. Subsequently, Young sought to return the car and not pay off the note because Ace made false representations concerning the car's mileage at the time of sale. Which of the following best describes the legal implications in these circumstances?

a. Neither Young nor Rich is liable on the note solely because Young is a minor.

b. Young's attempt to return the car, in and of itself, released Rich of any liability.

c. The fraud perpetrated upon Young is a valid defense to Rich's guaranty.

d. There are no valid defenses for Rich and Young and the only recourse is to seek to reduce the amount owed based upon a counterclaim for fraud.

**Items 19 and 20 are based on the following information:**

Matson loaned Donalds $1,000 at 8% interest for one year. Two weeks before the due date, Matson called upon Donalds and obtained his agreement in writing to modify the terms of the loan. It was agreed that on the due date Donalds would pay $850 to Cranston, to whom Matson owed that amount, and pay the balance plus interest to his son, Arthur, to whom he wished to make a gift.

19. Which of the following statements is legally valid with respect to the events described above?

a. Because Matson never received the interest on the Donalds loan, he will not have to include it in his gross income for federal income tax purposes.

b. Matson has irrevocably assigned the debt to Cranston and Arthur.

c. In the event of default by Donalds, Cranston must first proceed against him before seeking recourse against Matson.

d. Neither of the agreements between Matson and Donalds needs to be in writing.

20. Under the modified terms of the loan, Cranston or Arthur have what legal standing?

a. Cranston is a creditor beneficiary and Arthur is a donee beneficiary.

b. Cranston has the right to prevent Matson's delegation if he gives timely notice.

c. If Cranston is to be able to proceed against Donalds, he must have received notice of Donalds' promise to pay him the $850 prior to the due date.

d. Arthur is an incidental beneficiary.

21. Menlow Corporation dismissed Gibson, its purchasing agent, for incompetence. It published a notice in the appropriate trade journals which stated: "This is to notify all parties concerned that Gibson is no longer employed by the Menlow Corporation and the corporation assumes no further responsibility for his acts." Gibson called on several of Menlow's suppliers with whom he had previously dealt, and when he found one who was unaware of his dismissal, he would place a substantial order for merchandise to be delivered to a warehouse in which he had rented space. Menlow had rented warehouse space in the past when its storage facilities were crowded. Gibson also called on several suppliers with whom Menlow had never dealt; he would present one of his old business cards to the secretary and then make purchases on open account in the name of Menlow. Gibson then sold all the merchandise delivered to the warehouse and absconded with the money. In this situation.

    a.   Gibson had continuing express authority to make contracts on Menlow's behalf with suppliers with whom he had previously dealt as Menlow's agent, if they were unaware of his dismissal.

    b.   The suppliers who previously had no dealings with Menlow **cannot** enforce the contracts against Menlow even if the suppliers were unaware of Gibson's lack of authority.

    c.   Menlow is liable on the Gibson contracts to all suppliers who had dealt with Gibson in the past as Menlow's agent.

    d.   Constructive notice via publication in the appropriate trade journals is an effective notice to all third parties regardless of whether they had dealt with Gibson or read the notice.

22. Alfred Matz negotiated with Basic Construction Company, Inc., to construct an apartment house. Desiring additional assurance of completion or payment of damages in the event of default, Matz insisted that a performance bond be posted. Basic obtained First Fidelity Surety Bonding Company as the surety on the undertaking. In addition to the normal terms of such contracts, First Fidelity insisted upon the right to complete the building in the event of default by Basic. The contract was drafted and signed by all the parties involved. Under the circumstances

    a.   Basic Construction is the third-party beneficiary of the contract.

    b.   If Basic Construction refuses to perform, Matz can obtain a court order obligating First Fidelity to complete construction.

    c.   First Fidelity has assumed the primary obligation to perform.

    d.   First Fidelity would be entitled to any and all rights that Matz would have against Basic in the event Basic defaults and First Fidelity pays.

23. James Fisk recently acquired Valiant Corporation by purchasing all of its outstanding stock pursuant to a tender offer. Fisk demanded and obtained the resignation of the existing board of directors and replaced it with his own slate of nominees. Under these circumstances

    a.   Fisk had no right to demand the resignation of the existing board members; their resignations are legally ineffective and they remain as directors.

    b.   If Valiant is listed on a national stock exchange, Fisk would have to file his tender offer with the Securities and Exchange Commission.

    c.   The former stockholders of Valiant are parties to a tax free reorganization; hence, they are **not**

subject to federal income tax on their gain, if any, on transferring their stock to Fisk.

    d.   If Valiant is engaged in interstate commerce, the acquisition is exempt under the antitrust laws because the Securities and Exchange Commission has jurisdiction.

24. Martin Finance Corporation loaned David Small $2,500. Small agreed to repay in twelve monthly installments. After Small was late in making a payment, Martin indicated it needed additional protection and requested that Small obtain a surety. Small appealed to his long-time friend, Arthur Black, to help him. As a personal favor to Small, Black agreed and gave Small a written promise to answer for the debt in the event Small should default on the loan. Small defaulted and filed a voluntary petition in bankruptcy. Martin immediately demanded payment by Black. In this situation

    a.   Black's undertaking was **not** supported by consideration; hence, it is unenforceable.

    b.   Martin must wait until the bankruptcy proceeding has been concluded and the bankrupt's estate distributed to creditors.

    c.   The Statute of Frauds would **not** apply to Black's undertaking because he was a noncompensated surety.

    d.   Small's bankruptcy bars Martin from recovery against Black.

25. Mr. Jackson owns approximately 40% of the shares of common stock of Triad Corporation. The rest of the shares are widely distributed among over 2,000 shareholders. Jackson has had a number of personal problems related to other business ventures and would like to raise about $2,000,000 through the sale of some of his shares. He accordingly approached Underwood & Sons, an investment banking house in which he knew one of the principals, to purchase his Triad shares and distribute the shares to the public at a reasonable price through its offices in the United States. Any profit on the sales could be retained by Underwood pursuant to an agreement reached between Jackson and Underwood. In this situation

    a.   The securities to be sold probably do **not** need to be registered with the Securities and Exchange Commission.

    b.   Underwood & Sons probably is **not** an underwriter as defined in the federal securities law.

    c.   Jackson probably is considered the issuer under federal securities law.

    d.   Under federal securities law, **no** prospectus is required to be filed in connection with this contemplated transaction.

26. Norton owned and operated a trucking business. He was financially hard pressed and obtained a loan from the First State Bank "secured by his equipment and including all other chattels and personal property used in his business." The loan security agreement was properly filed in the county records office. In addition, Norton obtained a loan from the Title Mortgage Company; the loan was secured by a first mortgage on all the real property used in the trucking business. Norton is now insolvent and a petition in bankruptcy has been filed. Which of the following is a correct statement concerning the security interests in the properties?

    a.   If Title Mortgage failed to record its mortgage, the trustee in bankruptcy will be able to defeat Title's security interest.

    b.   Norton's central air conditioning and heating system is included in First State's security interest.

c. If Title Mortgage did **not** record its mortgage, First State is entitled to all fixtures, including those permanently annexed to the land.

d. A sale of all the personal and real business property by Norton to a bona fide purchaser will defeat First State's security interest unless First State recorded its security interest in both the appropriate real and personal property recordation offices.

27. Normally a principal will **not** be liable to a third party

a. On a contract signed on his behalf by an agent who was expressly forbidden by the principal to make it and where the third party was unaware of the agent's limitation.

b. On a contract made by his agent and the principal is **not** disclosed, unless the principal ratifies it.

c. For torts committed by an independent contractor if they are within the scope of the contract.

d. On a negotiable instrument signed by the agent in his own name without revealing he signed in his agency capacity.

28. Bonanza Real Estate Ventures is a limited partnership created pursuant to the law of a state which has adopted the Uniform Limited Partnership Act. It has three general partners and 1,100 limited partners living in various states. The limited partnership interests were offered to the general public at $5,000 per partnership interest. Johnson purchased a limited-partnership interest in the Bonanza Real Estate Ventures. As such, he

a. **Cannot** assign his limited-partnership interest to another person without the consent of the general partners.

b. Is entitled to interest on his capital contribution.

c. Is a fiduciary vis-a-vis the limited partnership and its partners.

d. Must include his share of the limited-partnership taxable profits in his taxable income even if he does **not** withdraw anything.

29. Snowmobile sales by manufacturers in a relevant market amount to about $10,000,000 annually. Sleekat, a manufacturer who sells its snowmobiles directly to dealers, has sales of about $4,000,000 annually in that market of which about $2,000,000 are to Sport Store. Sport Store has about 40% of the retail market and half of its sales are Sleekat vehicles. Four other manufacturers account for the other 60% of wholesale sales and three other dealers account for the other 60% of retail sales. Under these circumstances

a. Sleekat would probably commit an antitrust violation by acquiring all of the stock of Sport Store.

b. Sleekat would probably **not** commit an antitrust violation if it required Sport Store to limit its sales of Sleekat vehicles to persons resident in the defined market and provided that the dealership would be terminated for violation.

c. Sleekat could require Sport Store to sell only Sleekat vehicles and **no** competing vehicles and probably **not** violate the antitrust laws.

d. Sleekat could avoid any possible violation of the antitrust laws by acquiring the assets of Sport Store.

30. Inns Corporation operated a major hotel in a metropolitan city. An annual festival week brought many tourists to the city resulting in peak demand for accommodations. The local Tourism Bureau, of which Inns was an active member, embarked on a campaign to increase tourist trade in the area and asked all suppliers of goods to hotels and restaurants to contribute 1% of sales revenue to the bureau. Bureau members also were of the opinion that higher prices could be charged during the festival week without hurting the tourist trade. Which of the following actions would most likely violate the antitrust laws?

a. Rental of Inns' main ballroom on the key day of the festival at a price below that offered by other hotels.

b. The raising of rates on hotel rooms during festival week when other hotels also raise their rates.

c. Inns' notification to its purchasing officer to confine its purchases to suppliers contributing to the Tourism Bureau as agreed with other bureau members.

d. Inns' policy of purchasing soap products from only one manufacturer even though there were offers of lower prices for similar goods from other manufacturers.

31. Your client, Ace Auto Sales, sold a 1974 Skylark Magnificent to Marcus on the installment basis. Marcus signed an installment agreement for the balance due ($2,000) on the purchase price. Ace's policy was **not** to file a financing statement in the appropriate recordation office. Marcus subsequently sold the car to Franks without disclosing the debt owed to Ace. Franks purchased the car in good faith, knowing nothing about the debt owed by Marcus to Ace. Marcus is bankrupt. Wallace, a general creditor of Marcus has asserted rights to the car in question. Under the circumstances

a. Marcus takes title free and clear of any claims because Ace did **not** file.

b. Ace can defeat the claim of Franks in that Franks is a mere third party beneficiary.

c. Ace's rights against Marcus under the contract of sale are unimpaired despite the lack of filing.

d. In the final analysis Wallace will prevail.

32. General Cosmetics, a limited partnership created pursuant to the Uniform Limited Partnership Act, is in liquidation. Some of the limited partners are also creditors of the partnership. Under the circumstances, how should the liquidation be accomplished?

a. First satisfy all creditors, including any creditors who are also limited partners, in order of priority as provided by law.

b. Distribute any excess remaining after the satisfaction of creditors to limited partners with the exception of undistributed profits to which the general partners may be entitled.

c. Satisfy all outside creditors, excluding any limited partners who are also creditors, and then satisfy limited partners for all their claims.

d. Satisfy all partners whether general or limited for their original capital contributions after all creditors have been satisfied.

33. Nashville Baseball Corporation has a contract that provides it with exclusive rights to supply baseballs to the National and American Baseball Leagues as long as it meets the price and quality of baseballs offered by competitors. Excelsior Corporation offered a superior baseball at a reduced price. Nashville met the quality and price proposal submitted by Excelsior and retained its exclusive suppliership. Under these circumstances

a. If Nashville meets the price and quality offer of Excelsior, it has **not** violated the federal antitrust laws.

b. Nashville has obtained an exclusive dealing

arrangement which will be tested under the provisions of the Clayton Act.

c. Nashville is not engaged in interstate commerce because it sells all its baseballs to the league buyers in Tennessee.

d. Nashville has not violated the antitrust laws because it must meet competition from other suppliers.

34. Laser Corporation lent $5,000 to Mr. Jackson, a member of its board of directors. Mr. Jackson was also vice-president of operations. The board of directors, but not the stockholders, of Laser authorized the loan on the basis that the loan would benefit the Corporation. The loan made to Mr. Jackson is

a. Proper.
b. Improper because Mr. Jackson is an employee.
c. Improper because Mr. Jackson is a director.
d. Improper because Mr. Jackson is both a director and an employee.

35. Cutler sent Foster the following offer by mail:

I offer you 150 Rex portable electric typewriters, model J-I at $65 per typewriter, FOB your truck at my warehouse; terms 2/10, net/30. I am closing out this model, hence the substantial discount. Accept all or none.

(Signed) Cutler

Foster immediately wired back:

I accept your offer re the Rex electric typewriters, but will use Red Ball Express Company for the pickup, at my expense of course. In addition, if possible, could you have the shipment ready by Tuesday at 10:00 AM because of the holidays?

(Signed) Foster

a. The purported acceptance is invalid since it states both additional and different terms than those contained in the offer.

b. A purported acceptance which ordered 50 Rex electric typewriters would be valid.

c. Assuming the acceptance to be valid, it will not be effective until received by Cutler.

d. A purported acceptance which read, "Shipment must be ready by Tuesday at 10:00 AM or forget it." would constitute a counteroffer.

36. Miller Corporation declared a common stock dividend of 1 common share for every 10 common shares outstanding. The owners' equity accounts of the corporation immediately prior to the declaration of the common stock dividend were as follows:

Stated capital (10,000 shares of common
stock issued and outstanding, $1 par
value per share)                          $10,000
Earned surplus (retained earnings)          4,000

No other transactions are relevant. Immediately after the issuance of the common stock dividend, stated capital will amount to

a. $11,000.
b. $10,000.
c. $9,000.
d. $1,000.

37. Visco Sales, Inc., sent Nails Manufacturing Corporation the following telegram:

We need 2,000 two-pound boxes of your best grade two-inch roofing nails. Ship at once.

Visco Sales, S. Peters,
V.P. of Purchasing

a. The telegram is too indefinite and uncertain to constitute an offer.

b. Acceptance by Nails will not take place until receipt of the shipment by Visco.

c. The telegram is not an offer, but a mere invitation to do business.

d. The telegram constitutes a signed writing which would be enforceable against Visco under the Statute of Frauds, assuming the nails would cost $500 or more.

38. Marvin purchased a new 1975 automobile from Excellent Auto Sales. The car was fully warranted by the manufacturer, Specific Motors, for one year or 20,000 miles whichever occurred sooner. There was no warranty disclaimer by either the manufacturer or the retailer. The car contained a hidden defect insofar as the retailer was concerned, i.e., one that could not be discovered with reasonable care except during manufacture. The defect caused Marvin to have a serious accident which damaged the car and injured him. Which of the following statements is true regarding the status of Marvin's contract?

a. Marvin is not privity of contract with Specific Motors.

b. Excellent Auto has no liability to Marvin in that it could not have discovered the defect.

c. The Uniform Commercial Code abolished the privity requirement in cases such as this.

d. Marvin may recover only for the damage to the car and the replacement of the defective parts.

39. Boswell Woolen Yarns, Inc., is one of your audit clients. It has been a member of the Woolen Yarns Manufacturers Association of America which has represented 75% of the woolen yarn manufacturers of America for the past ten years. Until recently, the association has served primarily as a public relations and lobbying agent for its members. Now, as a result of severe inflation and competition from manufacturers of other types of fabrics, e.g., super nylon, orlon, etc., it has been proposed by the association and the overwhelming majority of its members that the association provides its members with suggested minimum and maximum prices to be charged and maximum production levels for each member. If the plan is implemented

a. The association and its members, including your client, have engaged in an illegal contract, combination, or conspiracy in restraint of trade.

b. There are no antitrust implications regarding such an arrangement as long as the parties are not compelled to join in the plan.

c. And the association is appointed by its members as their agent to engage in such activities, the arrangement will not be considered a violation of the antitrust laws even if its members could not have done so themselves.

d. Meeting competition from other non-wool manufacturers is a complete defense against any alleged antitrust violations.

40. Charles Lands offered to sell his business to Donald Bright. The assets consisted of real property, merchandise, office equipment, and the rights under certain contracts to purchase goods at an agreed price. In consideration for receipt of the aforementioned assets, Bright was to pay

$125,000 and assume all business liabilities owed by Lands. Bright accepted the offer and a written contract was signed by both parties. Under the circumstances, the contract

a. Represents an assignment of all the business assets and rights Lands owned and a delegation of whatever duties Lands was obligated to perform.

b. Must be agreed to by all Lands' creditors and the parties who had agreed to deliver goods to Lands.

c. Frees Lands from all liability to his creditors once the purchase is consummated.

d. Is too indefinite and uncertain to be enforced.

41. Delray Corporation has a provision in its corporate charter as follows: "Holders of the noncumulative preferred stock shall be entitled to a fixed annual dividend of 8% before any dividend shall be paid on common stock." There are no further provisions relating to preferences or statements regarding voting rights. The preferred stock apparently

a. Is noncumulative, but only to the extent that the 8% dividend is not earned in a given year.

b. Is nonvoting unless dividends are in arrears.

c. Has a preference on the distribution of the assets of the corporation upon dissolution.

d. Is not entitled to participate with common stock in dividend distributions beyond 8%.

42. Busby & Nelson, a general partnership, is a small furniture manufacturing company located in a southwestern state. It sells most of its products to fine furniture stores in Chicago, Los Angeles, and New York. It employs 50 skilled workmen and 10 other employees. Busby & Nelson has elected not to be covered under the state law which provides for elective workmen's compensation coverage because its safety standards are excellent, and there has not been a serious employee injury for several years. Busby & Nelson

a. Would not be held liable for workmen's compensation to an injured employee if the injury was due to the employee's negligence.

b. Is obligated to pay workmen's compensation benefits to its employees even though such coverage was optional.

c. Is subject to lawsuits for damages by injured employees and may not assert the common-law defenses such as contributory negligence.

d. Cannot create any type of pension plan for the partners and its employees which will permit payments thereto to be deducted in whole or part for federal-income-tax purposes.

43. One of your CPA firm's clients, Destination Garages, Inc., has entered into an agreement with its principal competitor, Parking Unlimited, Inc., to eliminate cut-throat competition. They have agreed to charge a uniform hourly rate in the different areas in which they compete. The garages are mainly located in Metropolis, but some are located in another state which is just across the state line from Metropolis. It is agreed that the rates to be charged are (1) always to be reasonable and (2) to be based upon the rate structure charged by the leading parking lot operator in Central City, the capital of the state in which Metropolis is located. What is the status of the agreement between Destination Garages and Parking Unlimited in regard to federal antitrust law?

a. Because the garages are real property, antitrust law does not apply.

b. Because the "product" sold is a service, antitrust law does not apply.

c. Regardless of the fact that the prices agreed upon are aimed at avoiding cut-throat competition, are always to be reasonable to the public, and are based upon another company's rates, the prices agreed upon are, nevertheless, in violation of the antitrust law.

d. If Destination Garages can show that it was in fact merely meeting competition from other parking lots, it would have a complete defense against any alleged antitrust violation.

44. Lester Dunbar sold to Walter Masters real property on which Charles Endicott held a first mortgage which had been created at the time Dunbar purchased the property. Under the terms of the written purchase agreement, Masters expressly assumed the mortgage debt. Subsequent to the purchase, Masters defaulted in his payment of the mortgage debt. Endicott thereupon sought to enforce payment of the mortgage debt against Masters personally. Masters contends that Endicott should have proceeded against Dunbar, the original mortgagor, because he is primarily liable for the mortgage debt. Based upon the above facts

a. Masters is correct in his assertion.

b. Endicott lost all rights against Dunbar upon learning of the sale to Masters and having made no objection thereto.

c. Dunbar is, in fact, a surety and must satisfy the mortgage if Masters does not.

d. Upon default, Endicott must elect to proceed against one of the parties involved and by so doing has made a binding election, thereby releasing the other.

45. Haworth Discount Stores mailed its order to Eagle Recordings, Inc., for 100 eight-track cassette recordings of "Swan Songs" by the Paginations at $5.50 per cassette. Eagle promptly wired its acceptance, delivery to take place within two weeks from date of Haworth's order and terms of net 30 days. Before delivery was made by Eagle, the retail price of this recording by the Paginations fell to $4.95. Haworth Discount informed Eagle of this and pleaded with Eagle, "Because we have been good customers give us a break by either reducing the price to $4.95 so we can break-even or by allowing us to cancel the order." Eagle's sales manager called Haworth the next day and informed them the price would be $4.95 per cassette, not the price that appeared on the original invoice.

The modification of the initial Haworth-Eagle contract

a. Fails due to lack of consideration.

b. Need not satisfy the Statute of Frauds.

c. Must be written and signed by the parties to be valid if no consideration is given by the party seeking to rely upon the modification.

d. Is voidable by Eagle at any time prior to shipment of the 100 cassettes.

46. Lutz sold his moving and warehouse business, including all the personal and real property used therein, to Allen Van Lines, Inc. The real property was encumbered by a $300,000 first mortgage upon which Lutz was personally liable. Allen acquired the property subject to the mortgage. Two years later, when the mortgage outstanding was $260,000, Allen decided to abandon the business location because it had become unprofitable and the value of the real property was less than the outstanding mortgage. Allen moved to another location and refused to

pay the installments due on the mortgage. What is the legal status of the parties in regard to the mortgage?

    a.   Allen took the real property free of the mortgage.

    b.   Allen breached its contract with Lutz when it abandoned the location and defaulted on the mortgage.

    c.   Lutz must satisfy the mortgage debt in the event that foreclosure yields an amount less than the unpaid balance.

    d.   If Lutz pays off the mortgage, he will be able to successfully sue Allen because Lutz is subrogated to the mortgagee's rights against Allen.

**47.** John Ford signed a check for $1,000 on January 25, 1975, payable to the order of Charles Benson Manufacturing, a sole proprietorship. The check was dated February 1, 1975. Benson indorsed the check to Francis Factoring, Inc., by writing on the back of the check: "Pay only to Francis Factoring, Inc., Charles Benson." After Benson delivered the check to Francis Factoring, Francis Factoring immediately took the check to First National Bank, the drawee, and had the check certified. Francis Factoring then indorsed the check in blank to Hills Brokerage Corporation in payment of materials purchased.

**Requried:**

    1.   Did the indorsement, "Pay only to Francis Factoring, Inc.," stop the negotiability of the check and legally require the drawee bank to pay the proceeds of the check to Francis Factoring only? Explain.

    2.   Can Hills Brokerage qualify as a valid holder of the check with all the rights of a holder in due course? Explain.

    3.   Assuming Hills Brokerage qualifies as a holder in due course, can it successfully sue First National Bank if the bank refuses to honor the check on February 1? Explain.

    4.   Assuming Hills Brokerage qualifies as a holder in due course, can it successfully sue Ford for proceeds of the check if the bank refuses to honor it on February 1? Explain.

    5.   Assuming Hills Brokerage qualifies as a holder in due course, can it successfully sue Benson for the proceeds of the check if the bank refuses to honor it on February 1? Explain.

    6.   Assuming Hills Brokerage qualifies as a holder in due course, can it successfully sue Francis Factoring for the proceeds of the check if the bank refuses to honor it on February 1? Explain.

**48.** Taylor Corporation, incorporated and doing business in Delaware, is a manufacturing company whose securities are registered on a national securities exchange. On February 6, 1975, one of Taylor's engineers disclosed to management that he had discovered a new product which he believed would be quite profitable to the corporation. Messrs. Jackson and Wilson, the corporation's president and treasurer and members of its board of directors, were very impressed with the prospects of the new poduct's profitability. Because the corporation would need additional capital to finance the development, production, and marketing of the new product, the board of directors proposed that the corporation issue an additional 100,000 shares of common stock.

Wilson was imbued with such confidence in the corporation's prospects that on February 12, 1975, he purchased on the open market 1,000 shares of the corporation's common stock at $10 per share. This was before news of the new product reached the public in late

February and caused a rise in the market price to $30 per share. Jackson did not purchase any shares in February because he had already purchased 600 shares of the corporation's common stock on January 15, 1975, for $10 per share.

In late February, when the market price of the corporation's common stock was $30 per share, Wilson approached two insurance companies to discuss the proposed issuance of an additional 100,000 shares of common stock. In March, Wilson reported to the board of directors that negotiations had been successful and one of the insurance companies had agreed to purchase the entire 100,000 shares for $3,000,000. The insurance company signed an investment letter, and a legend restricting transfers was imprinted on the face of each certificate issued to it. Moreover, the appropriate stop-transfer instructions were given to the corporation's stock-transfer agent.

Due to unexpected expenses arising from a fire in his home, on April 16, 1975, Jackson sold at $35 per share on the open market the 600 shares of stock he purchased in January. Wilson continues to hold his 1,000 shares.

**Required:**

    What questions arising out of the federal securities laws are suggested by these facts? Discuss.

**49.** Fletcher, Dry, Wilbert, and Cox selected the limited partnership as the form of business entity most suitable for their purpose of investing in mineral leases. Fletcher, the general partner, contributed $50,000 in capital. Dry, Wilbert, and Cox each contributed $100,000 capital and are limited partners. Necessary limited-partnership papers were duly prepared and filed clearly indicating that Fletcher was the sole general partner and that the others were limited partners.

Fletcher managed the partnership during the first two years. During the third year, Dry and Wilbert overruled Fletcher as to the type of investment to be made, the extent of the commitments, and the major terms contained in the leases. They also exercised the power to draw checks on the firm's bank account. Finally, Fletcher withdrew and was replaced by Martin, a new and more receptive general partner. Cox did not join his fellow partners in these activities. However, his name was used without qualification and with his general knowledge and consent on the partnership stationery as part of the firm's name.

**Required:**

    Discuss the legal liability of Martin, Dry, Wilbert, and Cox, as individuals, to creditors of the partnership.

**50.** Whitlow and Wyatt, CPAs, has been the independent auditors of Interstate Land Development Corporation for several years. During these years, Interstate prepared and filed its own annual income tax returns.

During 1974, Interstate requested Whitlow and Wyatt to examine all the necessary financial statements of the corporation to be submitted to the Securities and Exchange Commission (SEC) in connection with a multistate public offering of one-million shares of Interstate common stock. This public offering came under the provisions of the Securities Act of 1933. The examination was performed carefully and the financial statements were fairly presented for the respective periods. These financial statements were included in the registration statement filed with the SEC.

While the registration statement was being processed by the SEC but prior to the effective date, the Internal Revenue Service (IRS) subpoenaed Whitlow and Wyatt to turn over all its working papers relating to Interstate for the years 1971-1973. Whitlow and Wyatt initially refused to comply for two reasons. First, Whitlow and Wyatt did not prepare Interstate's tax returns. Second, Whitlow and Wyatt claimed that the working papers were confidential matters subject to the privileged-communications rule. Subsequently, however, Whitlow and Wyatt did relinquish the subpoenaed working papers.

Upon receiving the subpoena, Wyatt called Dunkirk, the chairman of Interstate's board of directors and asked him about the IRS investigation. Dunkirk responded, "I'm sure the IRS people are on a fishing expedition and that they will not find any material deficiencies."

A few days later Dunkirk received written confirmation from the IRS that it was contending that Interstate had underpaid its taxes during the period under review. The confirmation revealed that Interstate was being assessed $800,000 including penalties and interest for the three years.

This $800,000 assessment was material relative to the financial statements as of December 31, 1974. The amount for each year individually exclusive of penalty and interest was not material relative to each respective year.

**Required:**
1. Discuss the additional liability assumed by Whitlow and Wyatt in connection with this SEC registration engagement.
2. Discuss the implication to Whitlow and Wyatt and its responsibilities with respect to the IRS assessment.
3. Could Whitlow and Wyatt have validly refused to surrender the subpoenaed materials? Explain.

51. In the course of your examination of the financial statements of Lomax Manufacturing, Inc., you discovered the following facts relating to a real-estate transaction by the company during the current year.

Lomax purchased from Dunbar Corporation four acres of land in a proposed industrial-park site for $45,000. At the closing, Dunbar delivered to Lomax a bargain and sale deed with a covenant against the grantor's acts. Guaranty Indemnity Company wrote a title insurance policy for $45,000 covering the transaction.

Lomax disclosed to you that it recently learned of a defect in its title to the four acres of land due to a restriction placed on the land by John Jason, a former owner. Jason had included in his warranty deed a covenant " . . . that the land should be used exclusively for residential purposes." Jason's warranty deed was to an owner preceding Dunbar and conveyed all of the land now included in the proposed industrial park as well as surrounding land which has been developed for residential purposes. As a result of this restriction the value of the land acquired by Lomax has decreased by $15,000 according to an independent appraisal. Guaranty Indemnity had failed to discover this restriction at the time Lomax acquired the property.

**Required:**
Discuss the right of Lomax against the following:
1. Dunbar Corporation.
2. Guaranty Indemnity Company.

52. Harry Fisk operates a local tuna cannery. On May 31, 1975, your client, Fair Food Wholesalers, Inc., purchased 100 cases of tuna for $12 per case, FOB Fisk's warehouse. The contract expressly stipulated that the tuna was to be first quality and all white meat in "solid chunks." It was further agreed that Fair Food had until June 10, 1975, to inspect the tuna before the transaction became final. Consequently, on May 31, 1975, Fair Food gave Fisk the following instrument:

---

FAIR FOOD WHOLESALERS, INC.                                    No. 1625

                                                               1-12
                                                               210

                                                        June 10, 1975

Pay to the
order of     *Bearer*                              $1,200.00

*Twelve hundred & no/100's*                              Dollars

                                        Fair Food Wholesalers, Inc.

                                        By *James Duff*
                                              James Duff, President

CENTURY BANK
2 Broadlane
Providence, R.I.

*For tuna purchase from
Harry Fisk per contract dated May 31, 1975*

---

Fisk had orally agreed not to transfer the above instrument until June 10 or at the time final acceptance was manifested by Fair Food if this was earlier.

Fisk disregarded this agreement and promptly transferred the instrument to one of his creditors, Ross, who was threatening to force Fisk into bankruptcy. Ross took the instrument in good faith and without notice of any claim or defense in satisfaction of indebtedness arising from previous sales to Fisk which were overdue. The instrument was not indorsed by Fisk.

On June 10, 1975, Fair Food sample tested the tuna and found that it was not first quality and that it was not all white meat in solid chunks. Fair Food promptly notified Century Bank to stop payment on the instrument. Century did so and Ross is seeking recovery against Fair Food. In addition, Fair Food notified Fisk that it rejected the shipment and that it was holding the tuna on Fisk's behalf awaiting instructions from Fisk for disposition.

**Required:**
What are Ross's rights, if any, against Fair Food and Century Bank on the instrument? Explain.

53. During its annual examination of the financial statements of Ramrod Corporation, Farr & Williamson, CPAs, discovered the following problem involving an account receivable from DeMars Corporation. As of December 31, 1974, DeMars was three months in arrears on purchases of $21,690 made in late September 1974. In addition, a letter dated November 30, 1974, indicated that DeMars would not be able to pay its outstanding obligations because an involuntary petition in bankruptcy had been filed on November 21, 1974. The trustee in bankruptcy has indicated that, based upon a conservative estimate, DeMars will pay 10 cents on the dollar.

Further investigation revealed that DeMars was one of Ramrod's oldest and most-cherished customers. Not only that, but Fairmont, Ramrod's president, was a close personal friend and golfing partner of Goodson, DeMars' president. As a result of this relationship, Goodson had telephoned Fairmont on November 12, 1974, and informed him that DeMars' other creditors were in the process of preparing and filing an involuntary bankruptcy petition against it and that its financial condition had badly deteriorated. It was agreed by the two parties that Ramrod should take a secured position on the $21,690 arrearage via the assignment of $21,690 of DeMars' accounts receivable. This was done and a financing statement was duly signed by the parties and filed on November 15, 1974.

Later in its examination of Ramrod's financial statements, Farr & Williamson learned of another problem related to DeMars. Because of the close relationship between the companies and their presidents, Fairmont has urged Ramrod's board of directors in early January 1974 to authorize him to sign the corporate name as surety for a $200,000 loan which DeMars was negotiating with Local Lending Corporation. The loan was to be secured by a first mortgage on DeMars' real property. The fair market value of the real property at that time was $200,000; however, because it was Local Lending's policy not to loan in excess of 75% of the security fair market value, it was insisting upon a satisfactory surety on the loan. Additionally, Local Lending was worried about DeMars' financial condition. On January 10, 1974, Fairmont was authorized to sign the corporate name as an accommodation indorser on the $200,000 loan which was consummated that day. The current fair market value of the real property is approximately $180,000. DeMars is in default and Local Lending has demanded that Ramrod satisfy the debt.

**Required:**
    a.   Will Ramrod be able to successfully assert the standing of a secured creditor in the bankruptcy proceeding in respect to the $21,690 account receivable? Explain.
    b.   Discuss the legal rights of the parties and how Ramrod should account for the $21,690 receivable from DeMars and the related assignment of $21,690 of DeMars' receivables if
        1.   Ramrod qualifies as a secured creditor in the bankruptcy proceeding.
        2.   Ramrod does not qualify as a secured creditor in the bankruptcy proceeding.
    c.   Is Ramrod liable on its accommodation indorsement on the $200,000 loan from Local Lending to DeMars? Explain.
    d.   Assuming Ramrod is liable on its accommodation indorsement, can Ramrod force Local Lending to first resort to its mortgage before proceeding against Ramrod? Explain.
    e.   Assuming Ramrod is liable on its accommodation indorsement and has paid Local Lending the balance due ($190,260) on the loan by Local Lending to DeMars, what rights and standing does Ramrod have in bankruptcy as a result? Explain.

54.   Barney & Co., CPAs, has been engaged to perform an examination of the financial statements of Waldo, Inc., for several years. The terms of the engagement have been set out in an annual engagement letter signed by both parties. The terms of each engagement included the following:

    This being an ordinary examination, it is not primarily or specifically designed, and cannot be relied upon, to disclose defalcations and other similar irregularities, although their discovery may result.

Three years ago Harold Zamp, head cashier of Waldo and an expert in computer operations, devised a previously unheard of method of embezzling funds from his employer. At first, Zamp's thefts were small but increased as time went on. During the current year, before Barney began working on the engagement, the thefts became so large that serious variances in certain accounts came to the attention of the controller. When questioned about the variances, Zamp confessed and explained his unique embezzlement scheme. Investigation revealed that Zamp had stolen $257,550. Zamp has no assets with which to repay the thefts.

Waldo submitted its claim for $257,550 to Multi-State Surety Company in accordance with the terms of the fidelity bond covering Zamp. Fulfilling its surety obligation, Multi-State paid the claim and now seeks to recover its losses from Barney.

In defense, Barney asserts, in the alternative, the following defenses:
    1.   Multi-State has no standing in court to sue because it was not a party to the contract (i.e., lacking in privity) between Barney and its client, Waldo.
    2.   Even if Multi-State had the standing to sue, its claim should be dismissed because Barney's engagements with Waldo did not specifically include the discovery of defalcations other than those which might arise in the process of an ordinary examination.
    3.   Even if Barney's contract had made it responsible for discoverable defalcations, it could not have discovered Zamp's defalcations with the exercise of reasonable care. Zamp's technique was so new, unique, and novel that no accounting firm could have discovered the defalcations in any event.

**Required:**
    In separately numbered paragraphs, discuss the validity of each of Barney's defenses.

55.   On June 1, 1975, Markum Realty, Inc., offered to sell one acre of land in an industrial park it owned to Johnson Enterprises, Inc. The offer was by mail and, in addition to the other usual terms, stated: "This offer will expire on July 2, 1975, unless acceptance is received by the offeror on or before said date."

Johnson decided to purchase the tract of land and on July 1, telegraphed its acceptance to Markum. The acceptance telegram was delayed due to the negligence of the telegraph company which had admitted that delivery was not made to Markum until July 3. Markum decided not to sell to Johnson because it had received a better offer, but it remained silent and did not notify Johnson of its decision.

When Johnson did not hear from Markum by July 11, its president called the president of Markum and inquired when Johnson might expect to receive the formalized copy of the contract the two companies had entered into. Markum's president responded that there was no contract.

**Required:**
    1.   Did a contract result from the above described dealings between Markum and Johnson? Discuss the legal implications of each communication between the parties in your explanation.
    2.   Assuming a contract did not arise, does Johnson have any legal recourse against the telegraph company? Explain.

# Business Law Review Answers — Second Examination

1. (a) An assignment of a lease is *not* the same as a sub-lease, and prohibition of one does *not* prohibit the other. There is nothing wrong with Unlimited's action.

2. (b) The facts in this case are not particularly important in determining the answer. An insurable interest merely means that someone stands to suffer a pecuniary (monetary) loss. In this case, the lessee (Digital) stands to lose the value of its leasehold improvements. Franklin, the lessor, has an insurable interest if it rents the building, but none if it sells the building.

3. (a) Since 1972 only the debtor's signature is required. The statement can be filed at any time, but the perfection of the security interest occurs as of the date of filing.

4. (c) Jean *can* convey her interest to anyone she likes, but the interest ends upon her death. The land is not part of her estate, but of Franklin's. Joan does not hold the land in trust, she simply has a life estate. Since George and Harry are joint *tenants,* the survivor inherits the decedent's interest.

5. (d) Jason is not bound because there is no accord and satisfaction.

6. (b) This is one of the many acts that requires unanimous consent of all partners.

7. (c) Answers (a) and (d) are wrong because the agreement stipulates that partners share profits and losses equally. Between (b) and (c) is a matter of calculation:

$176,000 Total
  65,000 Outside creditors
$111,000
 −25,000 Capital Kimball
 −20,000 Loan Kimball
 −15,000 Capital Thompson
$ 51,000 Net Available
÷     3
$ 17,000 to each partner
 25,000 Capital Kimball
 20,000 Loan Kimball
$ 62,000 Total to Kimball

Note: Do *not* confuse this with loss absorption calculations on the practice exam.

8. (b) Federal antitrust laws apply to partnerships, large or small, as well as to corporations. There is nothing voidable about the partnership, nor is Wilson entitled to a salary. There are none of the conditions here that require a writing pursuant to the Statute.

9. (d) An option especially an option with consideration is binding for the period stated.

10. (b) When an agent acts outside the direct scope of his employment, the principal is not liable.

11. (b) Barron cannot avoid its obligation on the grounds of Super's credit rating because its contract is with Chubb, and Chubb remains liable. There is consideration here ($25 for each case). There is also no variation in Barron's dates to perform; they simply have to deliver the dynamite. The contract is assignable as to rights and duties.

12. (c) Both Super and Barron are still bound, and if Demerest defaults, Barron is liable. Super has to agree to the assignment of duties by Barron to Demerest for novation to apply (and free Barron of liability).

13. (d) Employees cannot waive the coverage. Workmen's Compensation is sort of a "no fault" insurance, and this answer defines its purpose.

14. (a) A limited partner is somewhere between a general partner and a common stockholder in a corporation in terms of these types of situations. His priority is below an outside creditor (which would *not* be the case for a common stockholder-creditor of a corporation), but above the general partners.

15. (d) The agent is personally liable in cases of undisclosed principals. Should the principal become known, he too is liable.

16. (b) A limited partner interest is a security, and SEC filing is required. The dispute does not turn the limited partners into general partners, especially since the dispute is not over management of the company but over the raising of capital. Again, it is generally safe to apply the rules of corporations to limited partnerships.

17. (c) There is no violation, even if the competitors

can show damages. In fact, competitors showing damages is ridiculous: we *expect* competition to decrease the profits of competitors. Cutting prices to meet competition is *not* a violation of antitrust laws. Quoting low prices to obtain new business (b) is a questionable activity. Operating at a loss (d) does not change the violation; in fact, it strengthens it.

18. (c)  First of all, always find for the minor, eliminating answer (d). A guarantor, however, cannot use minority of the primary obligor as a defense. The guarantor has available to him only the normal contract defenses, such as fraud.

19. (d)  Only contracts for sale of *personal property* over $500 need be in writing. As far as answer (c) is concerned, Matson can assign Donald's debt to Cranston, but *Matson* still has a primary obligation to Cranston. Furthermore, he hasn't irrevocably assigned the debt to Cranston. Fraud (not misrepresentation) in the *execution* has to do with negotiable instruments.

20. (a)  This is definitional.

21. (b)  (c) The rule is: constructive notice (an ad in the paper) is sufficient notice for suppliers with whom the company had no prior dealings. Hence (b) is correct: new suppliers were notified by the ad (under the law) and Menlow has no liability. *Actual* notice is required for old suppliers, and since this was not done, Menlow is liable to these suppliers.

22. (d)  This is a standard surety arrangement. The surety "steps into the shoes" of the creditor in case of default.

23. (b)  All tender offers have to be filed. The former stockholders are hardly parties to a tax free reorganization since they simply sold their stock to Fish. Answer (d) is ridiculous; antitrust has nothing to do with securities laws.

24. (a)  The law is quite clear on this: a surety, *like any other contract*, must be supported by consideration to be valid.

25. (c)  Underwood is the underwriter, and Jackson is the issuer. Registration and prospectus filing are required.

26. (a)  The mortgage must be recorded (filed) to prevail against general creditors. The central air-conditioning and heating system is part of the real property. Similarly, fixtures permanently *annexed* to the land are not part of First State's security. First State's interest is not in any real property, and there is no necessity to file it in the appropriate real property recordation office.

27. (c)  (d) If the third party is unaware of the agent's limitation, the principal *is* liable. An undisclosed principal is *also* liable along with the agent. When the agent signs a negotiable instrument in *his own name*, the principal is not liable. Independent contractors are not really agents. The principal is not liable for his acts at all.

28. (d)  The limited partner is only an *investor* and has no fiduciary duties, and can sell his interest. He is not entitled to interest (any more than a common stockholder is), but the partnership income *does* flow through to each partner (limited or not) and is taxable to them.

29. (a)  A very popular exam question makes the distinction between acquiring the assets and acquiring the capital stock of a competitor, supplier or major customer. This answer (d) is always wrong. There is no difference in antitrust law between the two methods of acquisition. Any action to acquire Sport Store or to limit its activities would probably be a violation because of the relative magnitude of Sleekat's share of the market, Sleekat's share of Sport's sales, Sport's share of Sleekat's sales, and/or Sport's share of the market.

30. (c)  Normally, the follow the leader actions in (b) would be violations, but here, (c) is an even greater violation. This is the sort of 19th century railroad activity that would be clearly illegal. Follow the leader actions are difficult to prove because they frequently are justified price increases (as in the case here).

31. (c)  A seller of consumer goods need not file to perfect his interest. The interest is automatically perfected against everybody (including Marcus) *except* innocent purchasers for value (such as Franks).

32. (a)  The important word in this question is limited. A limited partnership is more like a corporation than a partnership. Limited partners are more like stockholders than partners, and their creditor status is as good as anyone else's. General partners have lower priorities than ordinary creditors.

33. (b)  This question is tricky, and choosing the correct answer is more a matter of exam technique than knowledge of law. None of the incorrect answers is obviously wrong, but (b) is the best answer because it hedges. It only says that the

arrangement will be tested under the Clayton Act; it does not say definitely whether Nashville is or isn't in violation.

34. (a)  There is nothing wrong with this loan.

35. (d)  The contract rules regarding acceptance or rejection relative to this example are: A *minor* change in the terms (a) does *not* constitute a rejection and counter offer. In fact, the minor change here is hardly even a change. A *major* change (b), (d) *does* constitute a rejection and counter offer. Acceptance (c) speaks upon *sending*, not receipt of acceptance.

36. (a)  This is more a practice exam question. The transaction credits capital $1,000 and debits retained earnings (earned surplus) $1,000.

37. (d)  Answers (a) and (c) are the same, so they must be wrong. Acceptance by Nails takes place at shipment, not receipt by Visco. The telegram is a signed writing and an enforceable contract, although the applicability of the Statute of Frauds is questionable. The statute states that certain contracts must be in writing to be enforceable; here the contract is in writing so the statute is not at issue. Answer (d), however, is still the best answer.

38. (a)  The UCC only relaxed privity, it did not abolish it. Marvin is not in priority with Specific, and Excellent does not have liability to Marvin. The liability may extend further than damage.

39. (a)  This is quite clearly a combination in restraint of trade. Even in cases where no meeting takes place, or no association exists, but the members of the industry "follow the leader" (particularly in regards to price *increases*), there are grounds for government action.

40. (a)  A contract is an assignment of rights and a delegation of duties. The bulk sales law, hinted at in answer (b), requires only *notice* to the creditors of a purchased business.

41. (d)  The distinction between cumulative and non-cumulative *only* has to do with dividends not earned. Answer (a) doesn't make sense. Absent agreement to the contrary, preferred stock is preferred for dividends, *not* distribution of assets, it is not voting, and it does *not* participate in profits beyond its dividend rate.

42. (c)  If a company chooses not to take Workmen's Compensation insurance, they are nevertheless still liable under the same conditions as normal Workmen's Comp., i.e., they do not have the contributory negligence defense available to them. Answer (d) has nothing to do with Workmen's Comp.

43. (c)  This is clearly a violation. Memorize answer (c); for future reference . . . it is a good summary of antitrust. If Destination had acted *alone* to meet competition, (d) would be correct. *Conspiracy* in restraint of trade is the issue.

44. (c)  The seller of the property becomes a surety, but only a *secondary* obligor, that is, he must satisfy the mortgage *after* the primary obligor has defaulted.

45. (b)  This is subsequent modification of a contract and needs no consideration, and need not satisfy the Statute of Frauds because it is for personal property of value less than $500. Note that the modification of a contract has to be in writing only if the original contract had to be. Although the total value of the sale originally was $550, the cassettes do not constitute a set, and the relevant figure to use in determining whether the statute is applicable is $5.50 per cassette, not the total $550.

46. (c)  Allen took the property subject to the mortgage, which means he is not liable for it (and Lutz is). Allen did not take the property free of the mortgage, but he has no obligation to Lutz.

47.      1) No — the "pay only to . . ." endorsement is effectively changed to "pay to the order of . . . ". Only the making of the check in words "pay only to . . ." destroys negotiability.
         2) Yes — the check was validly negotiated.
         3) Yes — the bank certified the check.
         4) No — the certification by the bank releases Ford of liability.
         5) No — the certification also releases all prior endorsers.
         6) Yes — the certification does not release subsequent endorsers.

48.      1. Private placement (insurance companies) no registration necessary.
         2. Wilson's acts are fraudulent. He traded on inside information before it was known to the public.
         3. Jackson's acts were also insider trading even though he had purchased the stock *before* the new product was known to anybody. The rule here is a buy and sell within 6 months.

49.      Martin, Dry, Wilbert, and Cox are all liable as general partners. Martin is an incoming general

partner, and, as such, he would have the same liability as a general partner in an ordinary partnership. In effect, the law states that he has unlimited joint and several liability. However, as to obligations incurred prior to his entry into the partnership, his liability cannot exceed his capital contribution.

Dry and Wilbert are liable as general partners because, in addition to the exercise of their rights and powers as limited partners, they also took part in the control of the business.

Cox's liability as a general partner rests upon the doctrine of estoppel or a specific provision under the Uniform Limited Partnership Act. The act provides that a limited partner whose name appears in the partnership name is liable as a general partner to partnership creditors who extend credit to the partnership without actual knowledge that he is not a general partner. Hence, unless a creditor knows of Cox's true status, Cox has unlimited liability to that creditor.

50.    1.    The CPA is broadly liable and must prove that he exercised due care.

51.    1.    None — Bargain and sale deed just covers

grantor's (Dunbar's) acts — not prior owners.

2.    Full — Guaranty guaranteed the title

52.    1.    Fair Food — full rights. Ross is a holder in due course even without endorsement because the instrument is bearer paper. Century Bank — none — the stop order was valid.

53.  1.    Ramrod should be able to collect the receivable — memorandum offsetting entry for assignment. Ramrod will probably not collect — write off to bad debts.
c.    Yes — they are a surety.
d.    No — surety is immediately liable.
e.    Subrogation — Ramrod steps into shoes of previous creditor.

54.    1.    Subrogation — once Multi-State pays, it steps into the shoes of Waldo (and can sue Barney). Privity of contract has been relaxed — it is no defense.

55.    1.    No — normally acceptance speaks on dispatching, but not if stipulated otherwise.
2.    Yes — the telegraph company is liable for its mistakes.

# Weakness Identification Key
# Second Examination

After you have corrected your answers from the sample examination, circle the numbers of the answers you had incorrect or found difficulty in answering. A large number of incorrect answers in any subject area indicates a weakness. Go back to the appropriate chapters in this book, consult another text, or check with your course instructor, to understand where your difficulty lies.

**Question Numbers**

|  | 1 - 9 | 10 - 18 | 19 - 27 | 28 - 36 | 37 - 45 | 46 - 55 |
|---|---|---|---|---|---|---|
| Contracts | 5, 9 | 11, 12 | 19, 20 | 35 | 37, 38, 40, 45 | 55 |
| Sales |  |  |  |  |  | 46 |
| Secured Transactions | 3 |  | 26 | 31 | 44 |  |
| Suretyship |  | 18, 22 | 24 |  |  |  |
| Bankruptcy |  |  |  |  |  | 53 |
| Commercial Paper |  |  |  |  |  | 47, 52 |
| Agency Law |  | 10, 15, 21 | 27 |  |  |  |
| Partnerships | 6, 7, 8 | 14, 16 |  | 28, 32 |  | 49 |
| Corporations |  |  |  | 34, 36 | 41 |  |
| Insurance | 2 |  |  |  |  |  |
| Federal Securities Regulations |  |  | 23, 25 |  |  | 48 |
| Accountant's Legal Responsibility |  |  |  |  |  | 50, 54 |
| Antitrust Laws |  | 17 |  | 29, 30, 33 | 39, 43 |  |
| Employees' Rights |  | 13 |  |  | 42 |  |
| Real Property | 1 |  |  |  |  | 51 |
| Wills, Estates and Trusts | 4 |  |  |  |  |  |

169